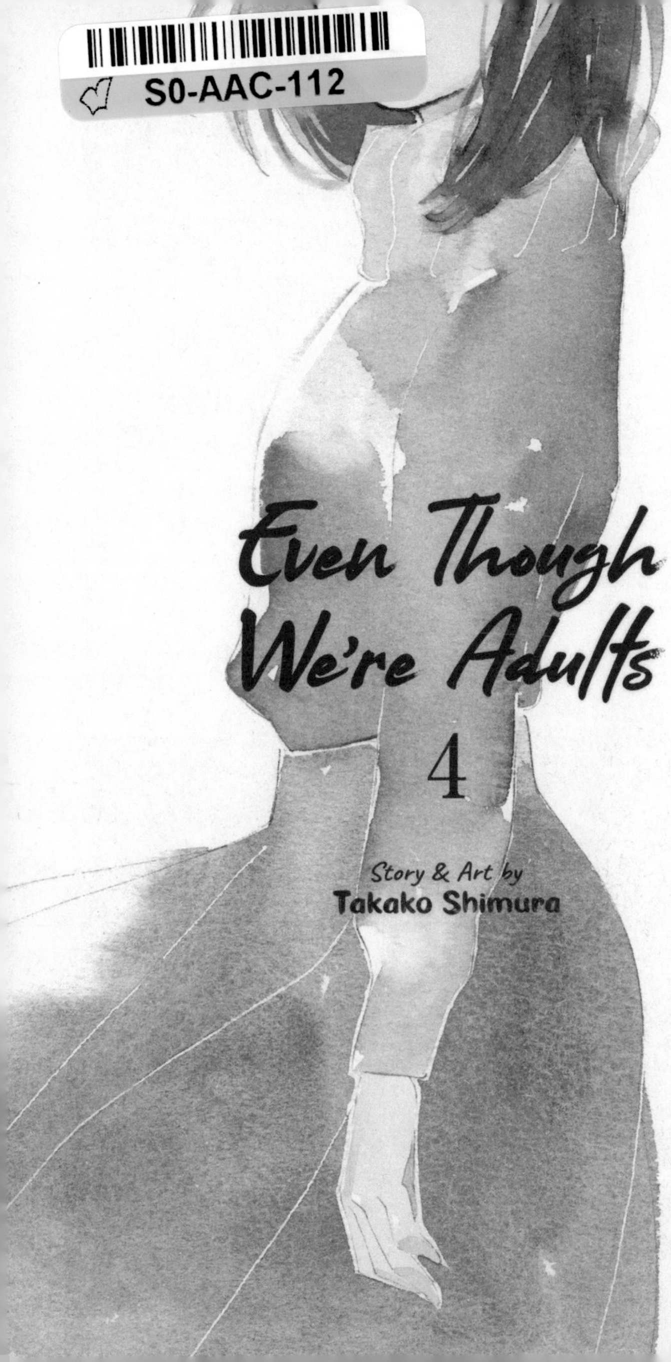

Even Though We're Adults

4

Story & Art by
Takako Shimura

CONTENTS

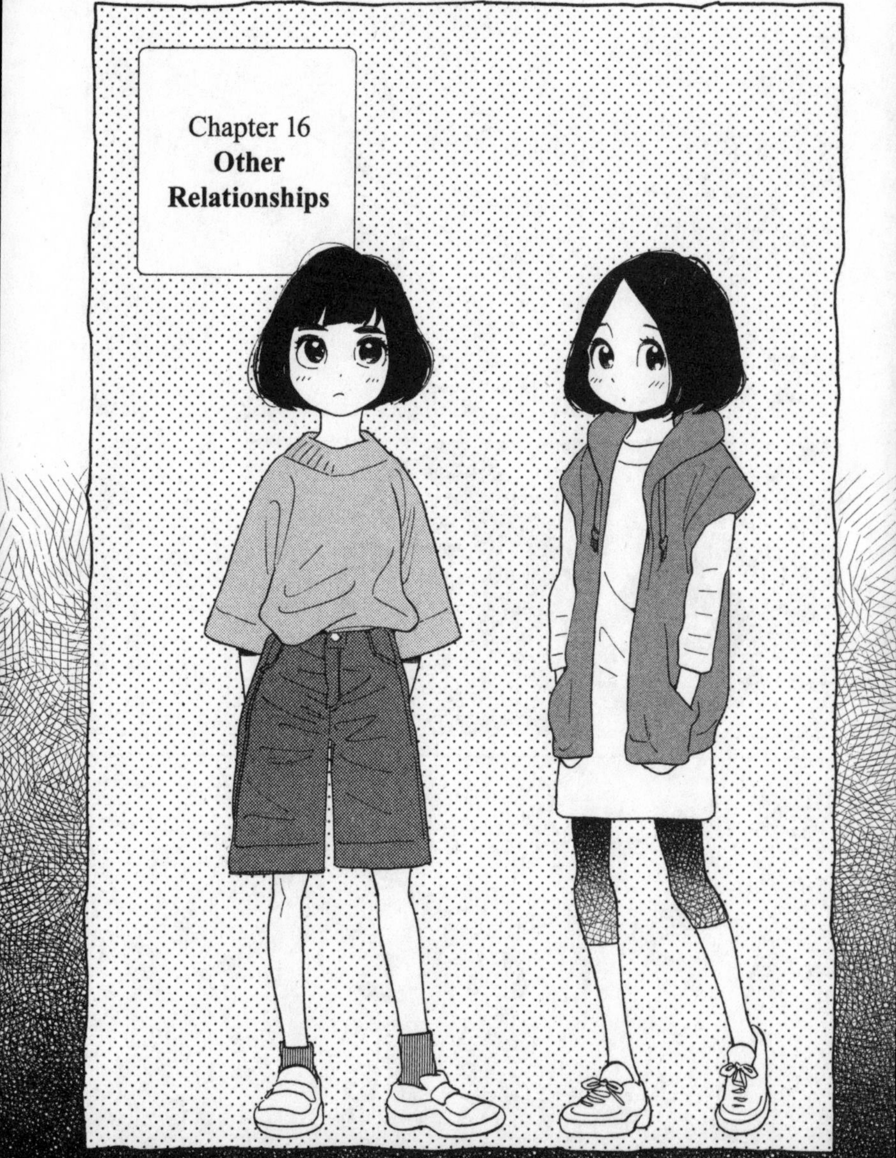
Chapter 16
Other
Relationships

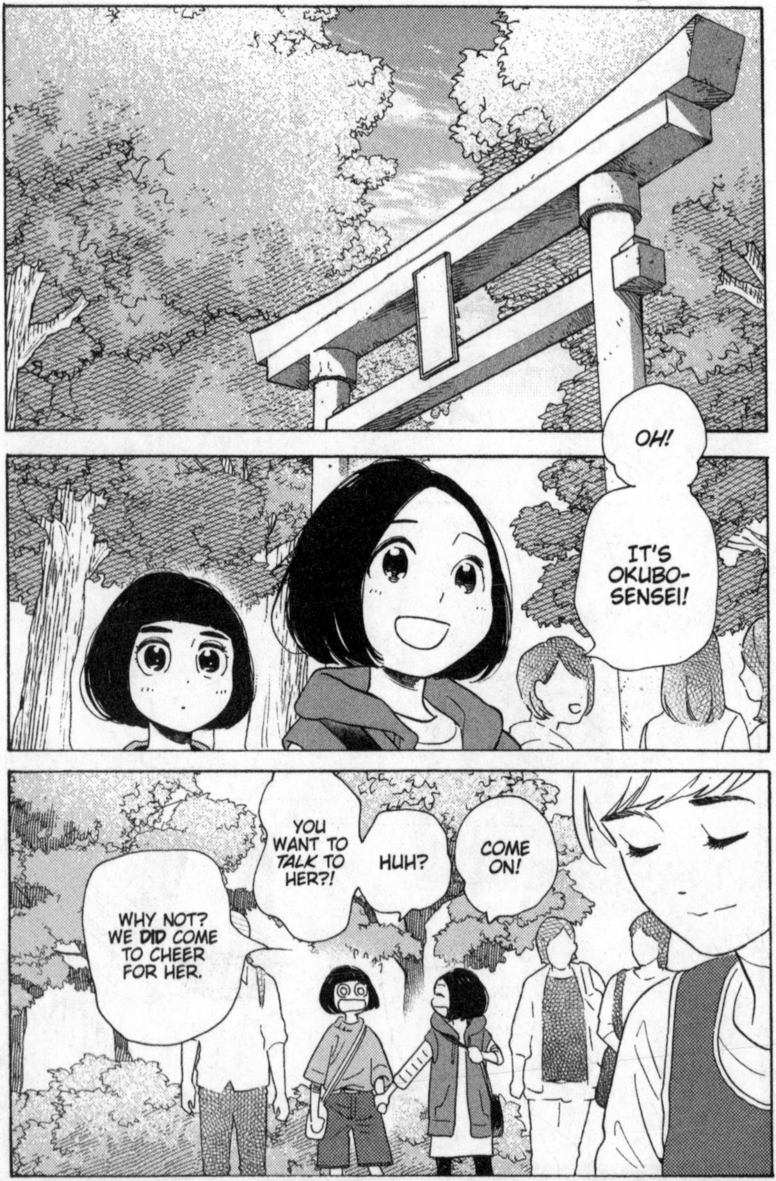
OH!
IT'S OKUBO-SENSEI!
COME ON!
HUH?
YOU WANT TO *TALK* TO HER?!
WHY NOT? WE **DID** COME TO CHEER FOR HER.

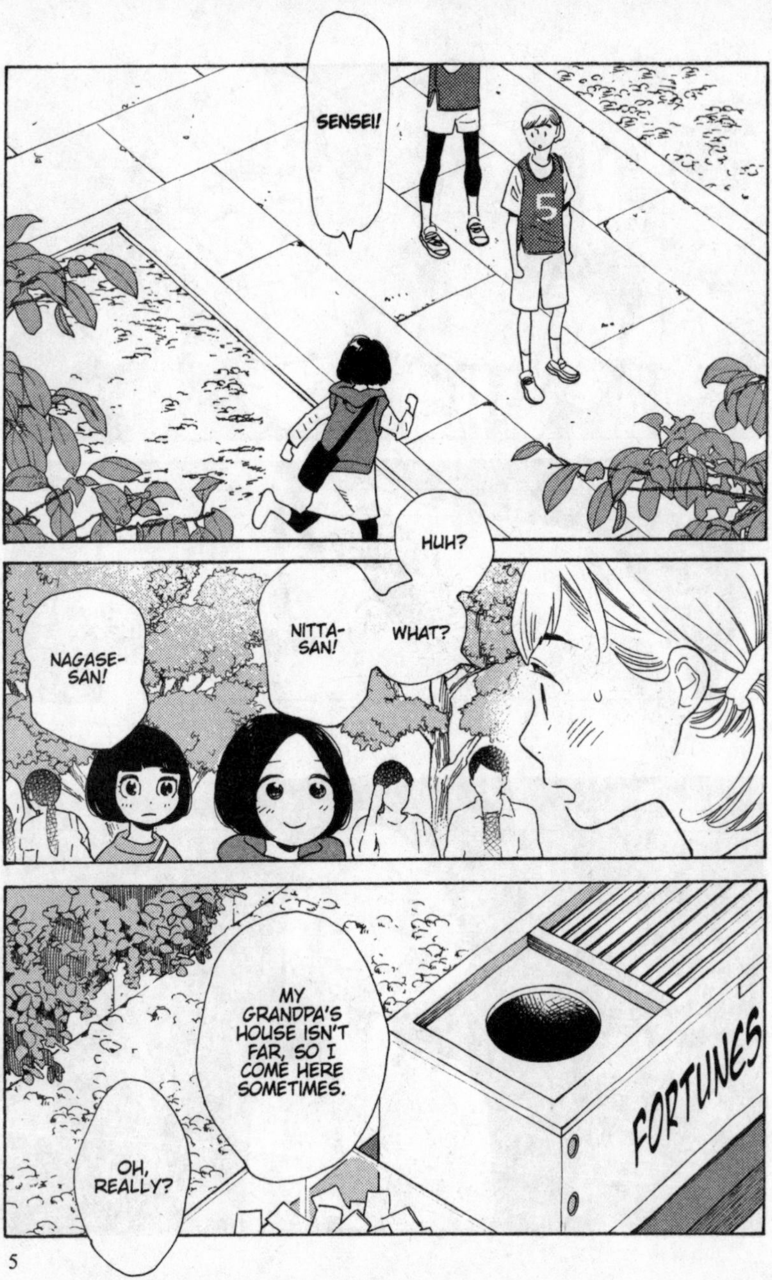
SENSEI!
HUH?
WHAT?
NITTA-SAN!
NAGASE-SAN!
MY GRANDPA'S HOUSE ISN'T FAR, SO I COME HERE SOMETIMES.
OH, REALLY?
FORTUNES

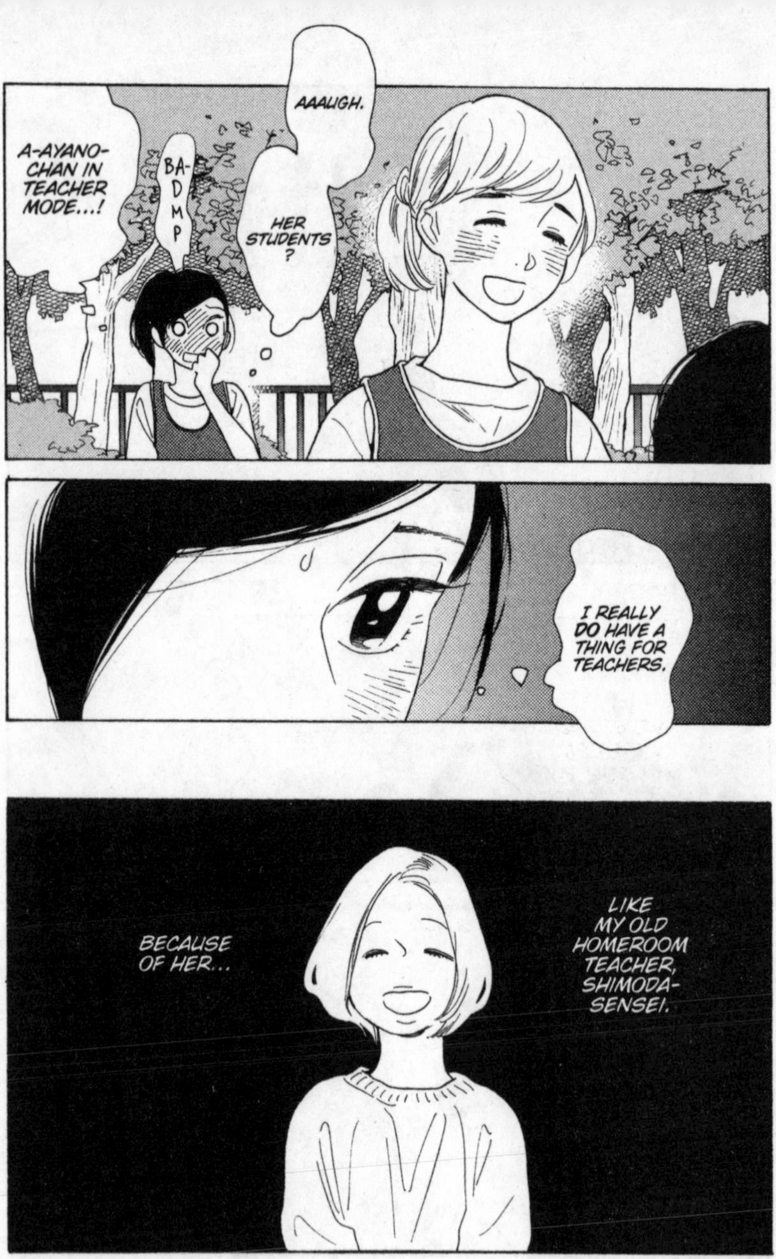
AAAUGH.
HER STUDENTS?
BA-DMP
A-AYANO-CHAN IN TEACHER MODE...!
I REALLY DO HAVE A THING FOR TEACHERS.
LIKE MY OLD HOMEROOM TEACHER, SHIMODA-SENSEI.
BECAUSE OF HER...

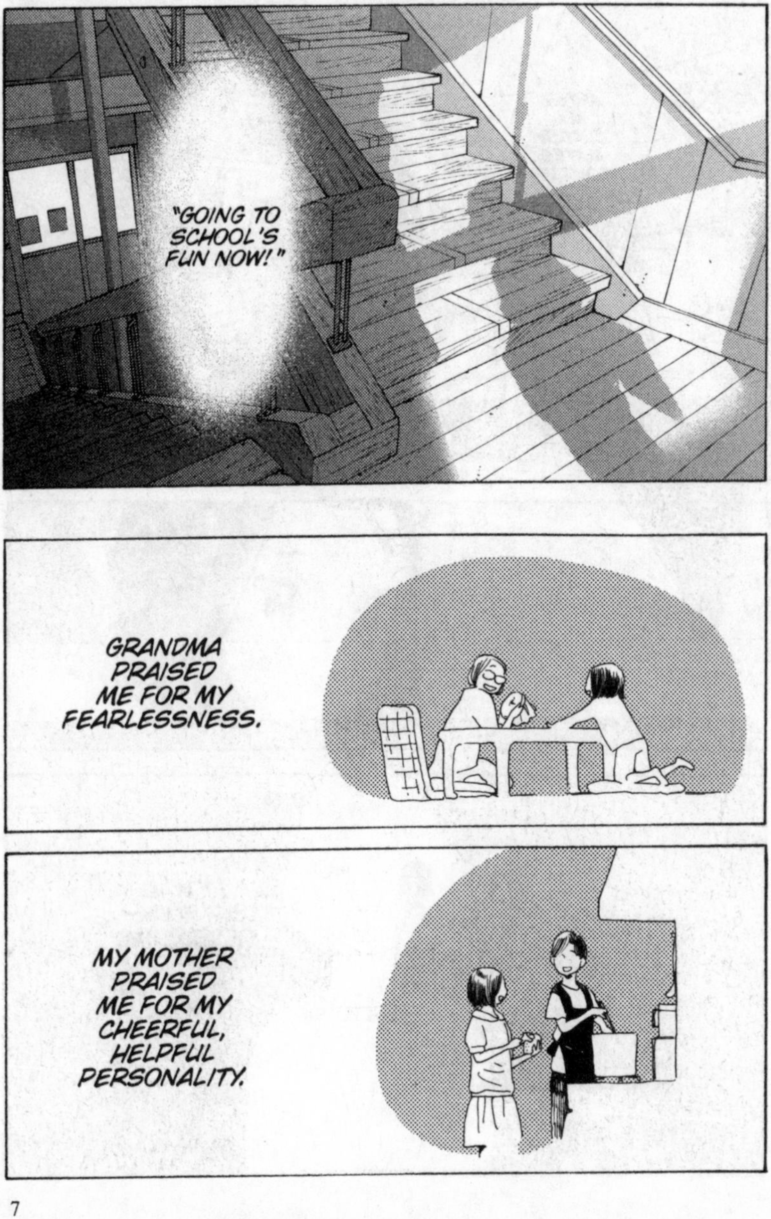
"GOING TO SCHOOL'S FUN NOW!"
GRANDMA PRAISED ME FOR MY FEARLESSNESS.
MY MOTHER PRAISED ME FOR MY CHEERFUL, HELPFUL PERSONALITY.

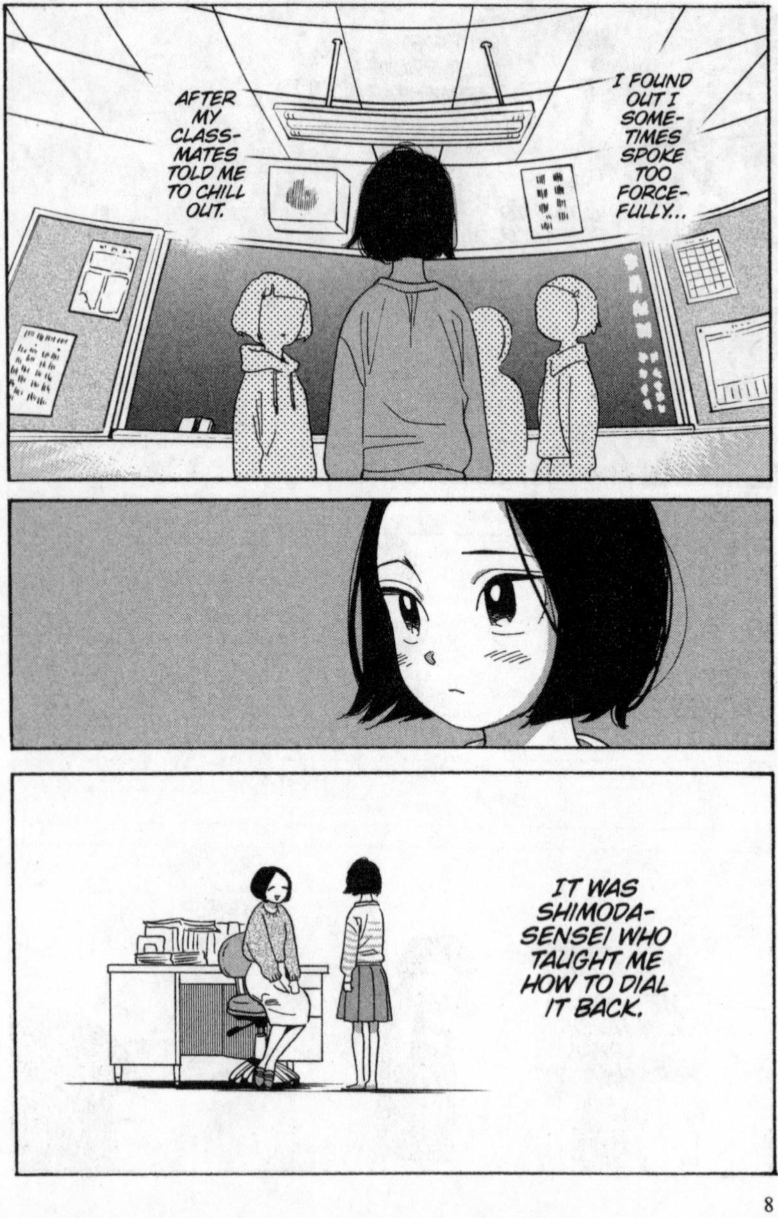
I FOUND OUT I SOME-TIMES SPOKE TOO FORCE-FULLY...
AFTER MY CLASS-MATES TOLD ME TO CHILL OUT.
IT WAS SHIMODA-SENSEI WHO TAUGHT ME HOW TO DIAL IT BACK.

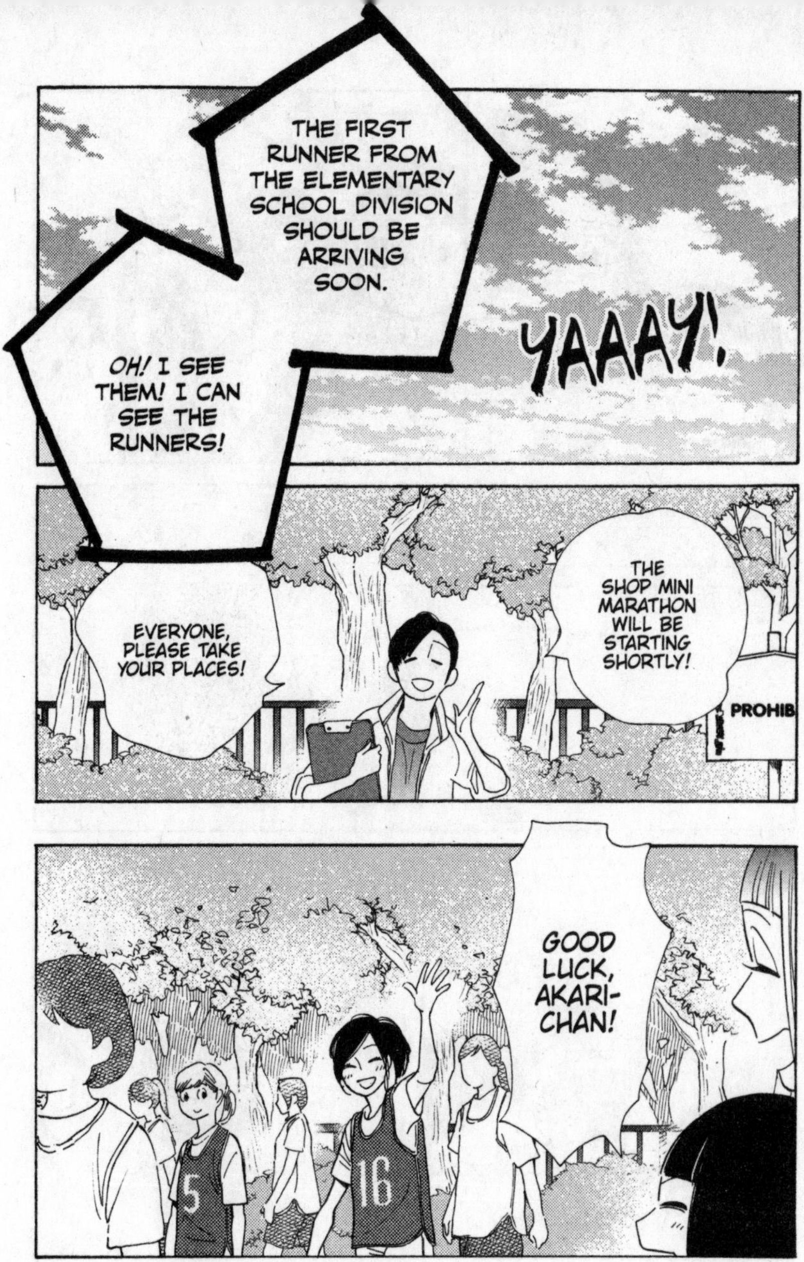
THE FIRST RUNNER FROM THE ELEMENTARY SCHOOL DIVISION SHOULD BE ARRIVING SOON.
YAAAY!
OH! I SEE THEM! I CAN SEE THE RUNNERS!
THE SHOP MINI MARATHON WILL BE STARTING SHORTLY!
PROHIB
EVERYONE, PLEASE TAKE YOUR PLACES!
GOOD LUCK, AKARI-CHAN!

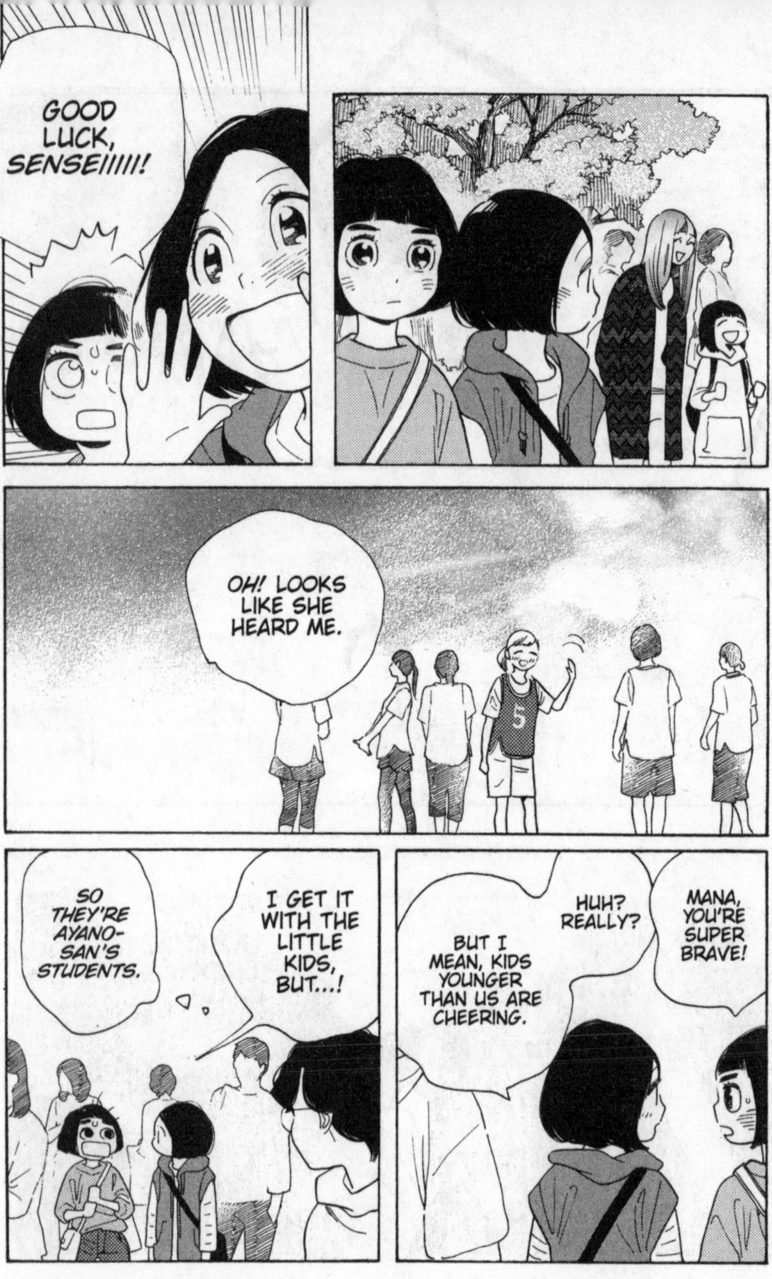
GOOD LUCK, SENSEI!!!!!!
OH! LOOKS LIKE SHE HEARD ME.
MANA, YOU'RE SUPER BRAVE!
HUH? REALLY?
BUT I MEAN, KIDS YOUNGER THAN US ARE CHEERING.
I GET IT WITH THE LITTLE KIDS, BUT...!
SO THEY'RE AYANO-SAN'S STUDENTS.

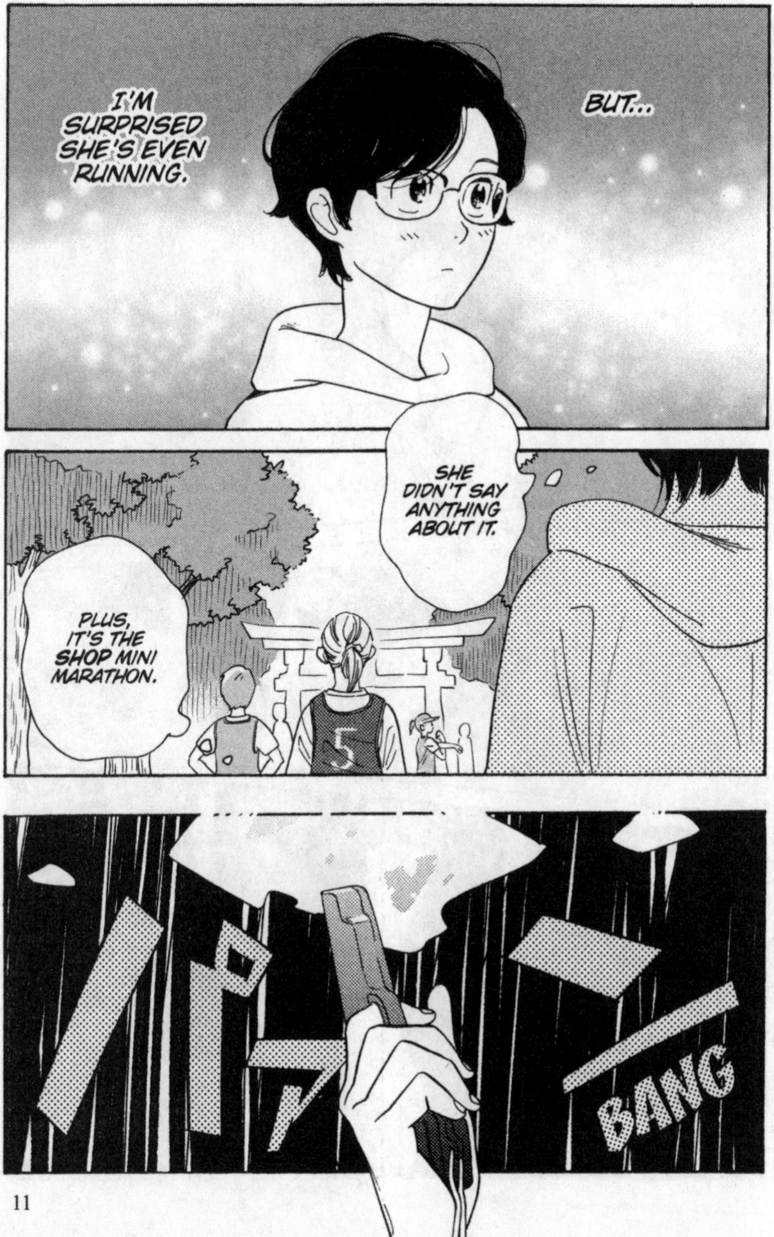
BUT...
I'M SURPRISED SHE'S EVEN RUNNING.
SHE DIDN'T SAY ANYTHING ABOUT IT.
PLUS, IT'S THE SHOP MINI MARATHON.
BANG

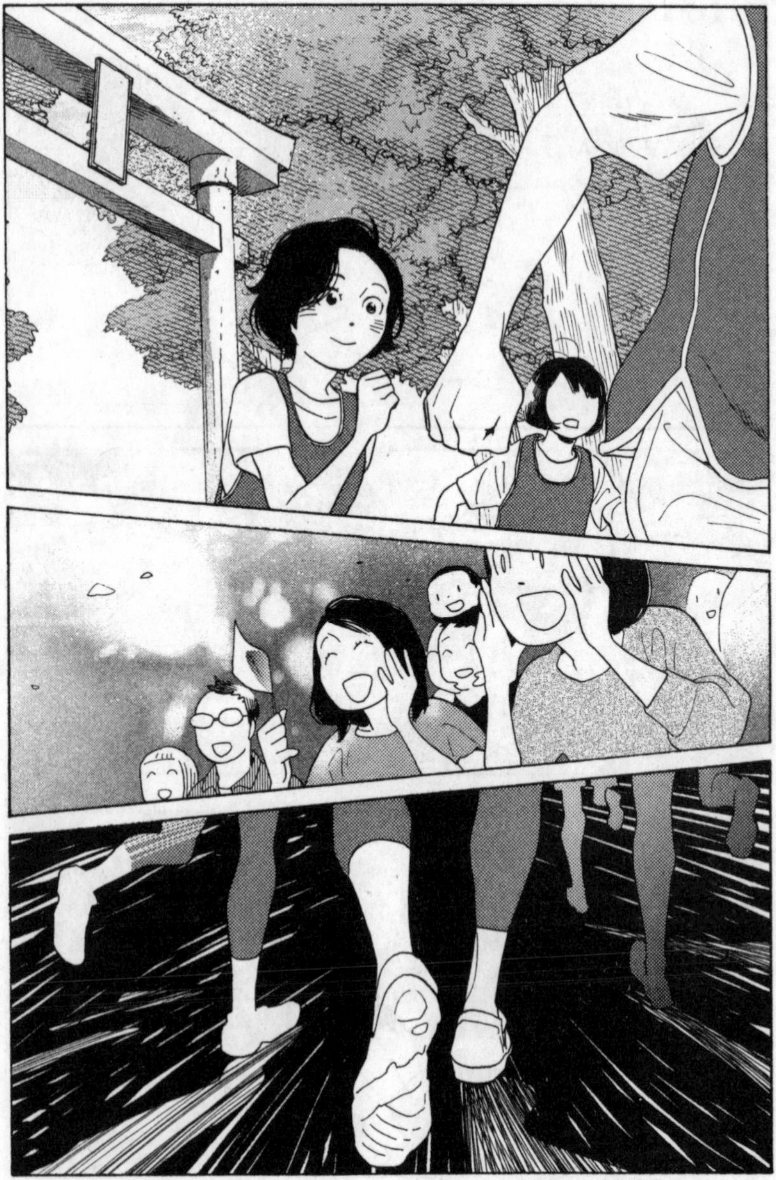

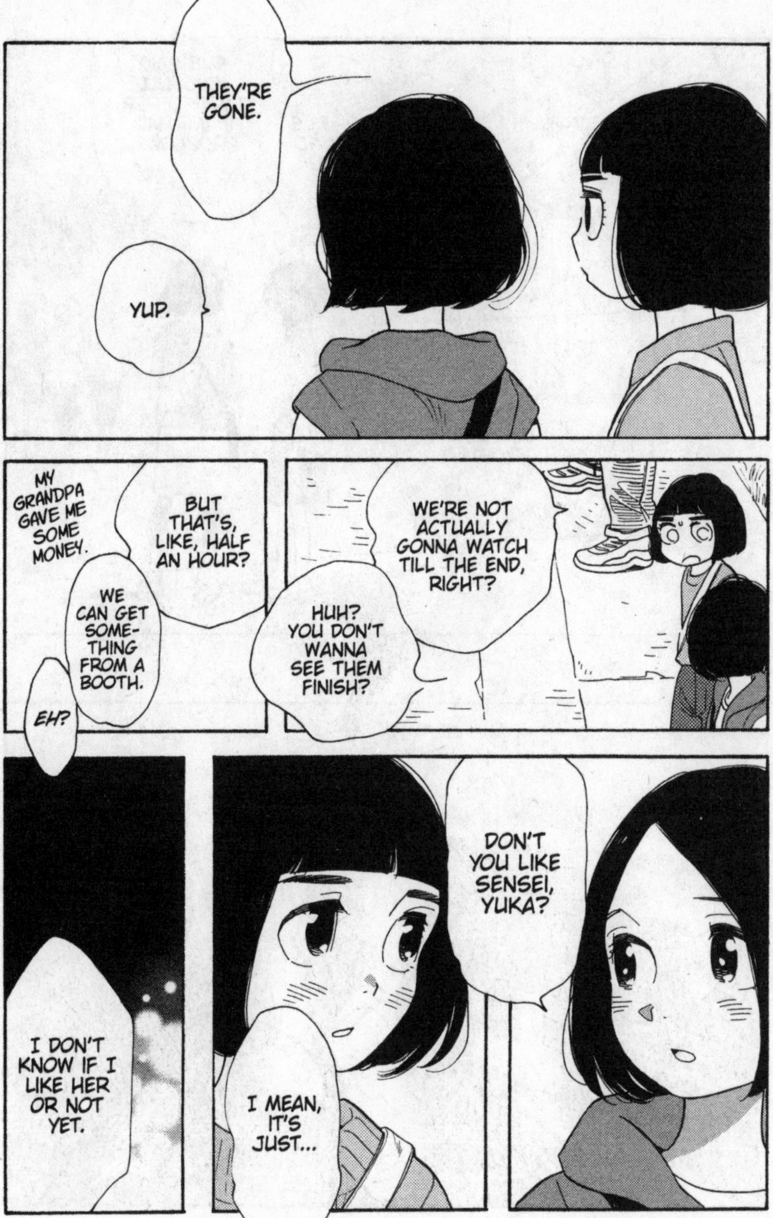
THEY'RE GONE.
YUP.
WE'RE NOT ACTUALLY GONNA WATCH TILL THE END, RIGHT?
HUH? YOU DON'T WANNA SEE THEM FINISH?
BUT THAT'S, LIKE, HALF AN HOUR?
MY GRANDPA GAVE ME SOME MONEY.
WE CAN GET SOME-THING FROM A BOOTH.
EH?
DON'T YOU LIKE SENSEI, YUKA?
I MEAN, IT'S JUST...
I DON'T KNOW IF I LIKE HER OR NOT YET.

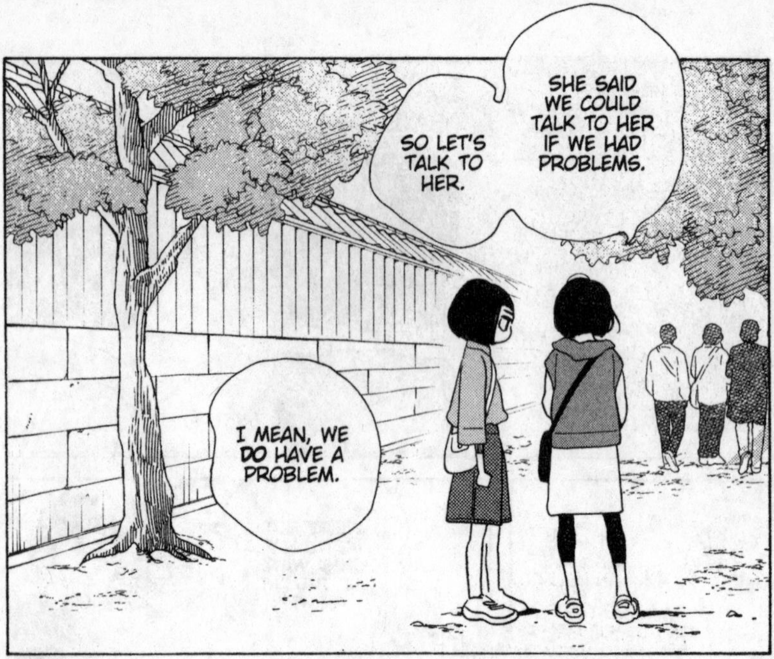
SHE SAID WE COULD TALK TO HER IF WE HAD PROBLEMS.
SO LET'S TALK TO HER.
I MEAN, WE DO HAVE A PROBLEM.

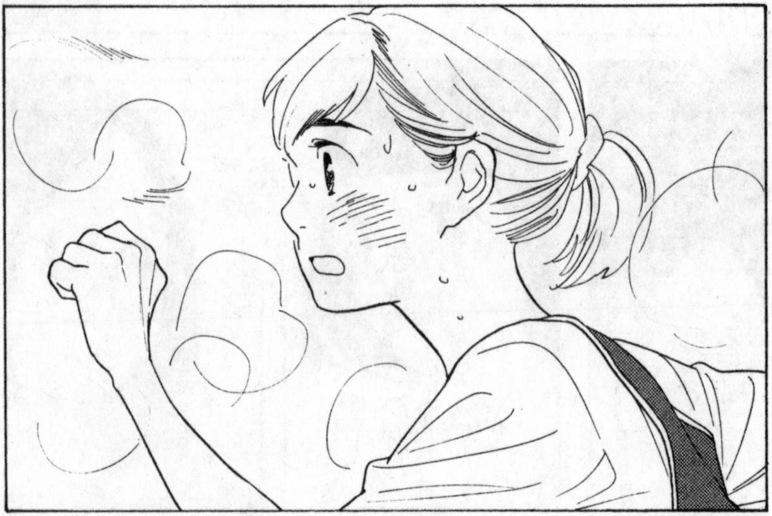

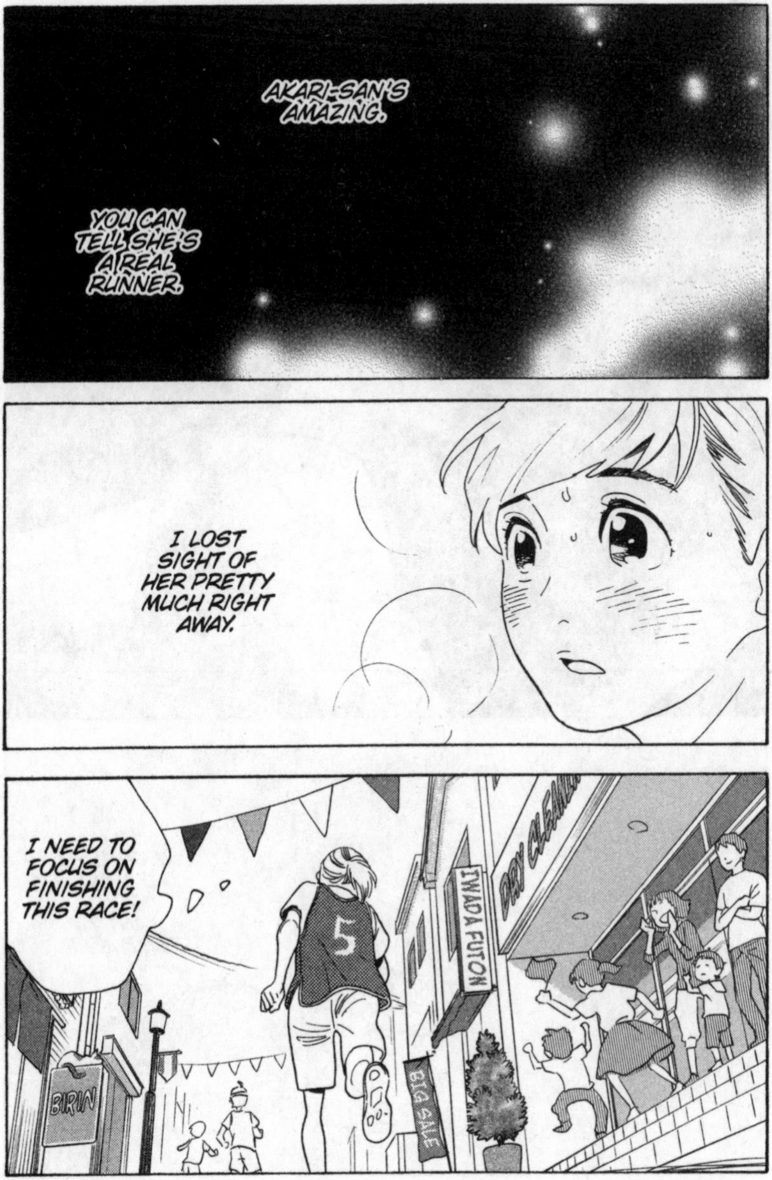
AKARI-SAN'S AMAZING.
YOU CAN TELL SHE'S A REAL RUNNER.
I LOST SIGHT OF HER PRETTY MUCH RIGHT AWAY.
IWADA FUTON
BIG SALE
I NEED TO FOCUS ON FINISHING THIS RACE!
BIRIN

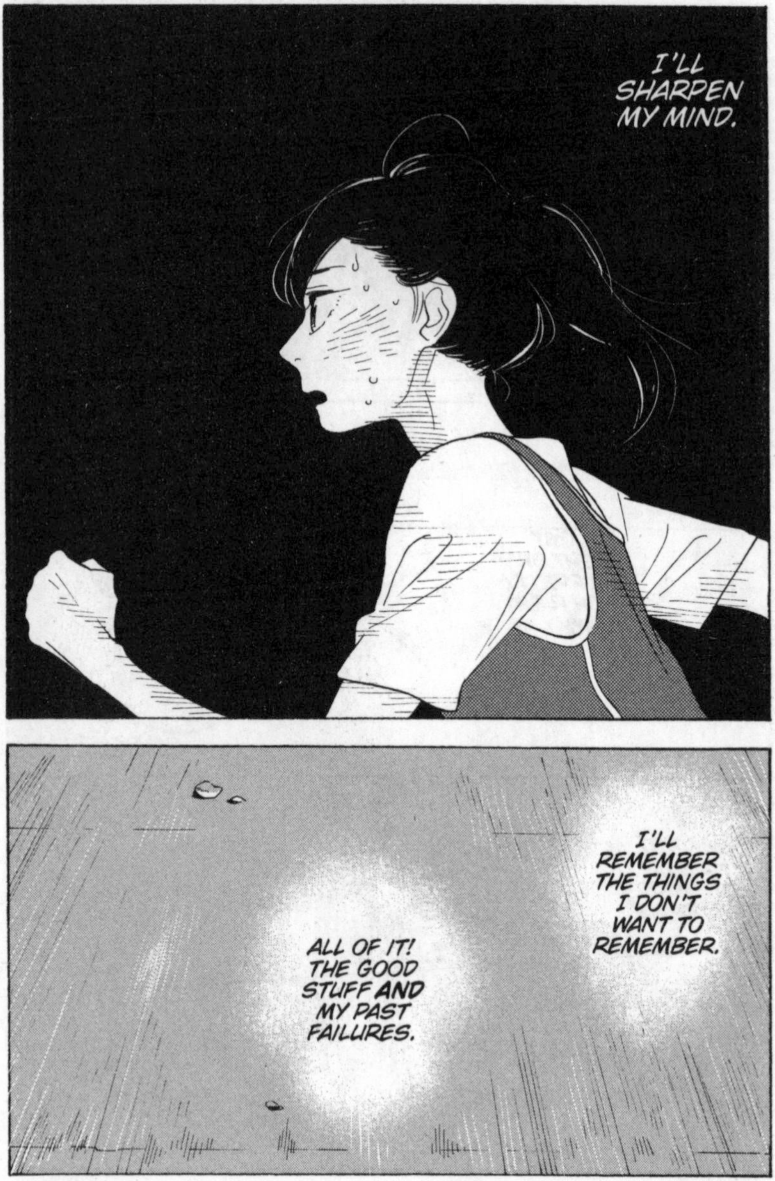
I'LL SHARPEN MY MIND.
I'LL REMEMBER THE THINGS I DON'T WANT TO REMEMBER.
ALL OF IT! THE GOOD STUFF AND MY PAST FAILURES.

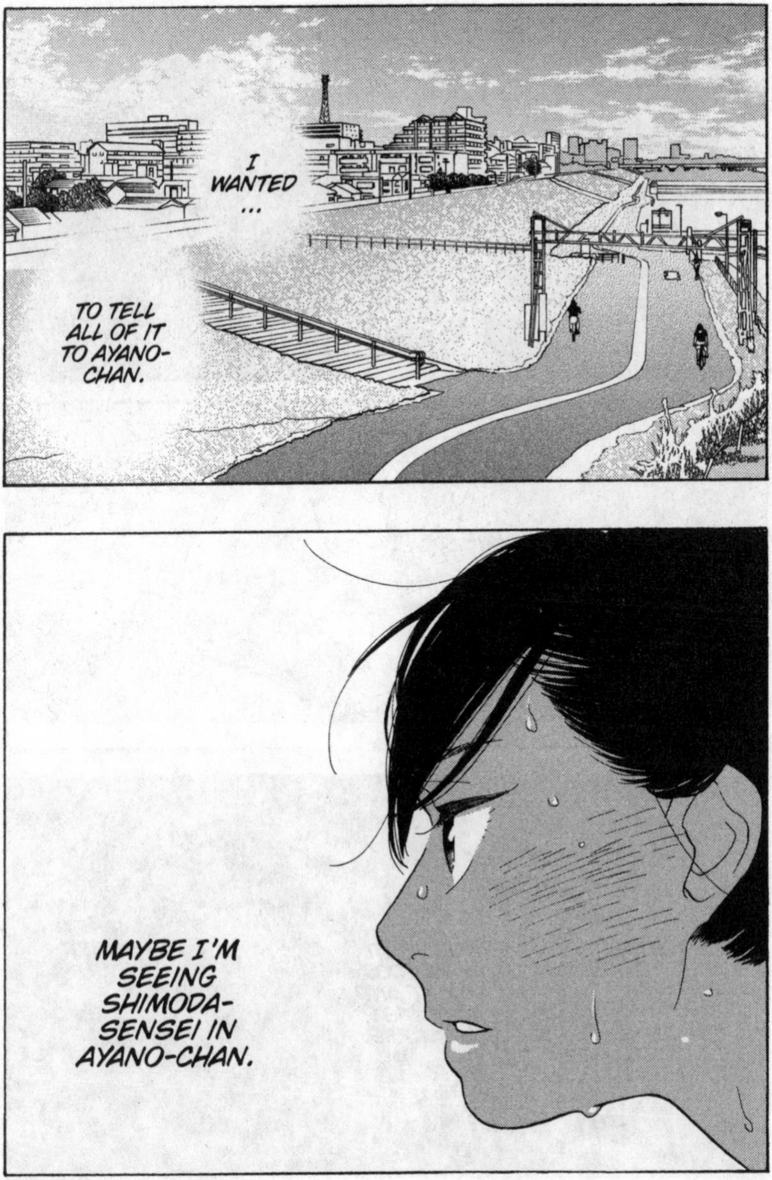
I WANTED ...
TO TELL ALL OF IT TO AYANO-CHAN.
MAYBE I'M SEEING SHIMODA-SENSEI IN AYANO-CHAN.

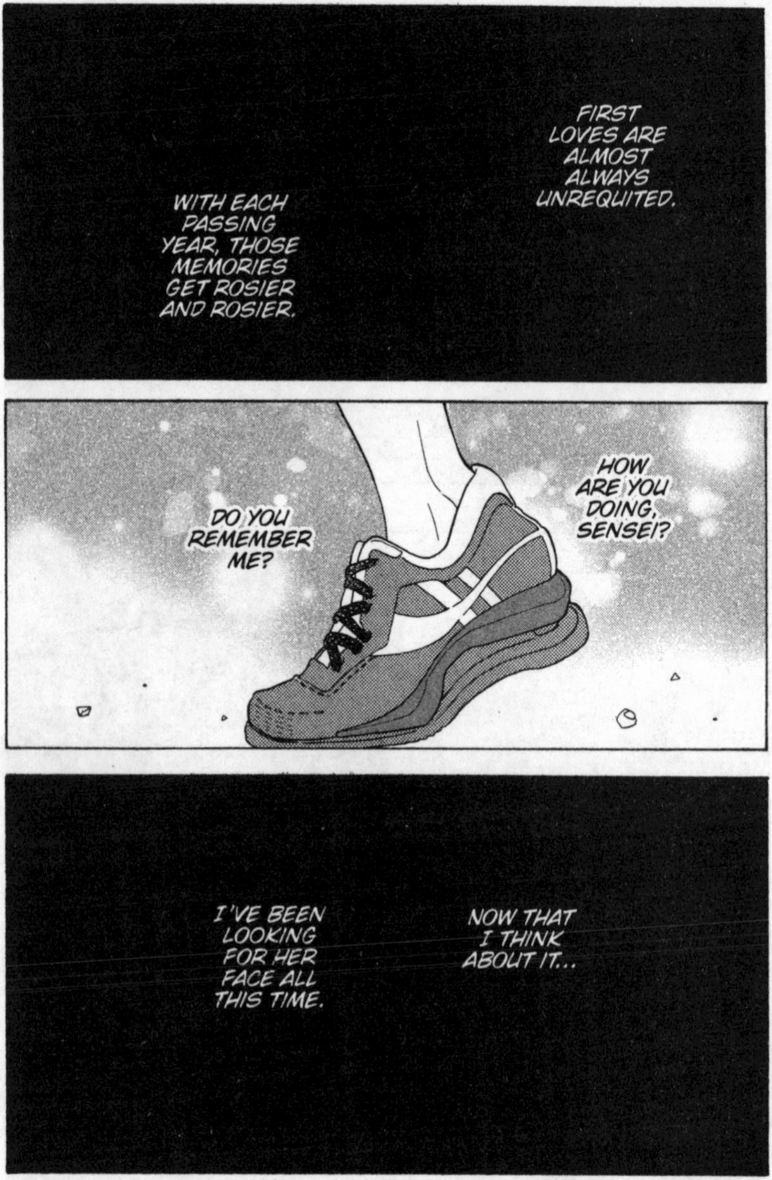
FIRST LOVES ARE ALMOST ALWAYS UNREQUITED.
WITH EACH PASSING YEAR, THOSE MEMORIES GET ROSIER AND ROSIER.
HOW ARE YOU DOING, SENSEI?
DO YOU REMEMBER ME?
NOW THAT I THINK ABOUT IT...
I'VE BEEN LOOKING FOR HER FACE ALL THIS TIME.

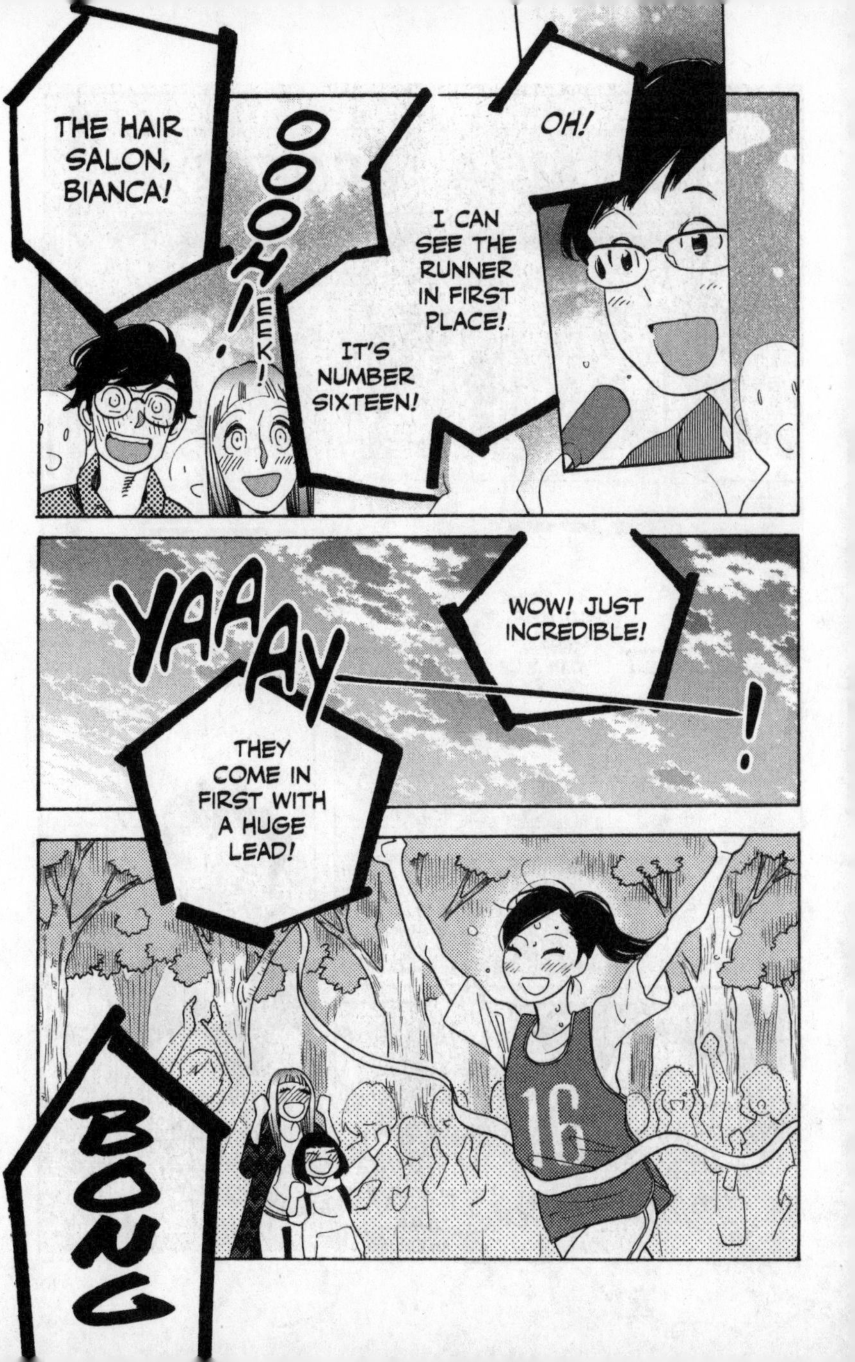
OH!
I CAN SEE THE RUNNER IN FIRST PLACE!
IT'S NUMBER SIXTEEN!
THE HAIR SALON, BIANCA!
OOOOH!
EEEK!
WOW! JUST INCREDIBLE!
YAAAAY!
THEY COME IN FIRST WITH A HUGE LEAD!
BONG

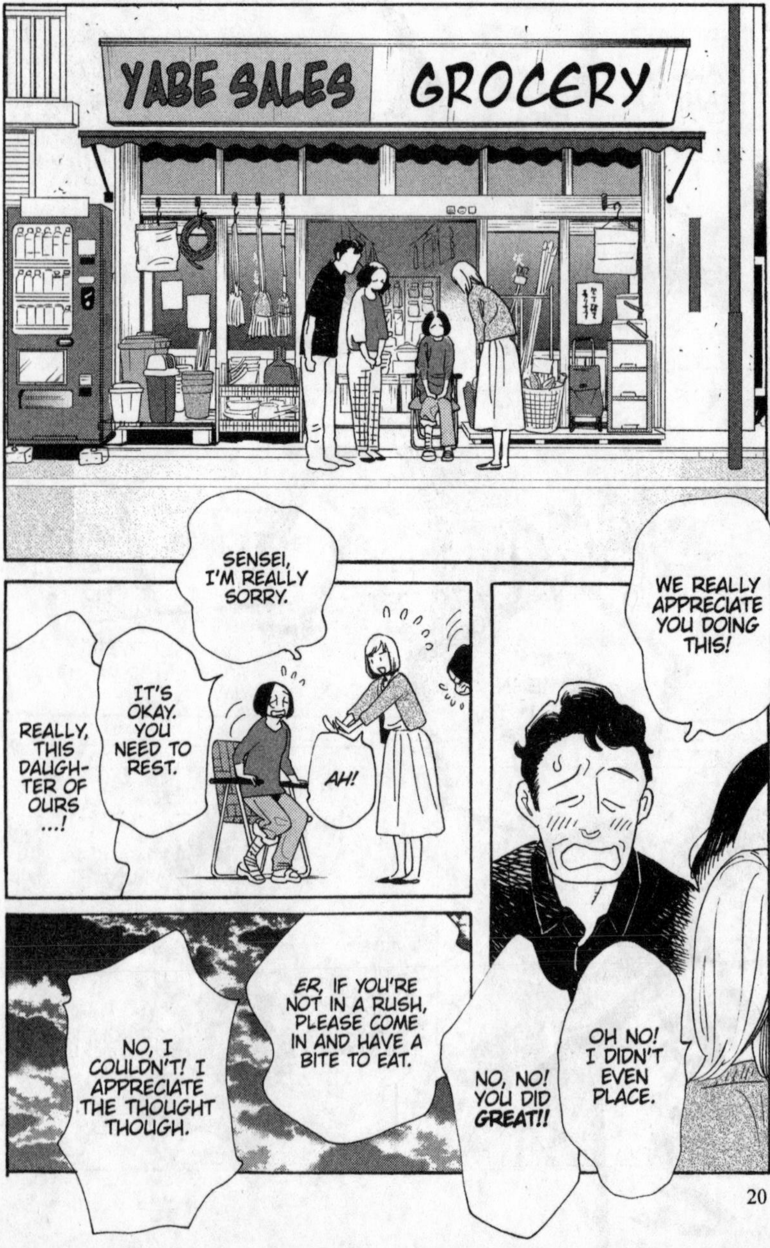
YABE SALES
GROCERY
WE REALLY APPRECIATE YOU DOING THIS!
SENSEI, I'M REALLY SORRY.
IT'S OKAY. YOU NEED TO REST.
AH!
REALLY, THIS DAUGHTER OF OURS ...!
OH NO! I DIDN'T EVEN PLACE.
NO, NO! YOU DID **GREAT!!**
ER, IF YOU'RE NOT IN A RUSH, PLEASE COME IN AND HAVE A BITE TO EAT.
NO, I COULDN'T! I APPRECIATE THE THOUGHT THOUGH.

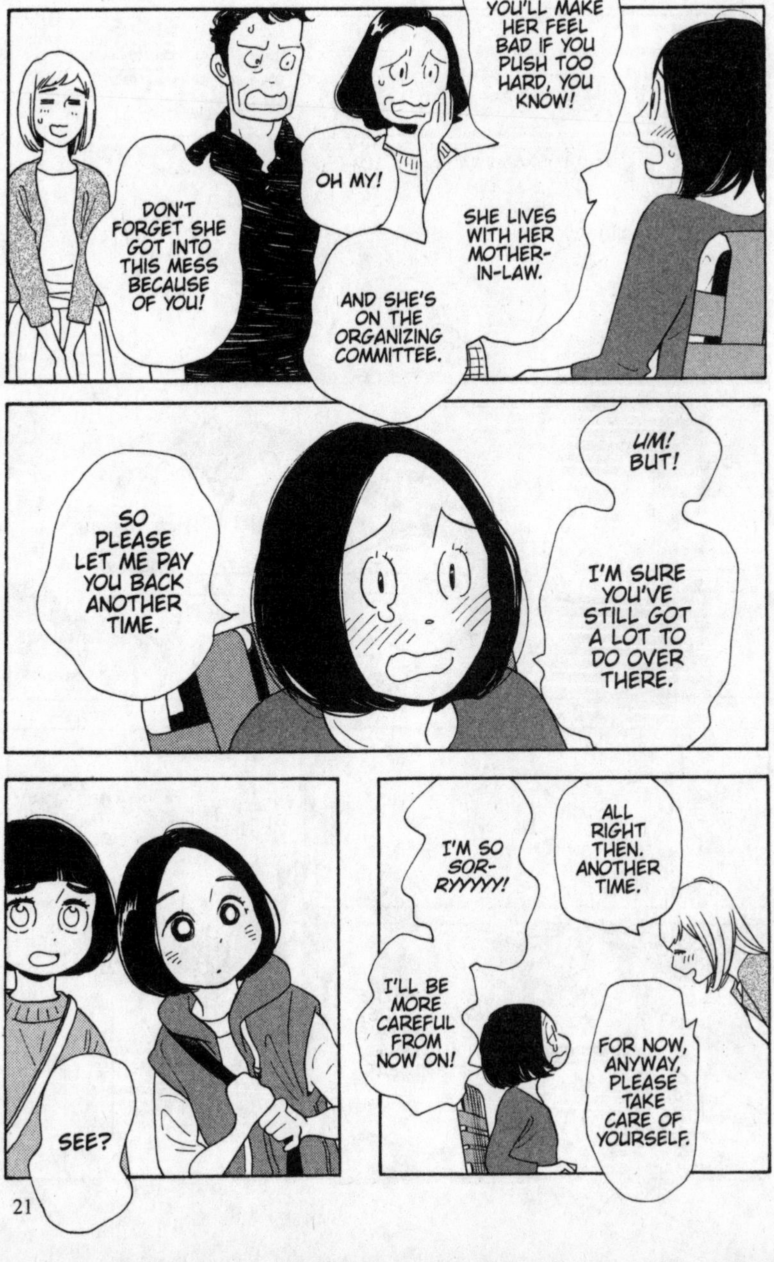
EXACTLY! YOU'LL MAKE HER FEEL BAD IF YOU PUSH TOO HARD, YOU KNOW!
SHE LIVES WITH HER MOTHER-IN-LAW.
AND SHE'S ON THE ORGANIZING COMMITTEE.
OH MY!
DON'T FORGET SHE GOT INTO THIS MESS BECAUSE OF YOU!
UM! BUT!
I'M SURE YOU'VE STILL GOT A LOT TO DO OVER THERE.
SO PLEASE LET ME PAY YOU BACK ANOTHER TIME.
ALL RIGHT THEN. ANOTHER TIME.
FOR NOW, ANYWAY, PLEASE TAKE CARE OF YOURSELF.
I'M SO *SOR-RYYYYY!*
I'LL BE MORE CAREFUL FROM NOW ON!
SEE?

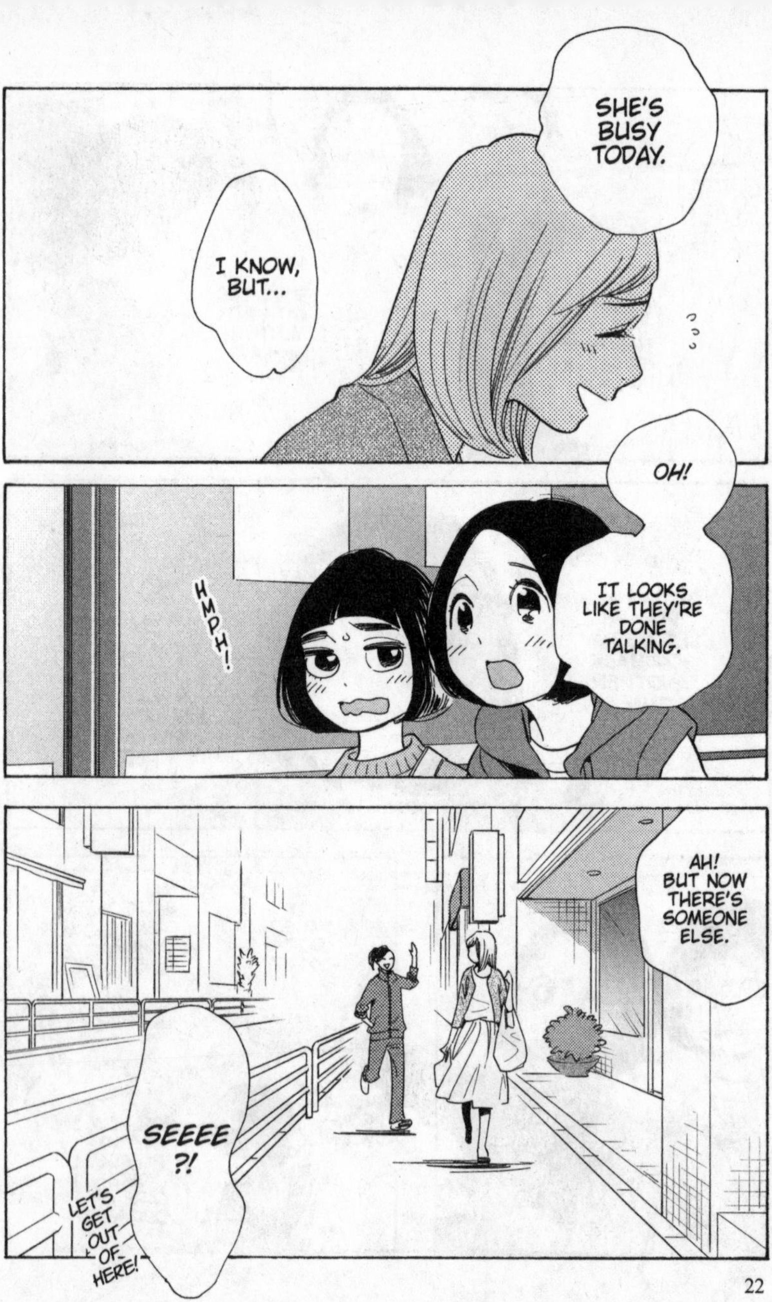
SHE'S BUSY TODAY.
I KNOW, BUT...
OH!
IT LOOKS LIKE THEY'RE DONE TALKING.
HMPH!
AH! BUT NOW THERE'S SOMEONE ELSE.
SEEEE?!
LET'S GET OUT OF HERE!

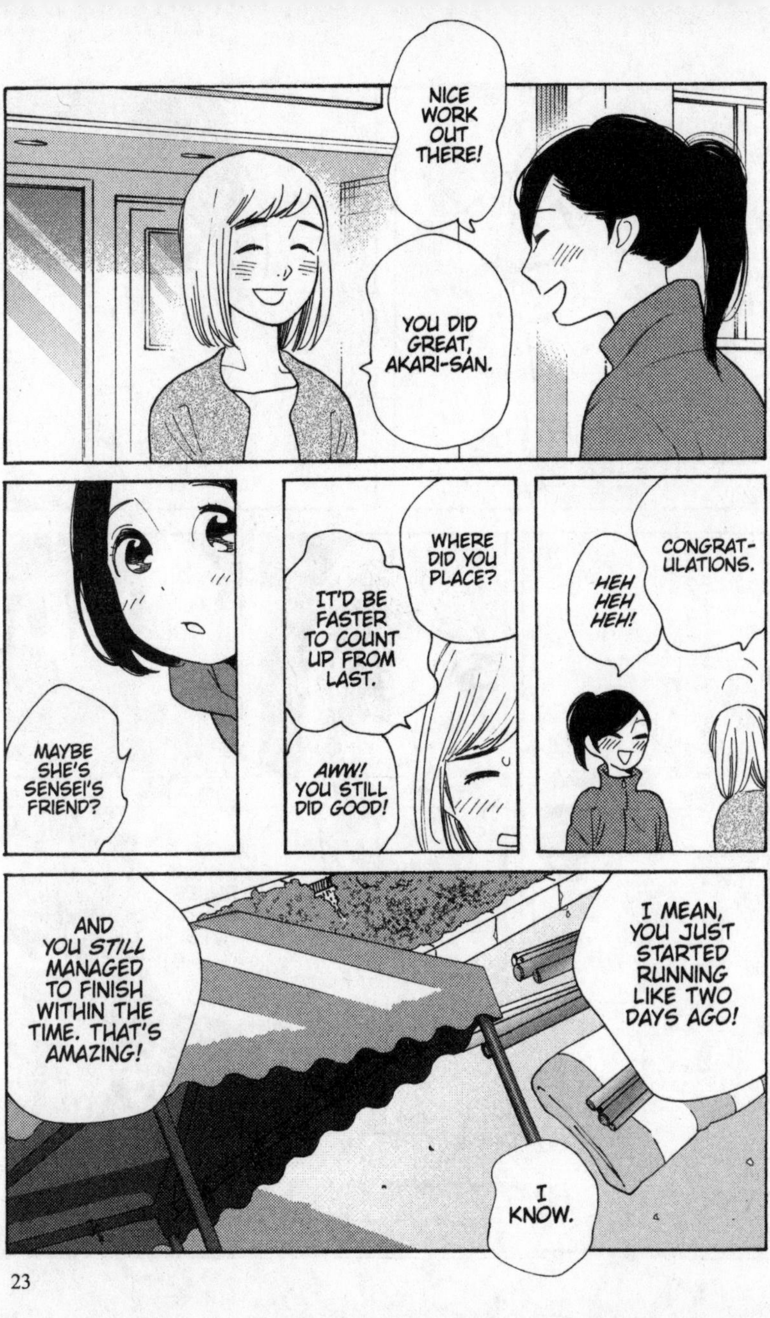
NICE WORK OUT THERE!
YOU DID GREAT, AKARI-SAN.
CONGRAT-ULATIONS.
HEH HEH HEH!
WHERE DID YOU PLACE?
IT'D BE FASTER TO COUNT UP FROM LAST.
AWW! YOU STILL DID GOOD!
MAYBE SHE'S SENSEI'S FRIEND?
I MEAN, YOU JUST STARTED RUNNING LIKE TWO DAYS AGO!
AND YOU STILL MANAGED TO FINISH WITHIN THE TIME. THAT'S AMAZING!
I KNOW.

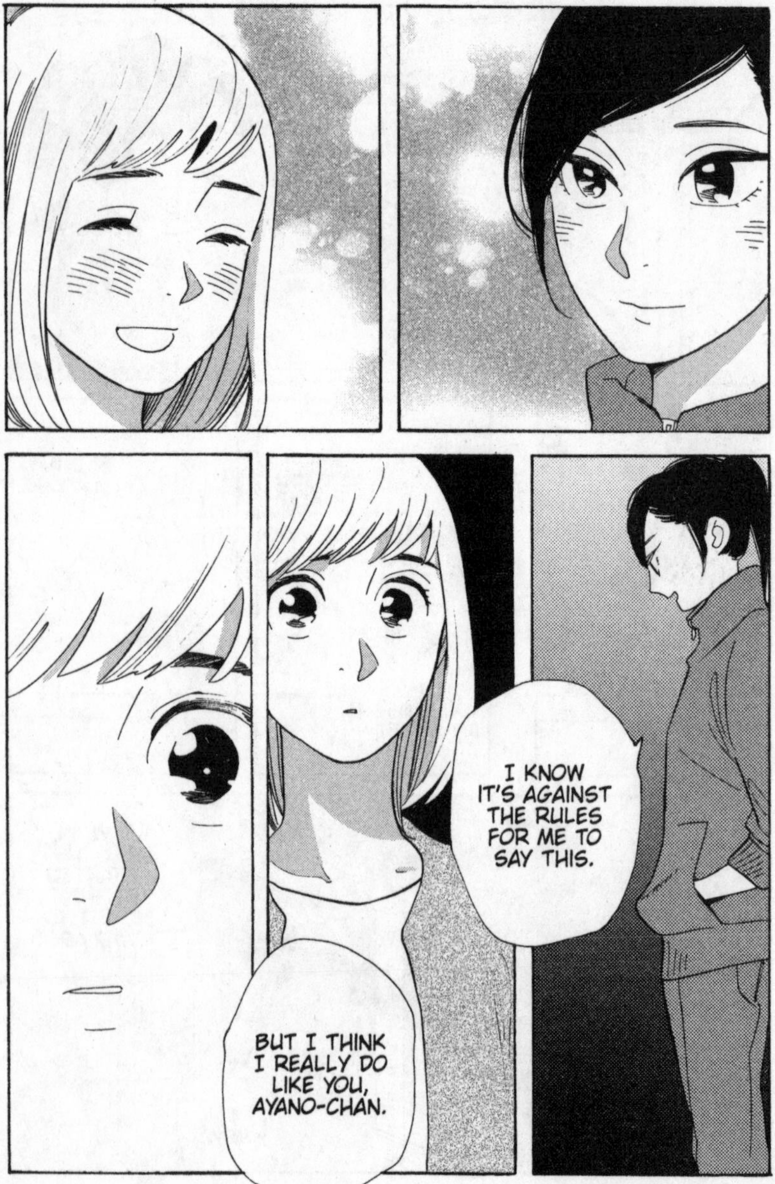
I KNOW IT'S AGAINST THE RULES FOR ME TO SAY THIS.
BUT I THINK I REALLY DO LIKE YOU, AYANO-CHAN.

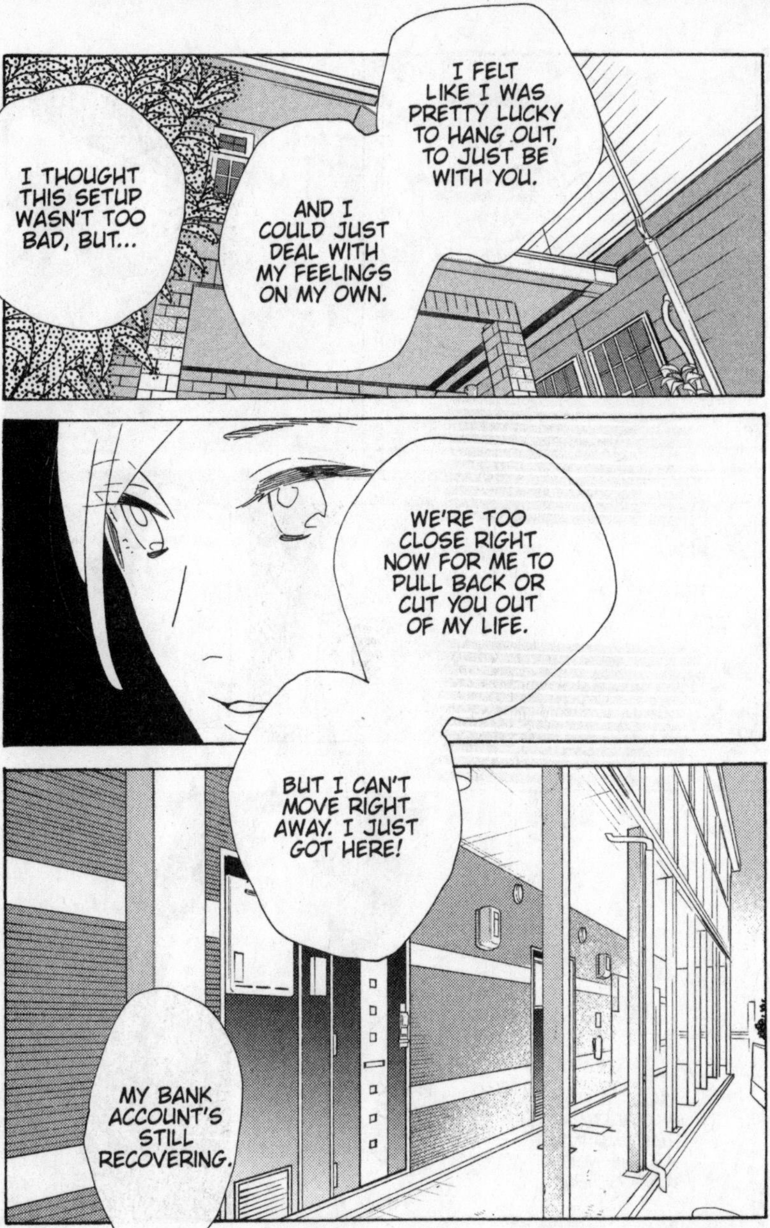
I FELT LIKE I WAS PRETTY LUCKY TO HANG OUT, TO JUST BE WITH YOU.
AND I COULD JUST DEAL WITH MY FEELINGS ON MY OWN.
I THOUGHT THIS SETUP WASN'T TOO BAD, BUT...
WE'RE TOO CLOSE RIGHT NOW FOR ME TO PULL BACK OR CUT YOU OUT OF MY LIFE.
BUT I CAN'T MOVE RIGHT AWAY. I JUST GOT HERE!
MY BANK ACCOUNT'S STILL RECOVERING.

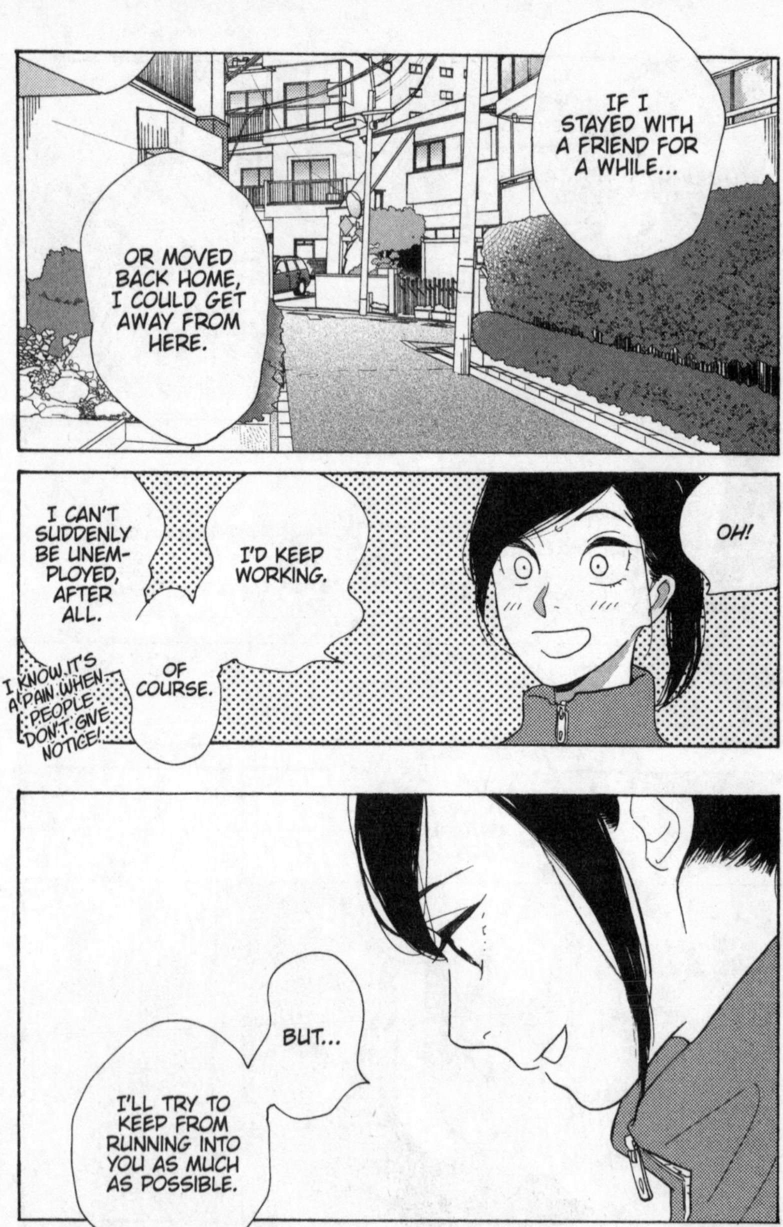
IF I STAYED WITH A FRIEND FOR A WHILE...
OR MOVED BACK HOME, I COULD GET AWAY FROM HERE.
OH!
I'D KEEP WORKING.
I CAN'T SUDDENLY BE UNEMPLOYED, AFTER ALL.
OF COURSE.
I KNOW IT'S A PAIN WHEN PEOPLE DON'T GIVE NOTICE!
BUT...
I'LL TRY TO KEEP FROM RUNNING INTO YOU AS MUCH AS POSSIBLE.

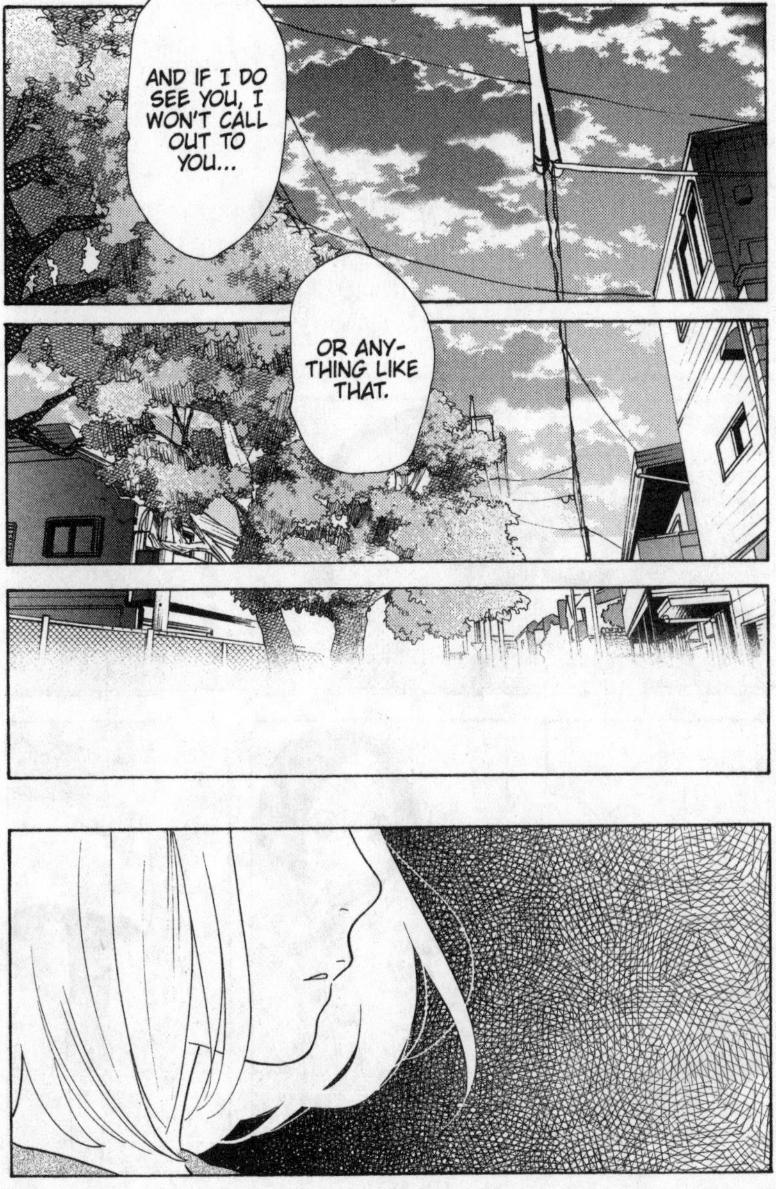
AND IF I DO SEE YOU, I WON'T CALL OUT TO YOU...
OR ANYTHING LIKE THAT.

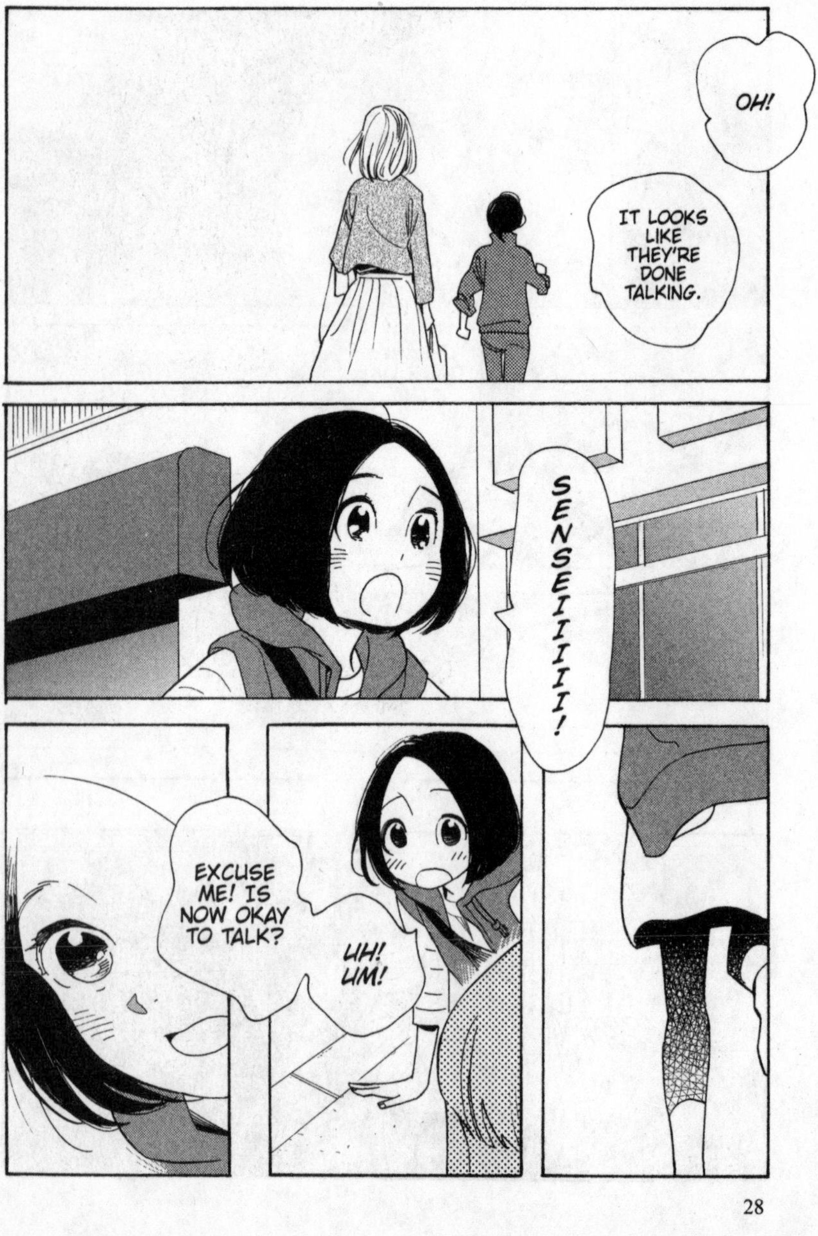
OH!
IT LOOKS LIKE THEY'RE DONE TALKING.
SENSEIIIIII!
EXCUSE ME! IS NOW OKAY TO TALK?
UH! UM!

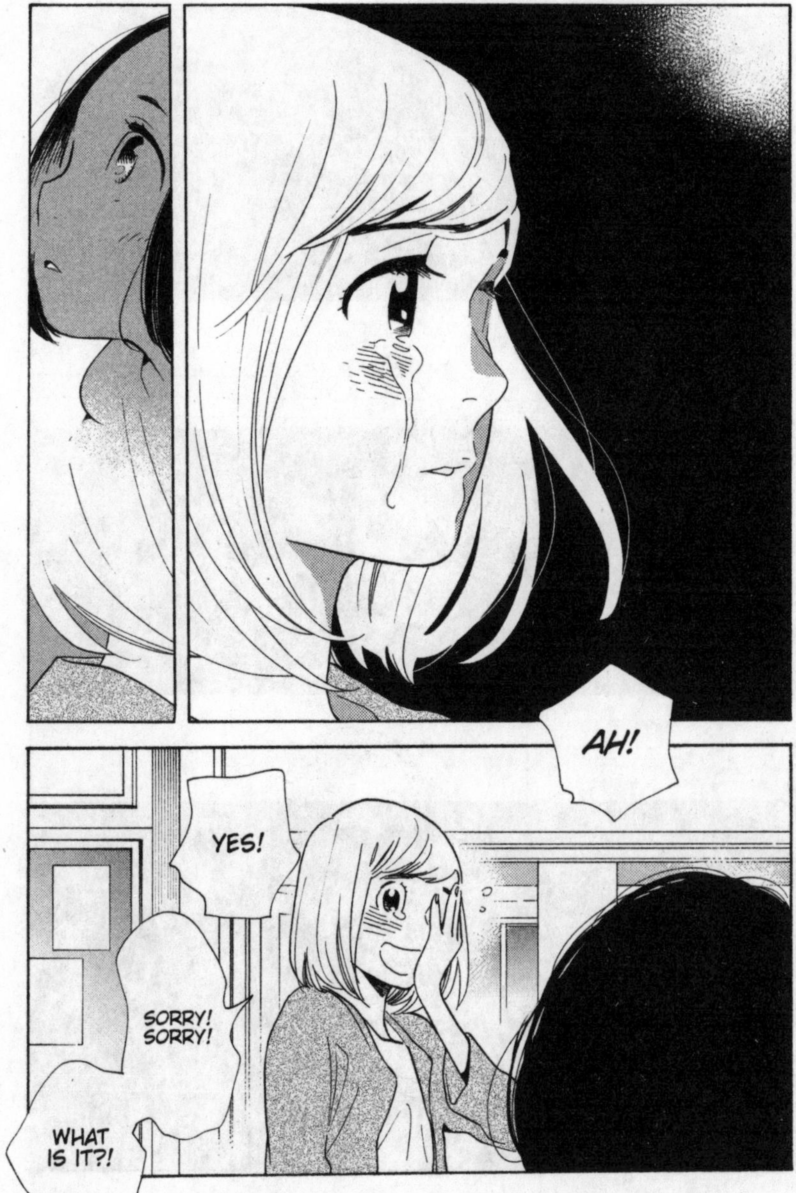
AH!
YES!
SORRY! SORRY!
WHAT IS IT?!

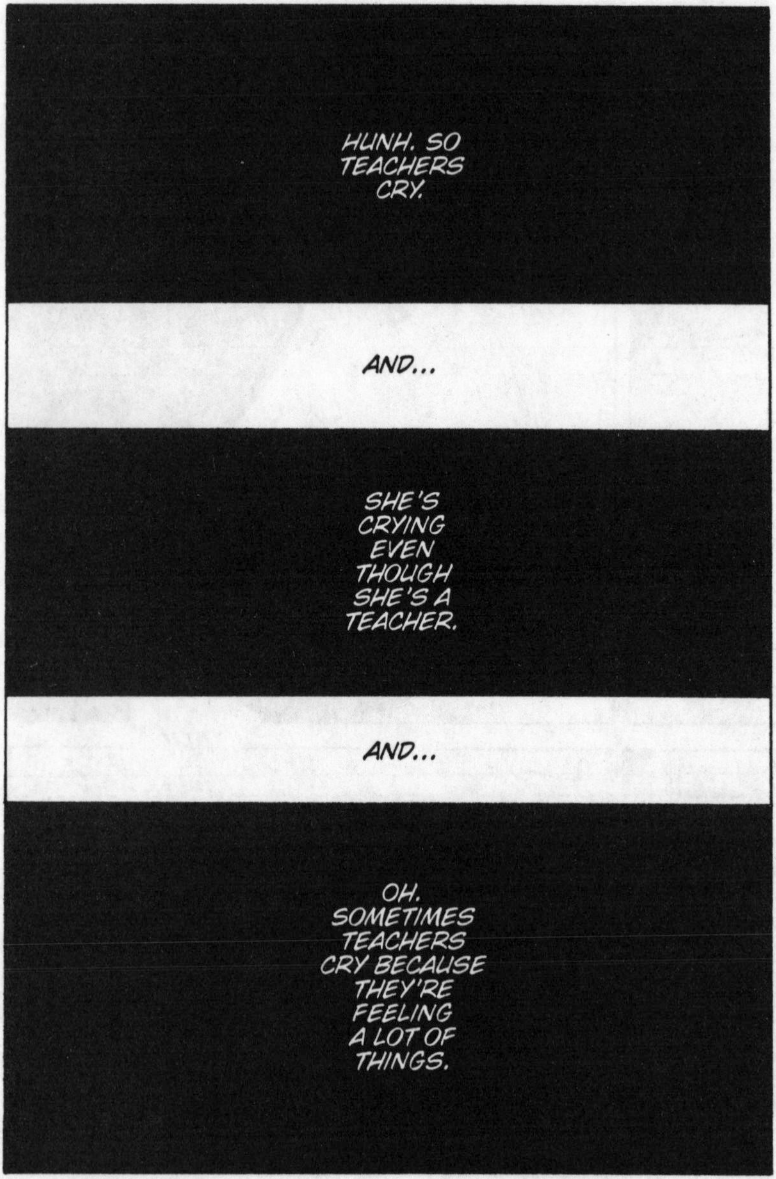
HUNH. SO TEACHERS CRY.
AND...
SHE'S CRYING EVEN THOUGH SHE'S A TEACHER.
AND...
OH. SOMETIMES TEACHERS CRY BECAUSE THEY'RE FEELING A LOT OF THINGS.

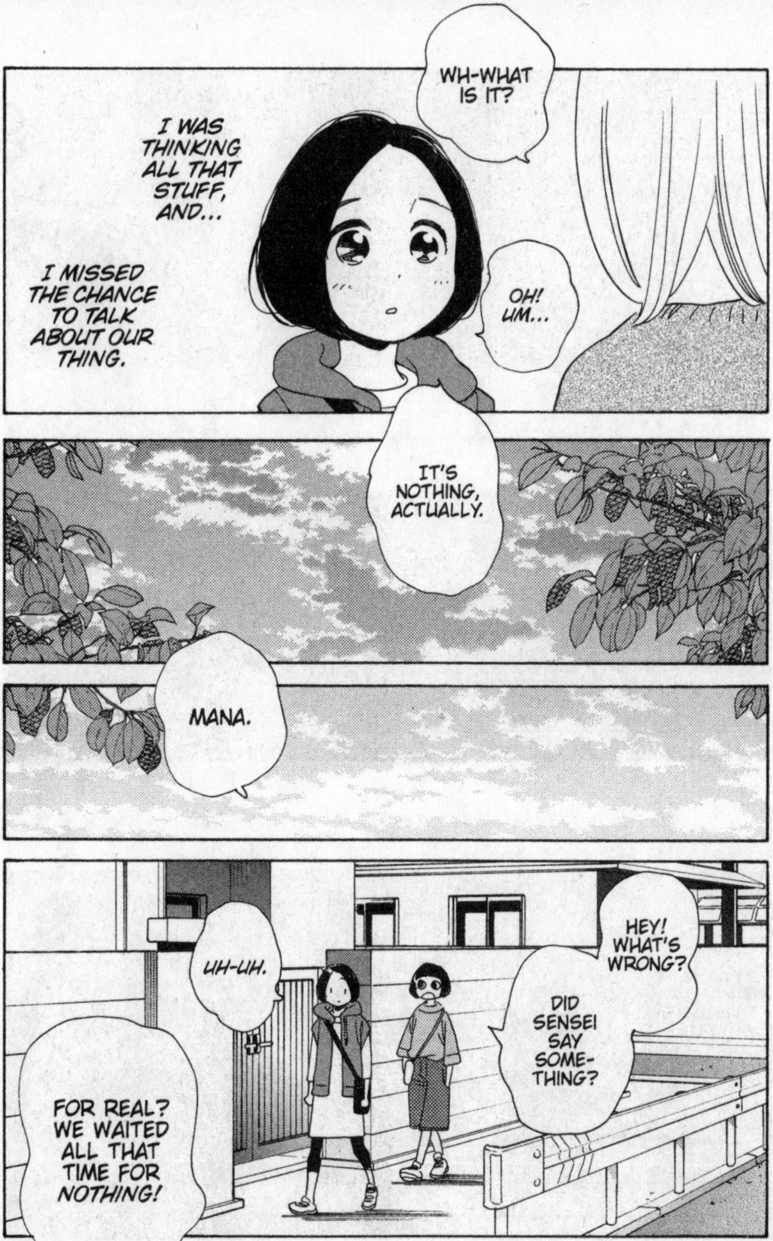
WH-WHAT IS IT?
I WAS THINKING ALL THAT STUFF, AND...
OH! UM...
I MISSED THE CHANCE TO TALK ABOUT OUR THING.
IT'S NOTHING, ACTUALLY.
MANA.
HEY! WHAT'S WRONG?
DID SENSEI SAY SOME-THING?
UH-UH.
FOR REAL? WE WAITED ALL THAT TIME FOR NOTHING!

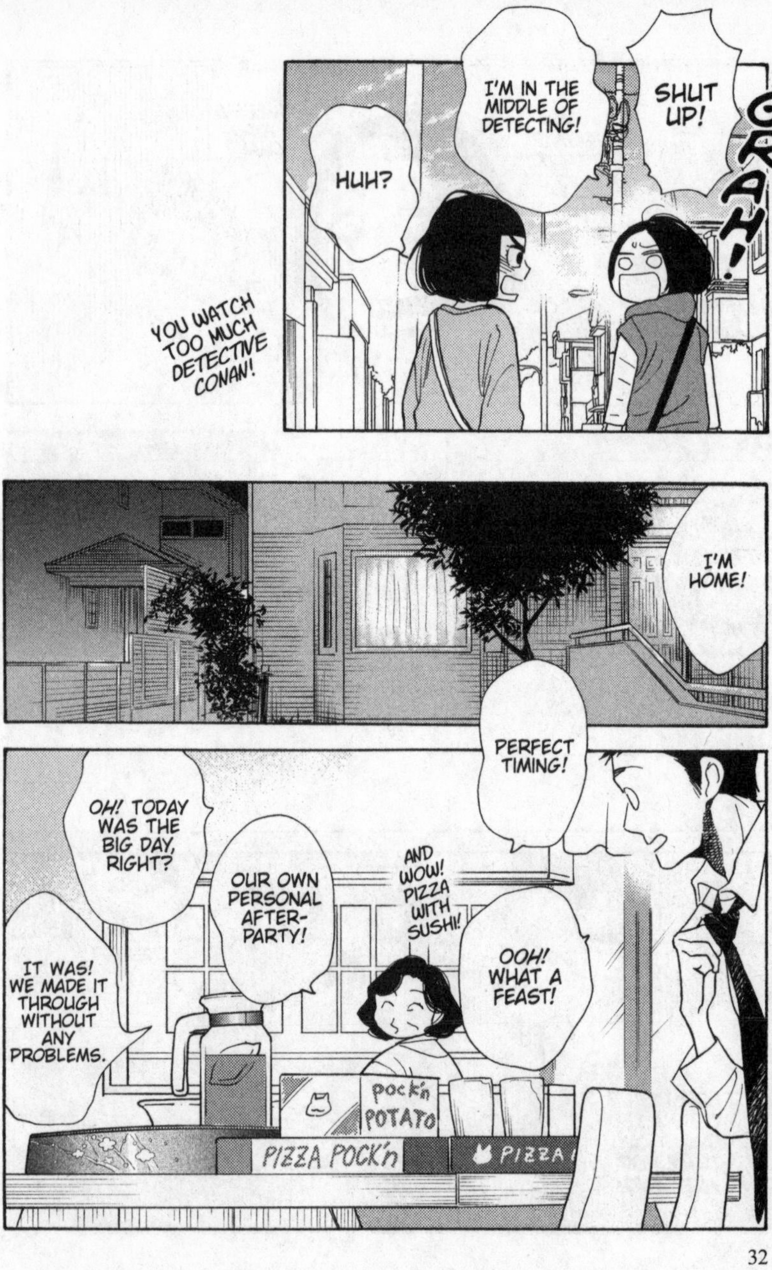
GRAH!
SHUT UP!
I'M IN THE MIDDLE OF DETECTING!
HUH?
YOU WATCH TOO MUCH DETECTIVE CONAN!
I'M HOME!
PERFECT TIMING!
OOH! WHAT A FEAST!
AND WOW! PIZZA WITH SUSHI!
OUR OWN PERSONAL AFTER-PARTY!
OH! TODAY WAS THE BIG DAY, RIGHT?
IT WAS! WE MADE IT THROUGH WITHOUT ANY PROBLEMS.
pock'n POTATO
PIZZA POCK'n
PIZZA

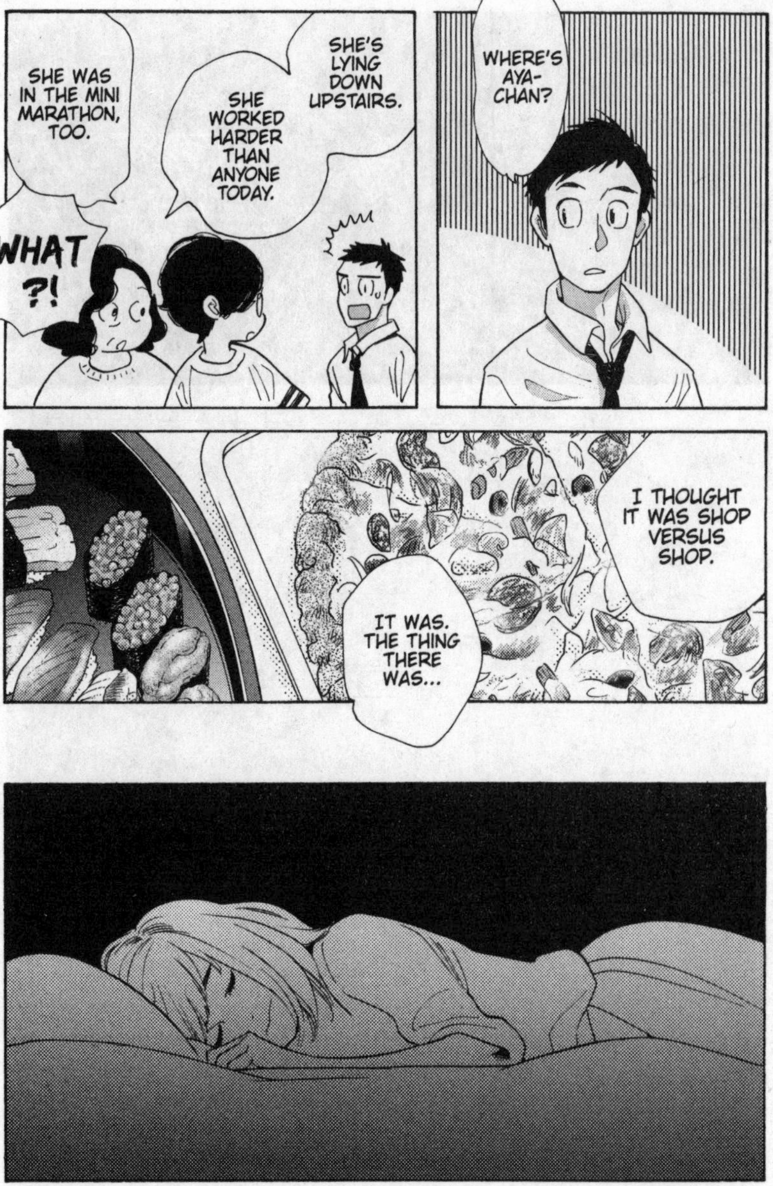
WHERE'S AYA-CHAN?
SHE'S LYING DOWN UPSTAIRS.
SHE WORKED HARDER THAN ANYONE TODAY.
SHE WAS IN THE MINI MARATHON, TOO.
WHAT?!
I THOUGHT IT WAS SHOP VERSUS SHOP.
IT WAS. THE THING THERE WAS...

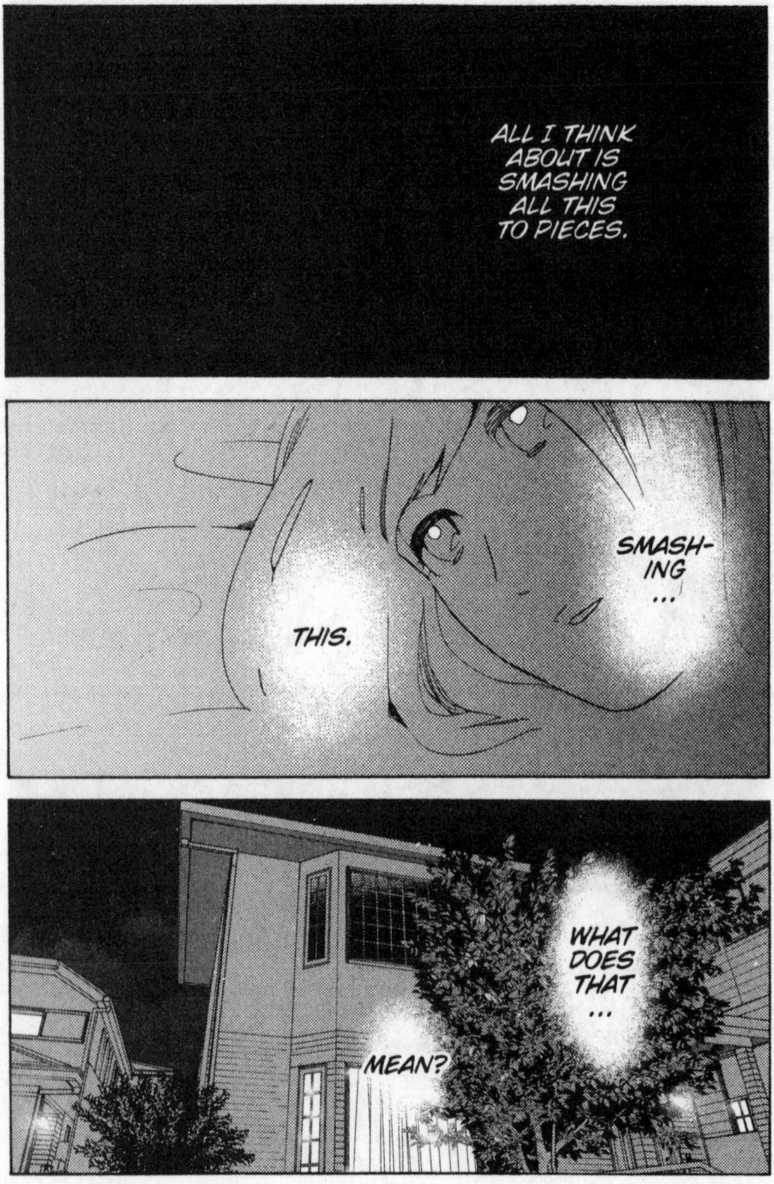
ALL I THINK ABOUT IS SMASHING ALL THIS TO PIECES.
SMASHING ...
THIS.
WHAT DOES THAT ...
MEAN?

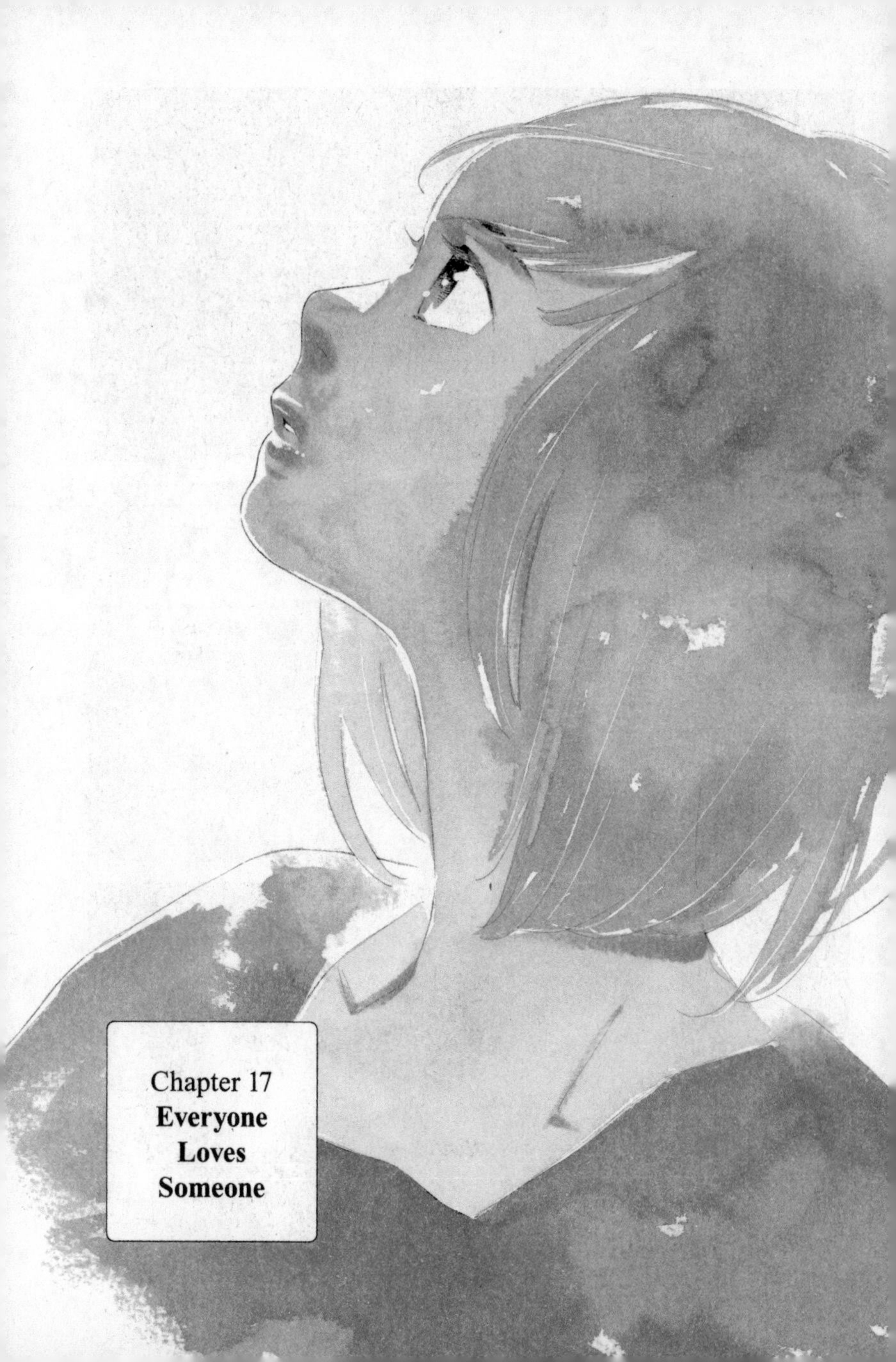
Chapter 17
Everyone Loves Someone

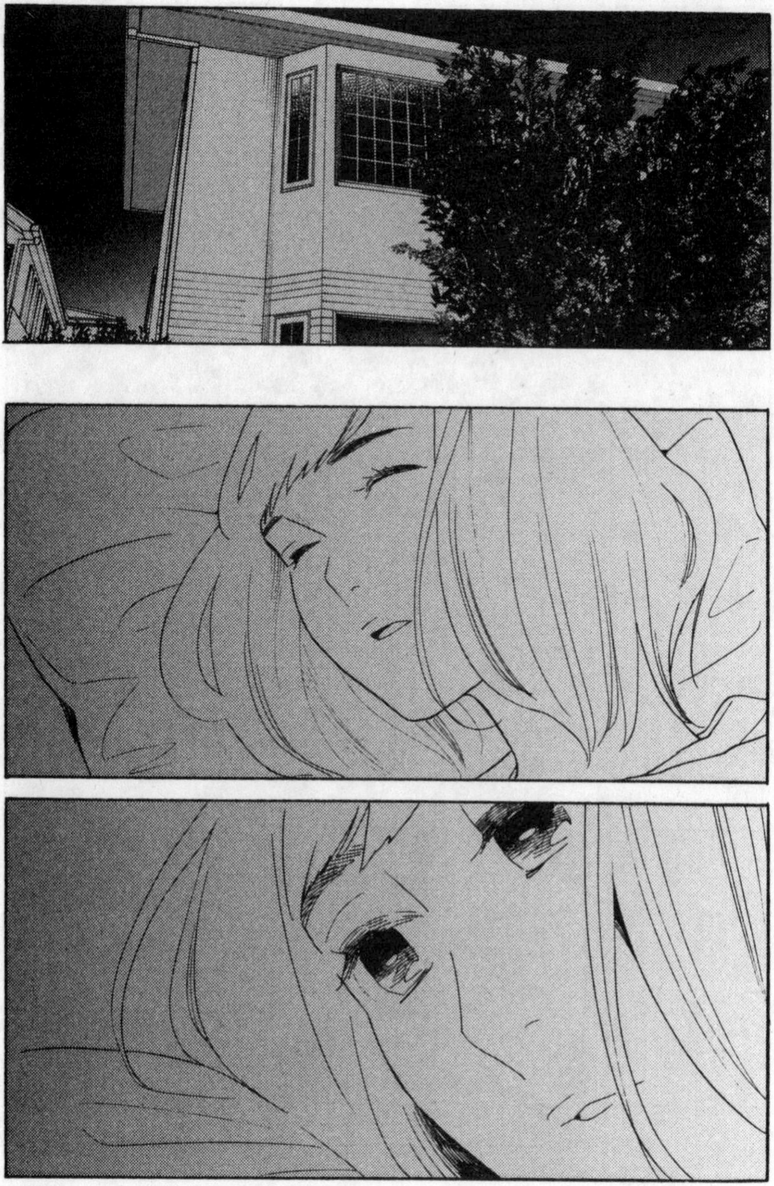

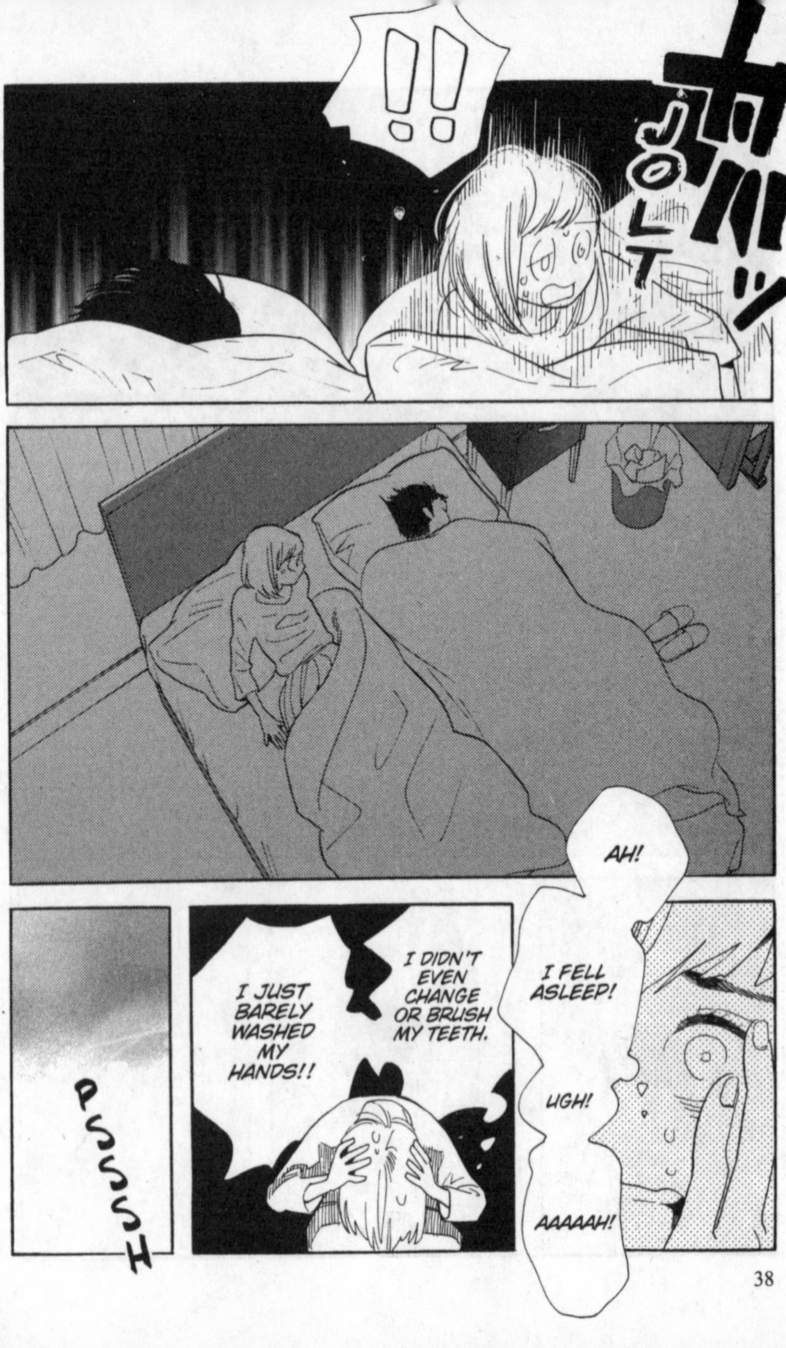
ガバッ
JOLT
!!
AH!
I FELL ASLEEP!
UGH!
AAAAAH!
I DIDN'T EVEN CHANGE OR BRUSH MY TEETH.
I JUST BARELY WASHED MY HANDS!!
PSSSH

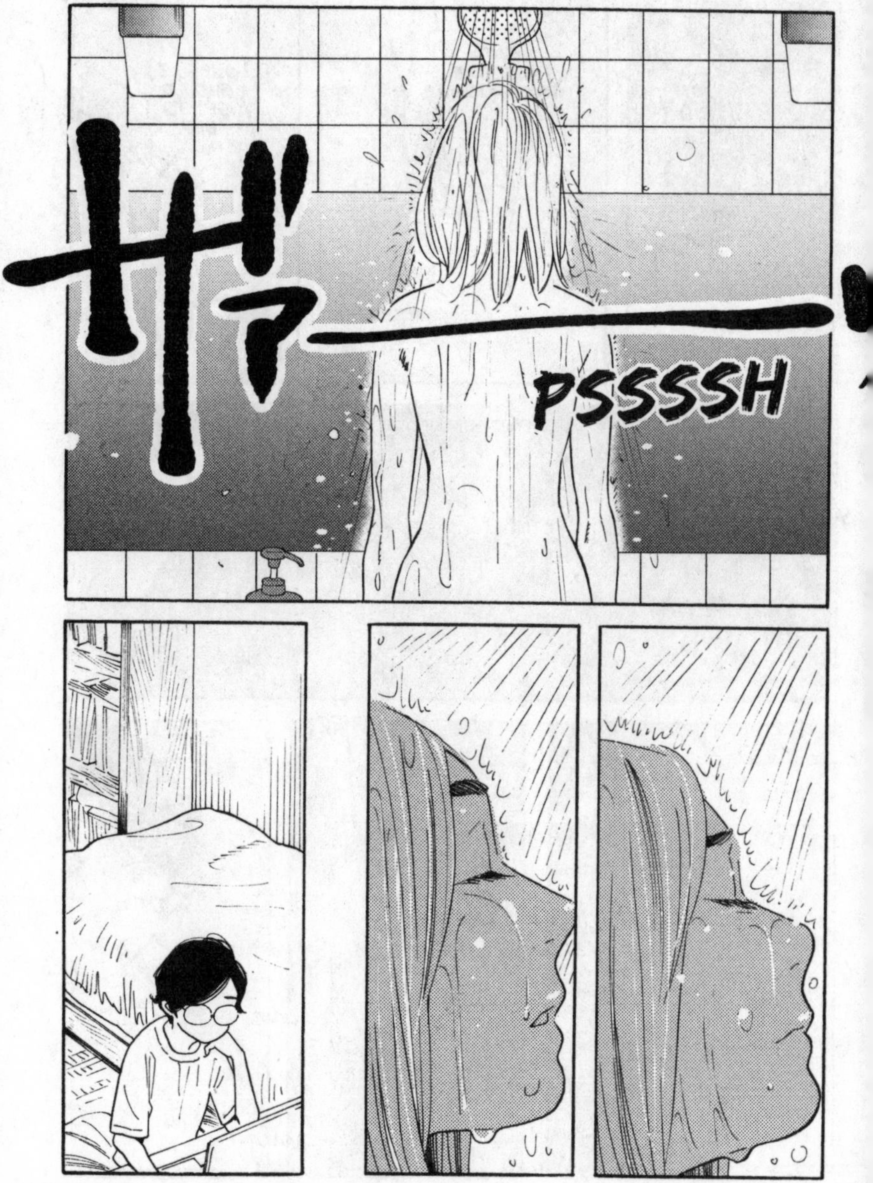
ザァ――
PSSSSH

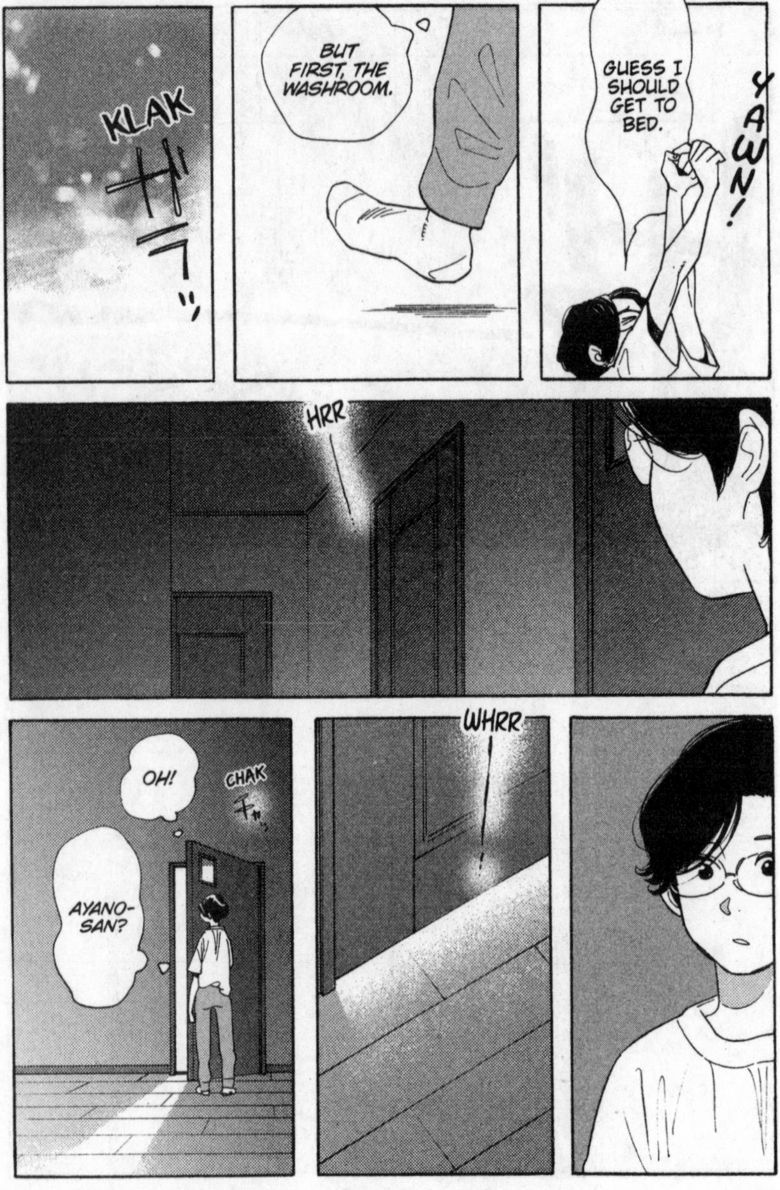
GUESS I SHOULD GET TO BED.
YAWN!
BUT FIRST, THE WASHROOM.
KLAK
HRR
WHRR
CHAK
OH!
AYANO-SAN?

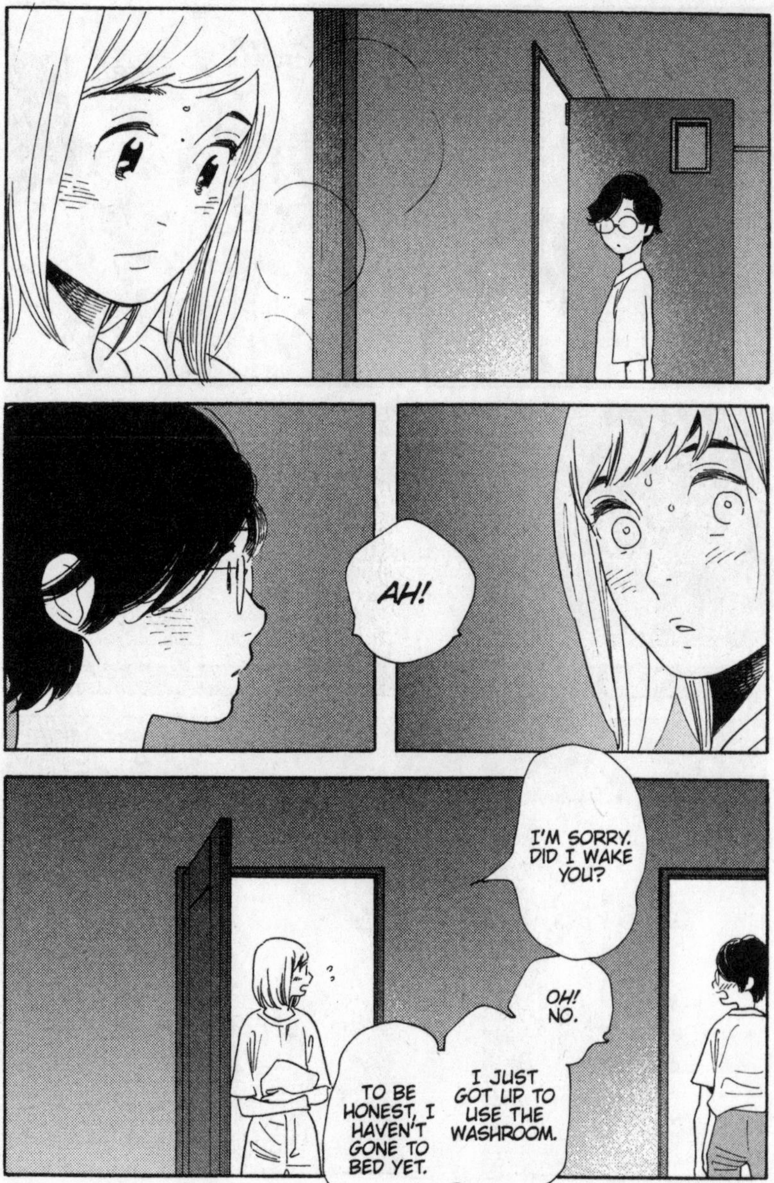
AH!
I'M SORRY. DID I WAKE YOU?
OH! NO.
I JUST GOT UP TO USE THE WASHROOM.
TO BE HONEST, I HAVEN'T GONE TO BED YET.

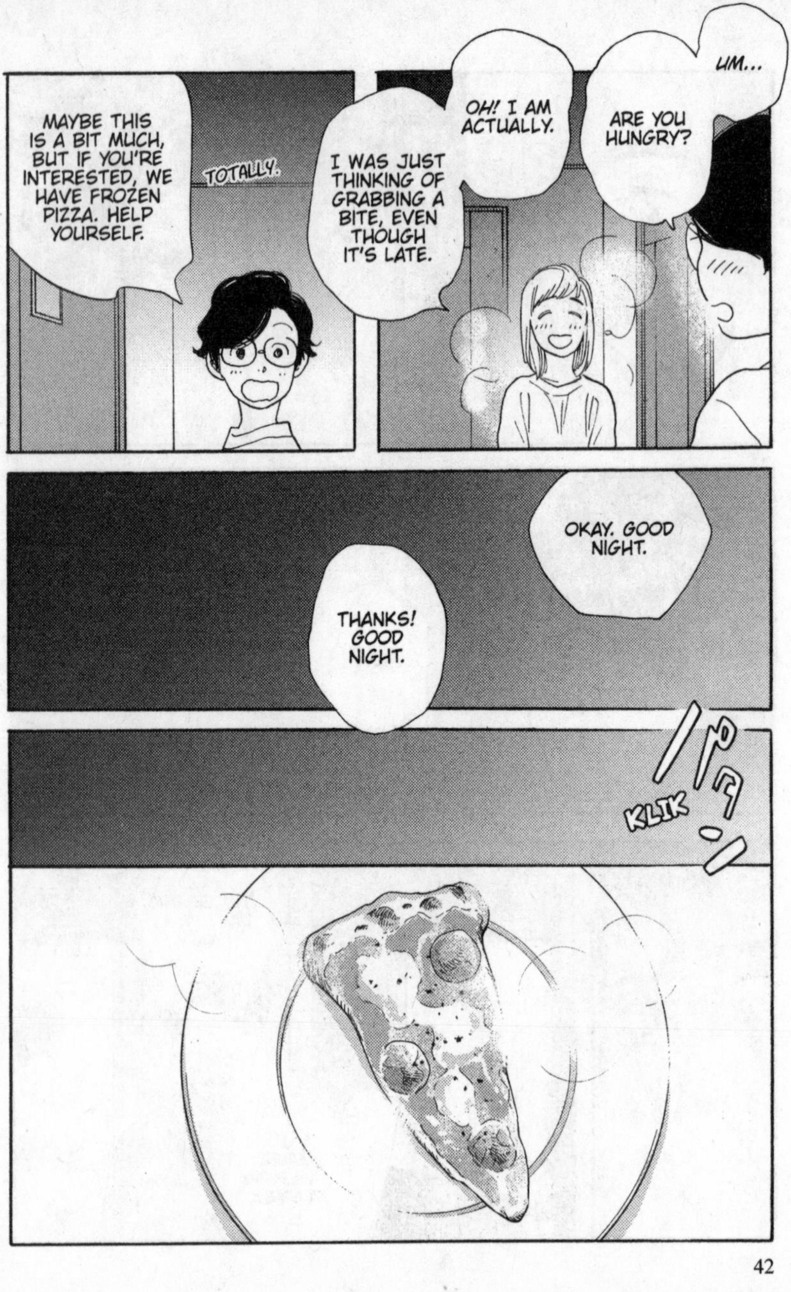
UM...
ARE YOU HUNGRY?
OH! I AM ACTUALLY.
I WAS JUST THINKING OF GRABBING A BITE, EVEN THOUGH IT'S LATE.
MAYBE THIS IS A BIT MUCH, BUT IF YOU'RE INTERESTED, WE HAVE FROZEN PIZZA. HELP YOURSELF.
TOTALLY.
OKAY. GOOD NIGHT.
THANKS! GOOD NIGHT.
KLIK

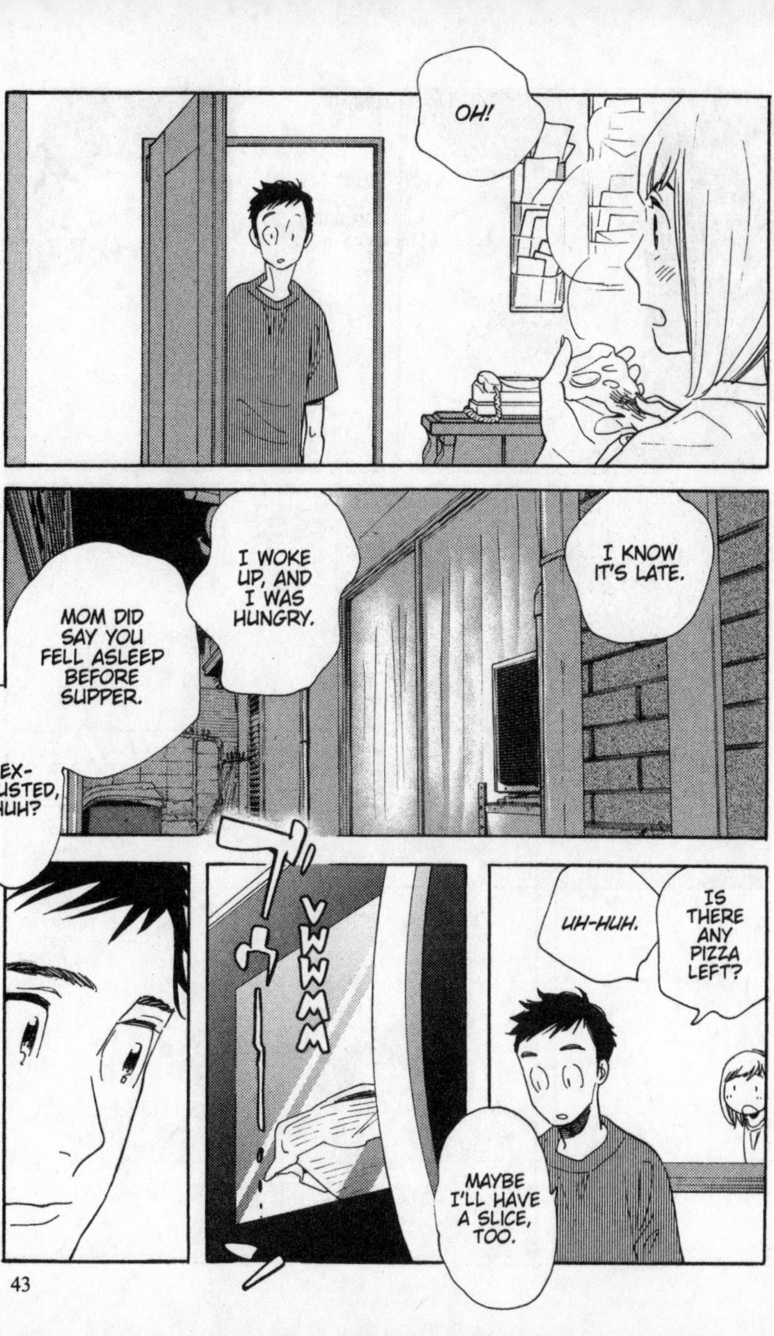
OH!
I KNOW IT'S LATE.
I WOKE UP, AND I WAS HUNGRY.
MOM DID SAY YOU FELL ASLEEP BEFORE SUPPER.
EX-HAUSTED, HUH?
IS THERE ANY PIZZA LEFT?
UH-HUH.
MAYBE I'LL HAVE A SLICE, TOO.
VWWWMM

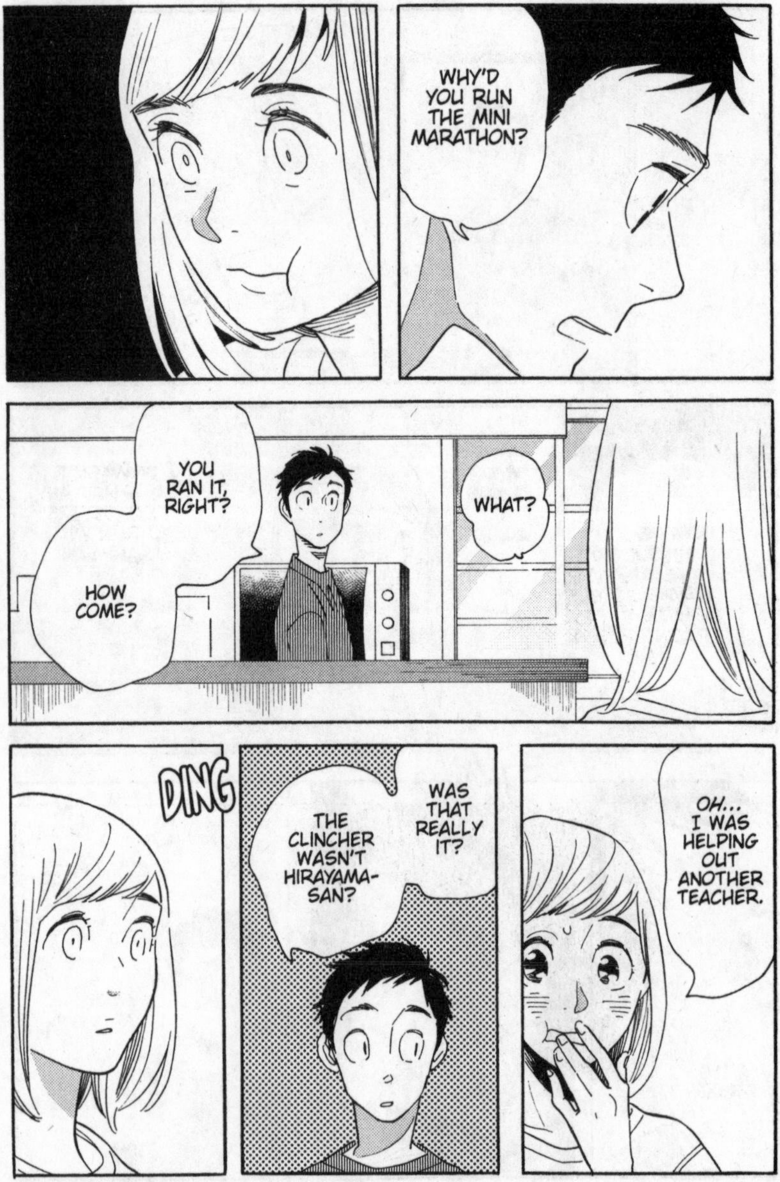
WHY'D YOU RUN THE MINI MARATHON?
WHAT?
YOU RAN IT, RIGHT?
HOW COME?
OH... I WAS HELPING OUT ANOTHER TEACHER.
WAS THAT REALLY IT?
THE CLINCHER WASN'T HIRAYAMA-SAN?
DING

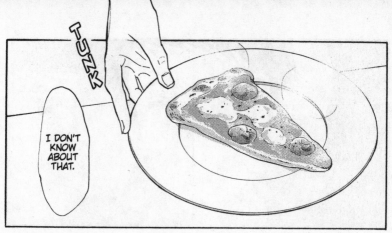

I DON'T KNOW ABOUT THAT.

IT WASN'T LIKE I HAD ANY REAL DESIRE TO RUN WITH AKARI-SAN.

BUT I DID FEEL RELIEVED MAYBE, TO SEE A FAMILIAR FACE RACING BESIDE ME.

MM-HMM.

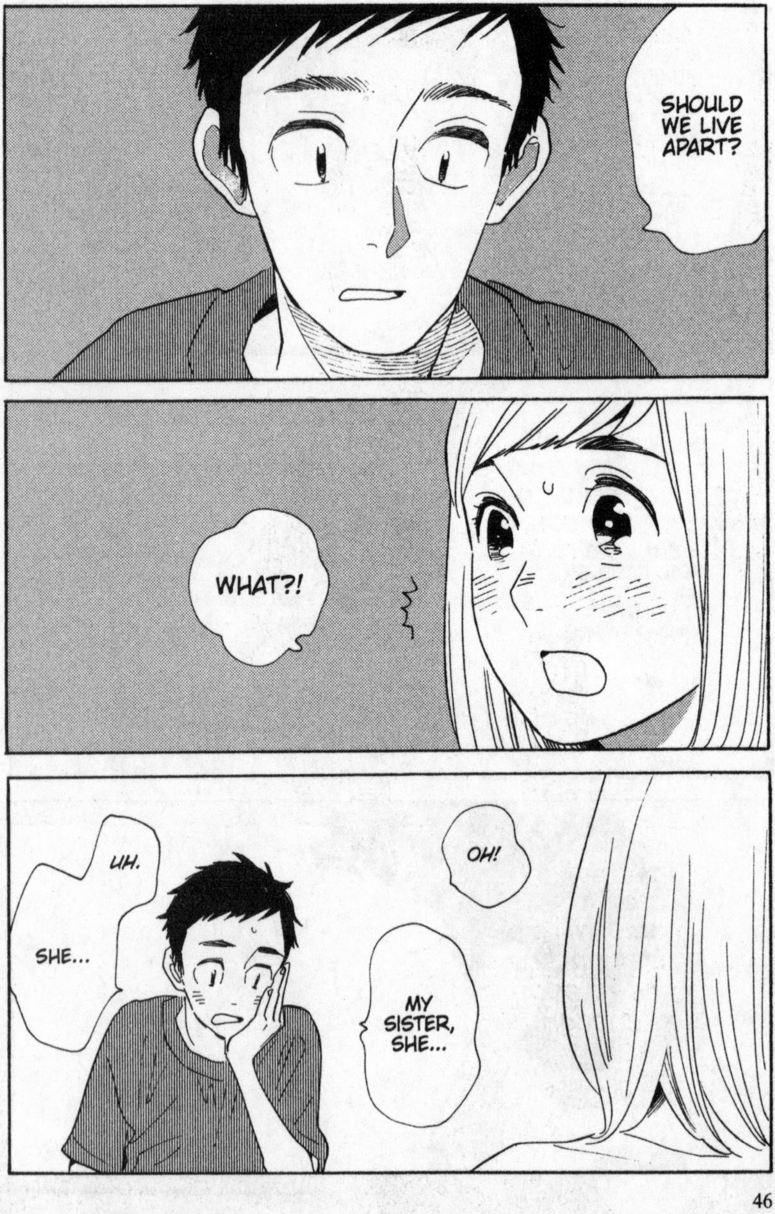
SHOULD WE LIVE APART?
WHAT?!
OH!
UH.
SHE...
MY SISTER, SHE...

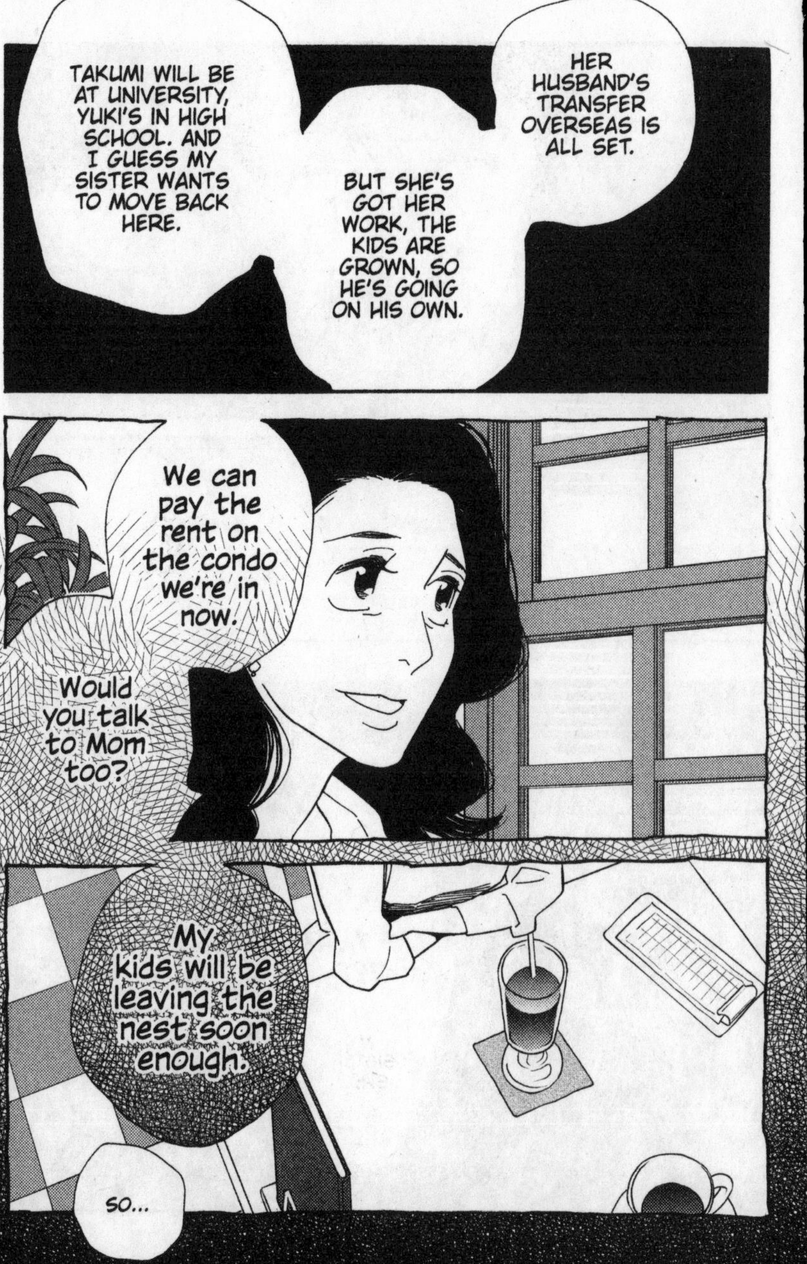
HER HUSBAND'S TRANSFER OVERSEAS IS ALL SET.
BUT SHE'S GOT HER WORK, THE KIDS ARE GROWN, SO HE'S GOING ON HIS OWN.
TAKUMI WILL BE AT UNIVERSITY, YUKI'S IN HIGH SCHOOL. AND I GUESS MY SISTER WANTS TO MOVE BACK HERE.
We can pay the rent on the condo we're in now.
Would you talk to Mom too?
My kids will be leaving the nest soon enough.
SO...

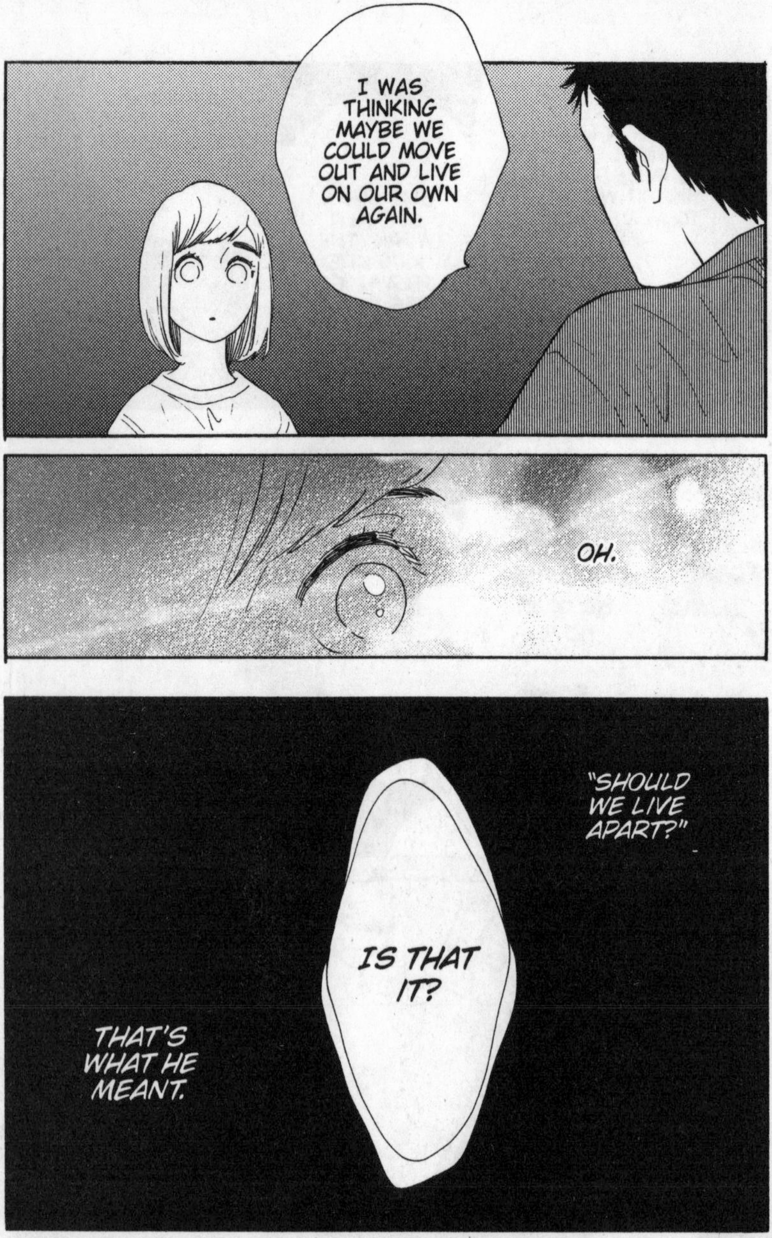
I WAS THINKING MAYBE WE COULD MOVE OUT AND LIVE ON OUR OWN AGAIN.
OH.
"SHOULD WE LIVE APART?"
IS THAT IT?
THAT'S WHAT HE MEANT.

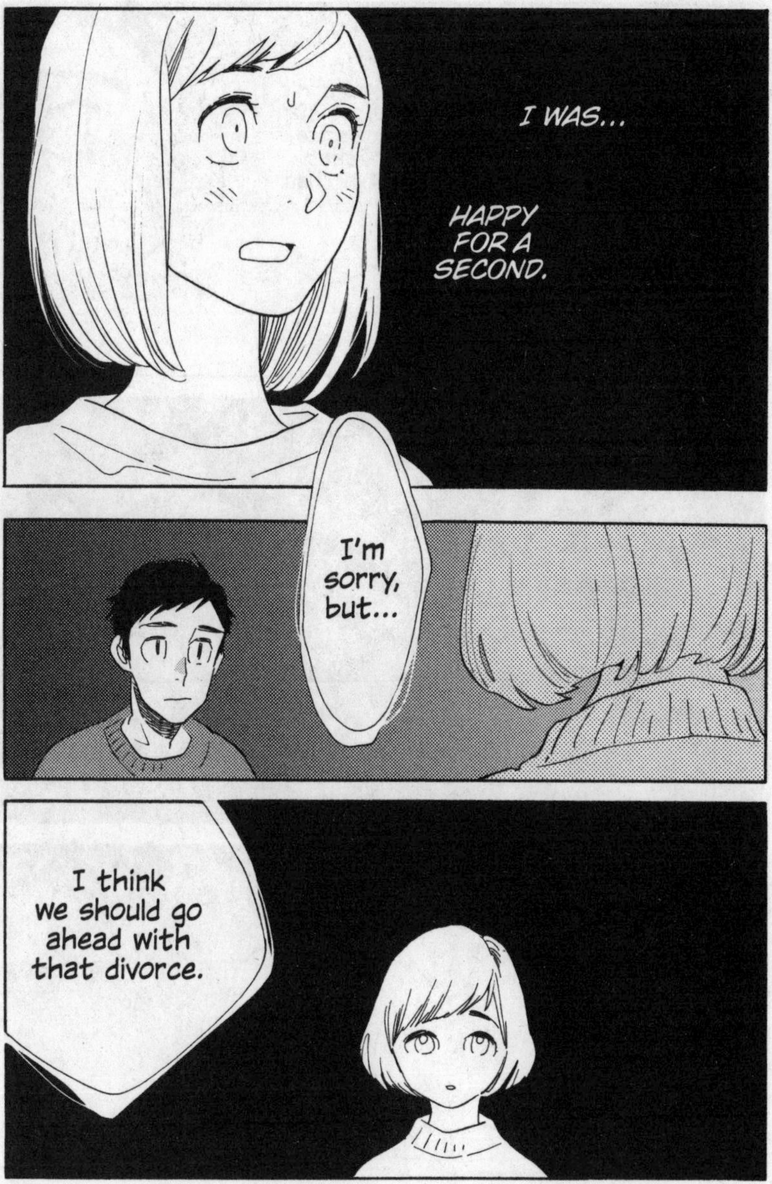
I WAS...
HAPPY FOR A SECOND.
I'm sorry, but...
I think we should go ahead with that divorce.

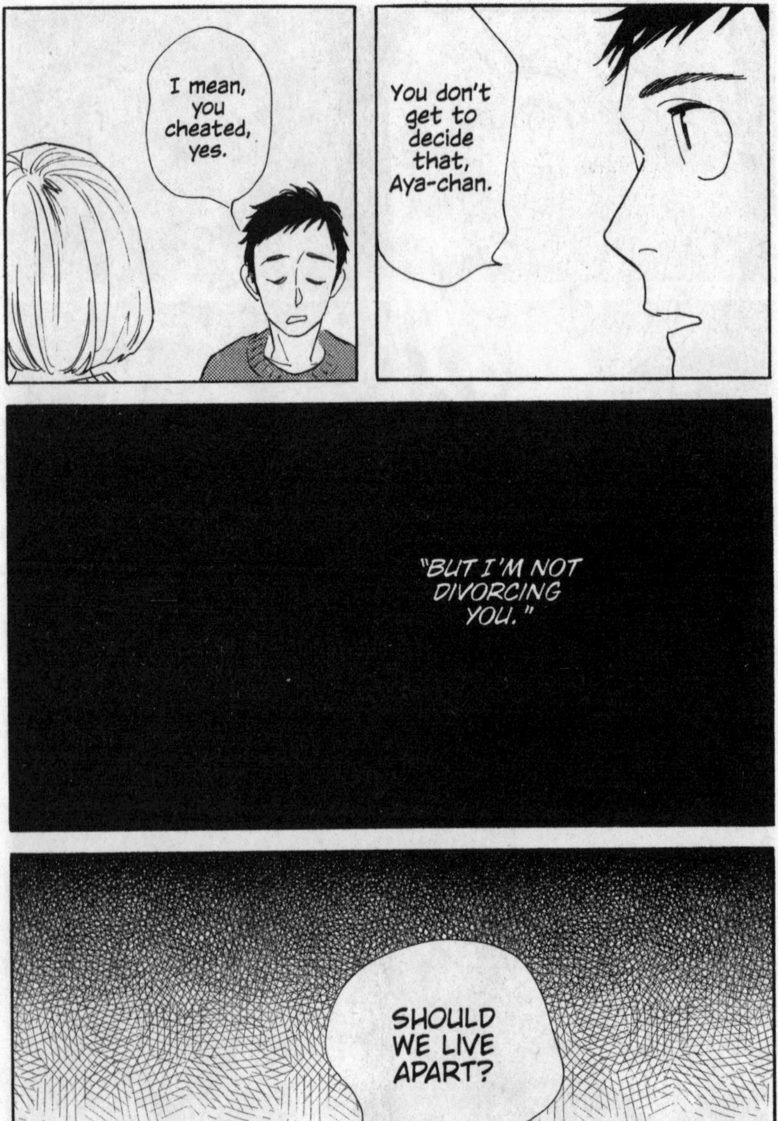
You don't get to decide that, Aya-chan.
I mean, you cheated, yes.
"BUT I'M NOT DIVORCING YOU."
SHOULD WE LIVE APART?

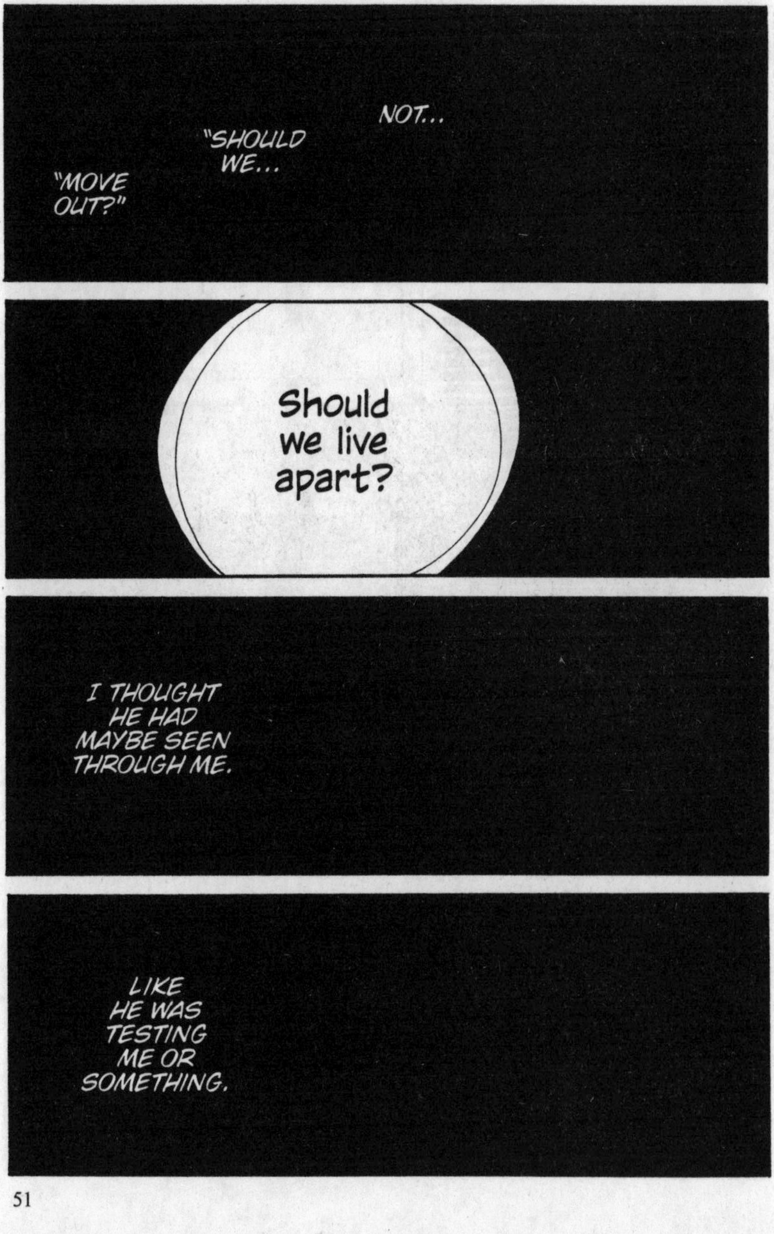
NOT...
"SHOULD WE...
"MOVE OUT?"
Should we live apart?
I THOUGHT HE HAD MAYBE SEEN THROUGH ME.
LIKE HE WAS TESTING ME OR SOMETHING.

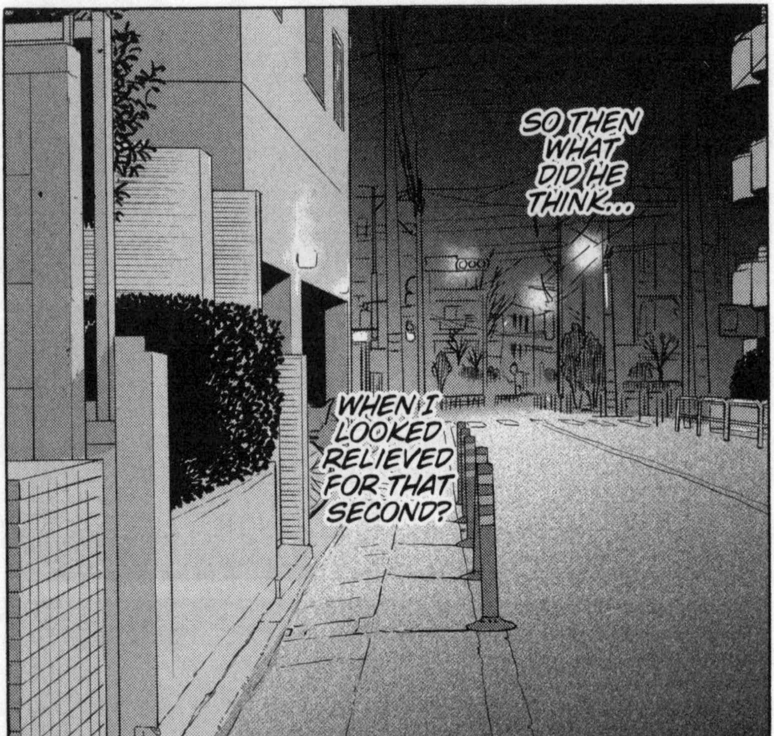
SO THEN WHAT DID HE THINK...
WHEN I LOOKED RELIEVED FOR THAT SECOND?
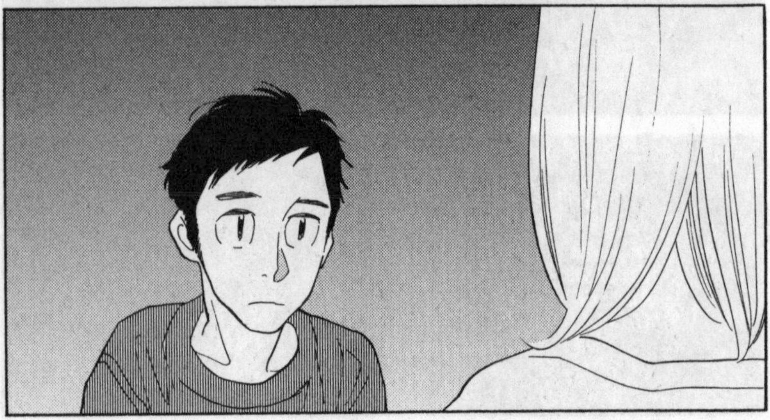

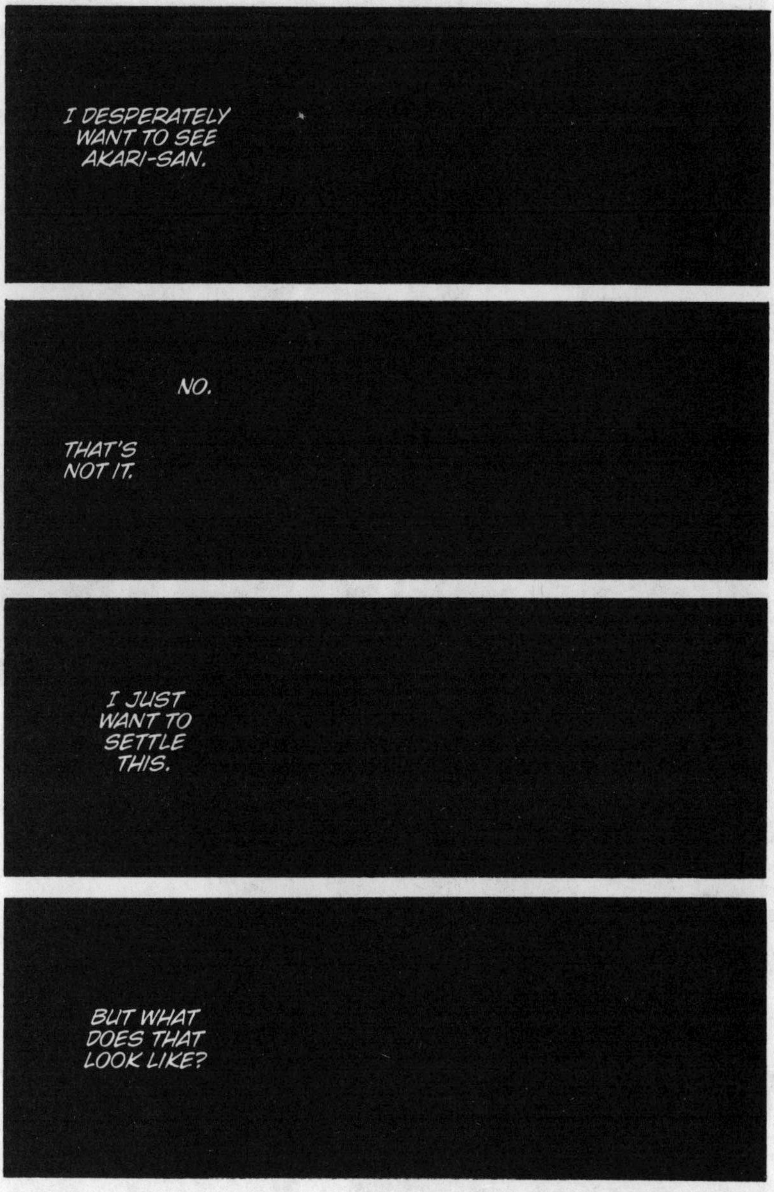

I DESPERATELY WANT TO SEE AKARI-SAN.
NO.
THAT'S NOT IT.
I JUST WANT TO SETTLE THIS.
BUT WHAT DOES THAT LOOK LIKE?

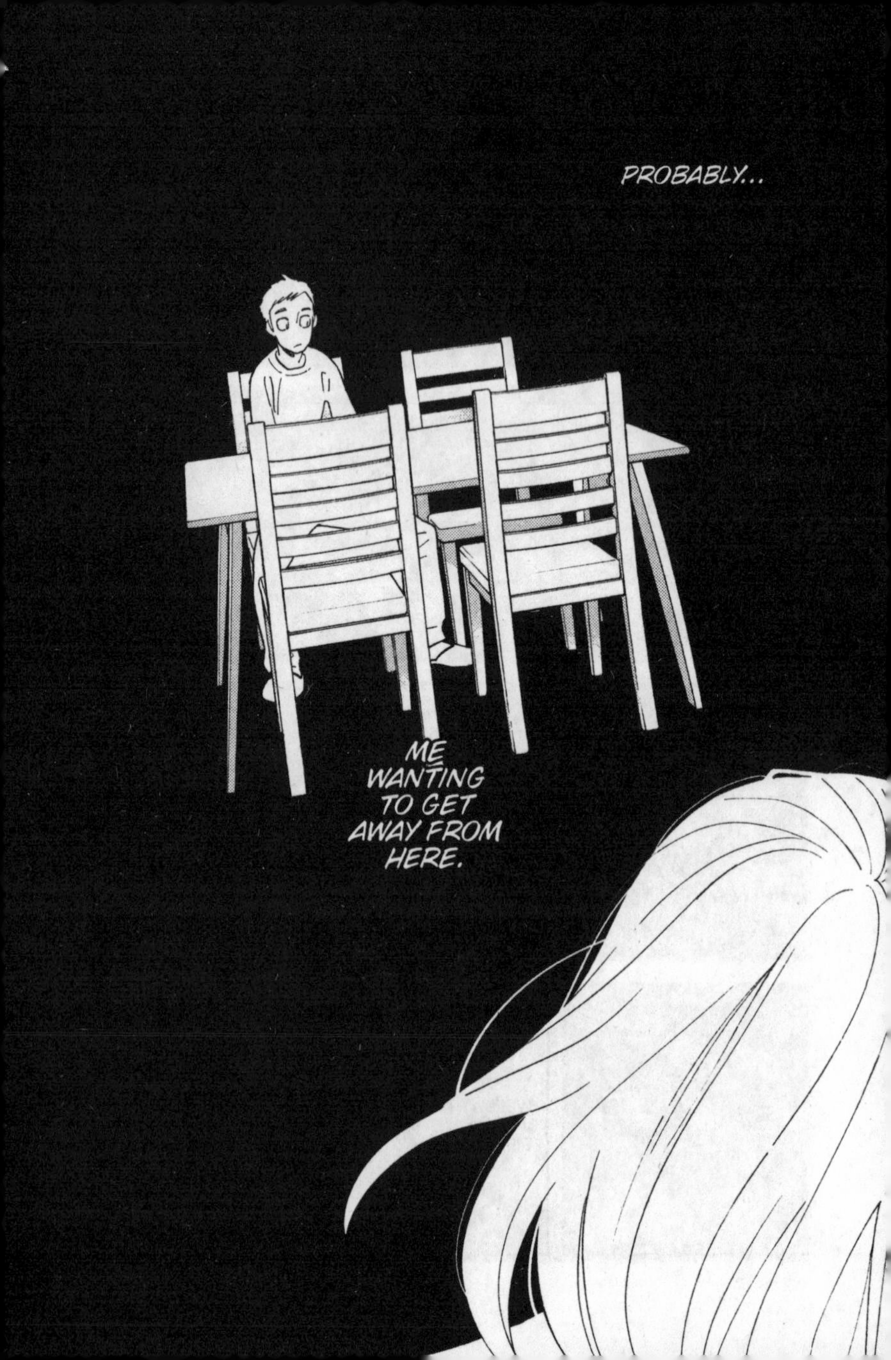
PROBABLY...
ME WANTING TO GET AWAY FROM HERE.

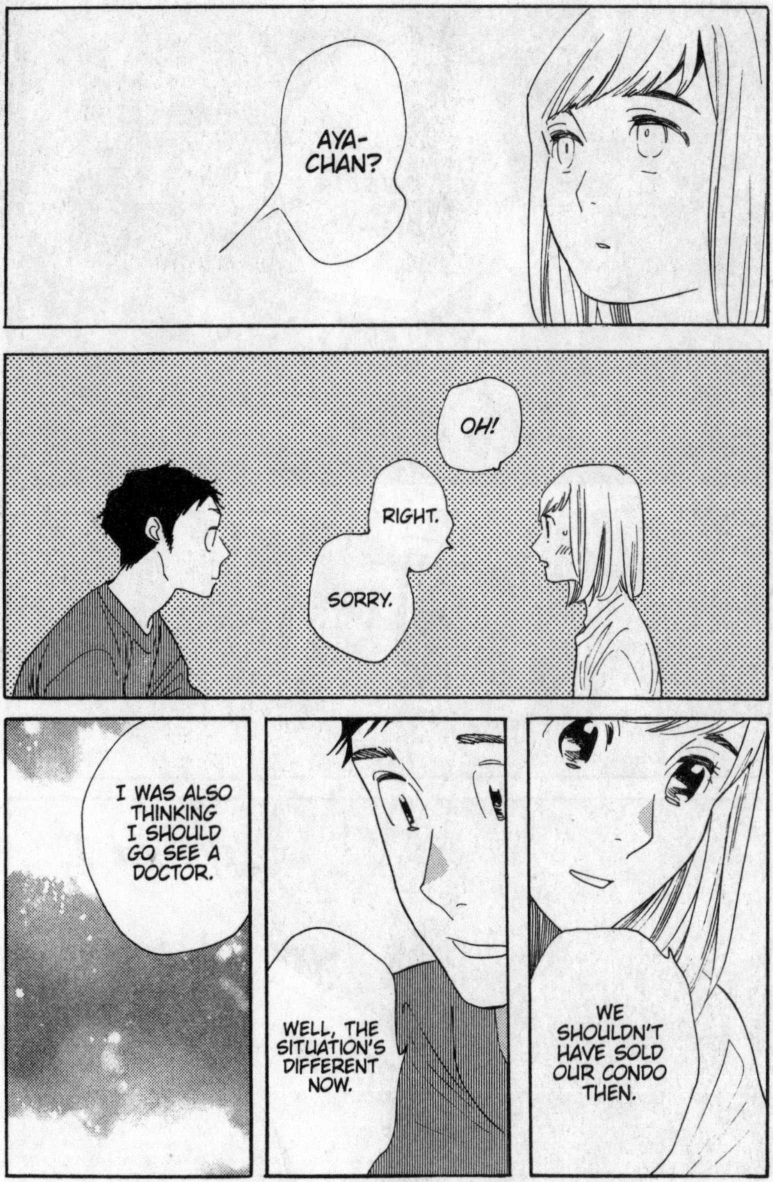
AYA-CHAN?
OH!
RIGHT.
SORRY.
WE SHOULDN'T HAVE SOLD OUR CONDO THEN.
WELL, THE SITUATION'S DIFFERENT NOW.
I WAS ALSO THINKING I SHOULD GO SEE A DOCTOR.

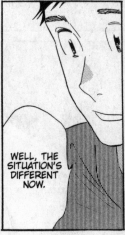

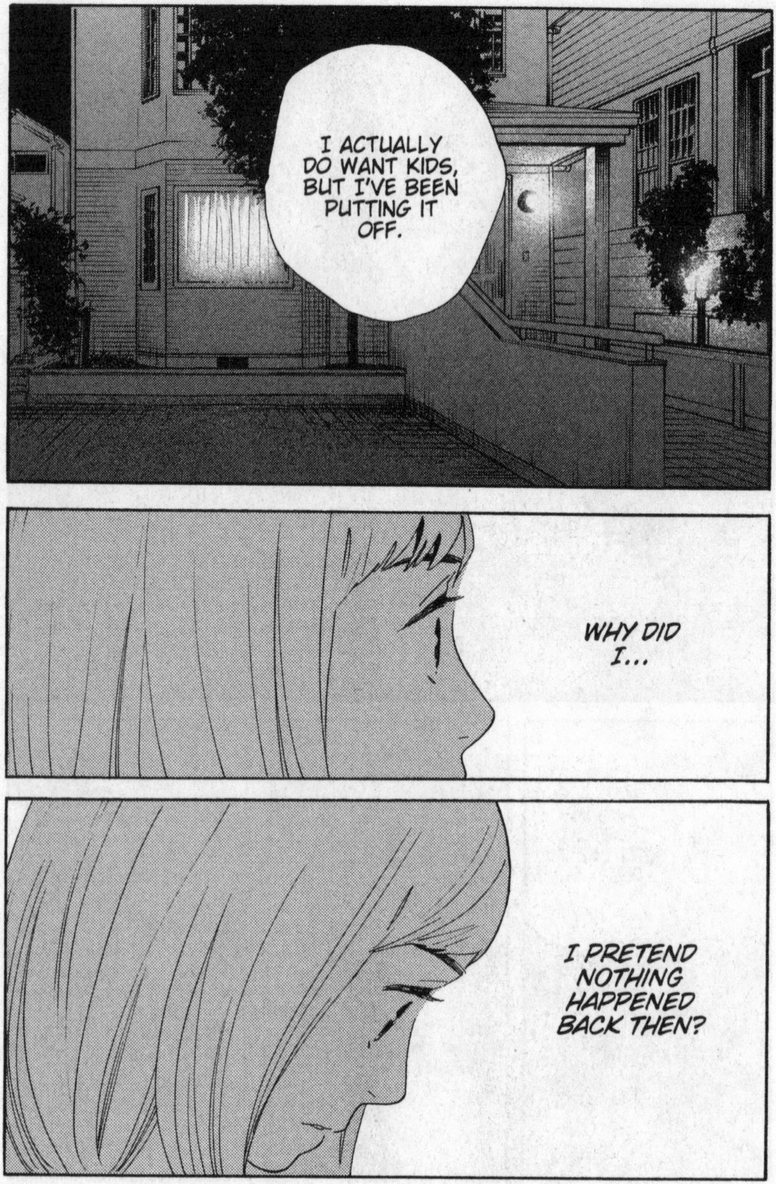
I ACTUALLY DO WANT KIDS, BUT I'VE BEEN PUTTING IT OFF.
WHY DID I...
I PRETEND NOTHING HAPPENED BACK THEN?

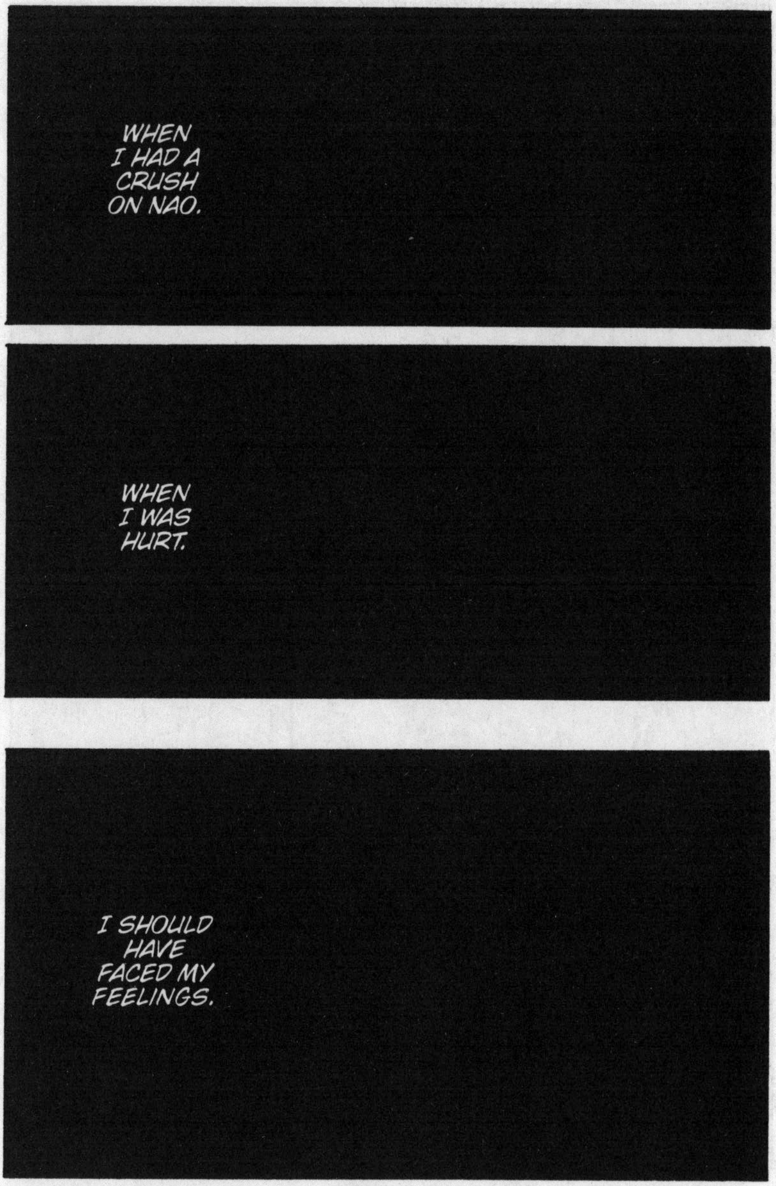
WHEN I HAD A CRUSH ON NAO.
WHEN I WAS HURT.
I SHOULD HAVE FACED MY FEELINGS.

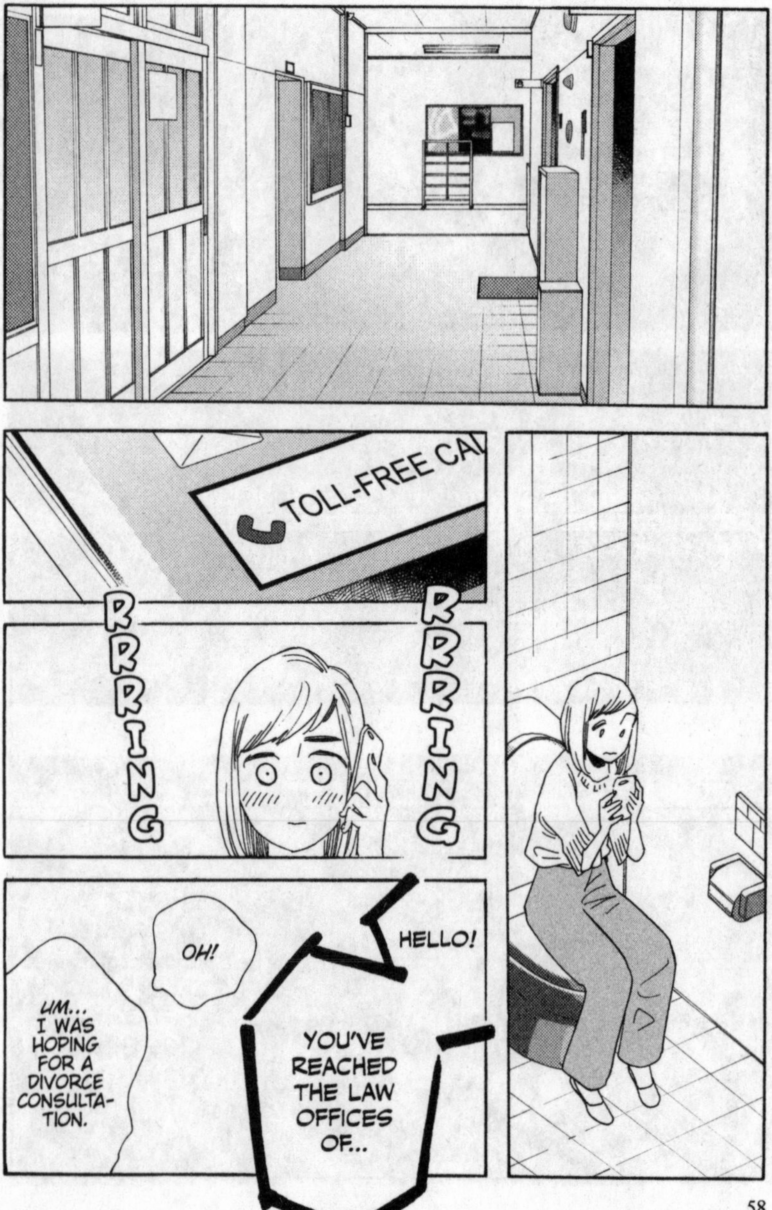
TOLL-FREE CA
RRRING
RRRING
HELLO!
YOU'VE REACHED THE LAW OFFICES OF...
OH!
UM... I WAS HOPING FOR A DIVORCE CONSULTA-TION.

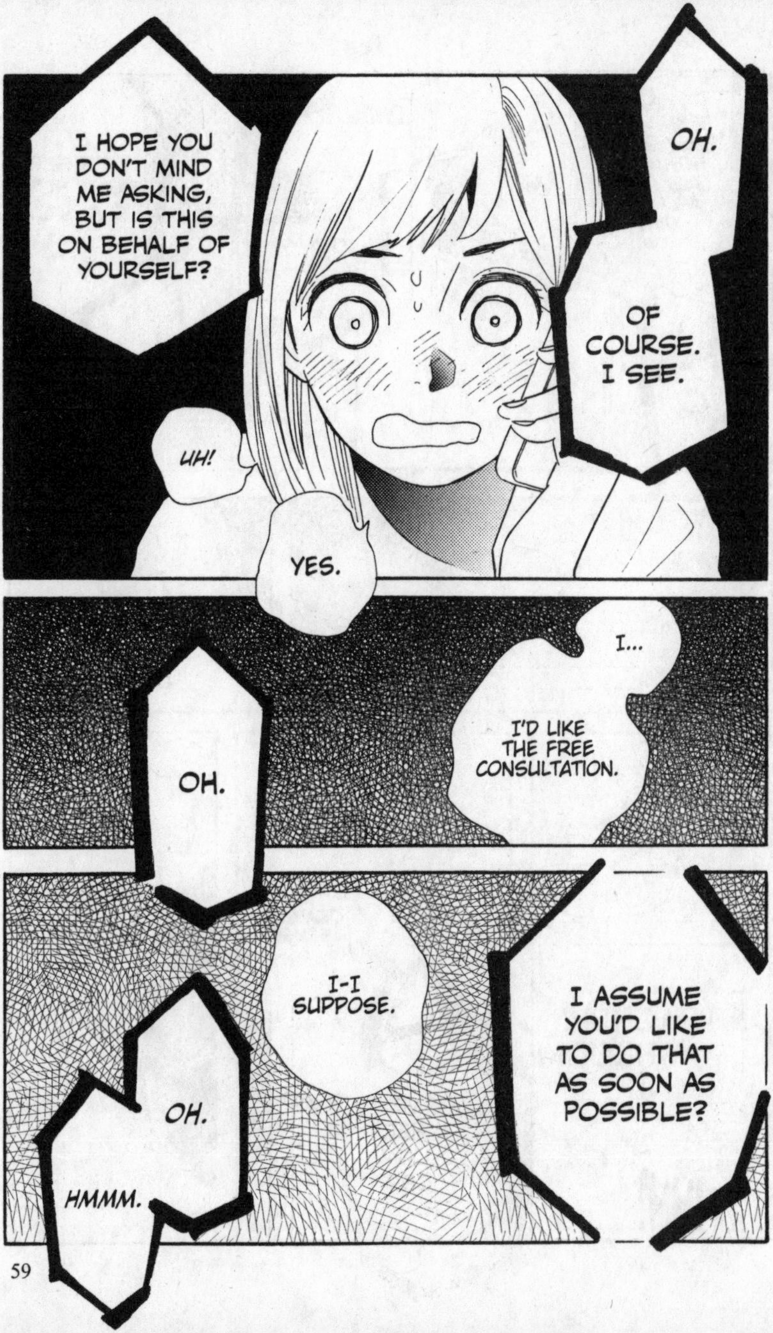
OH.
OF COURSE. I SEE.
I HOPE YOU DON'T MIND ME ASKING, BUT IS THIS ON BEHALF OF YOURSELF?
UH!
YES.
I...
I'D LIKE THE FREE CONSULTATION.
OH.
I ASSUME YOU'D LIKE TO DO THAT AS SOON AS POSSIBLE?
I-I SUPPOSE.
OH.
HMMM.

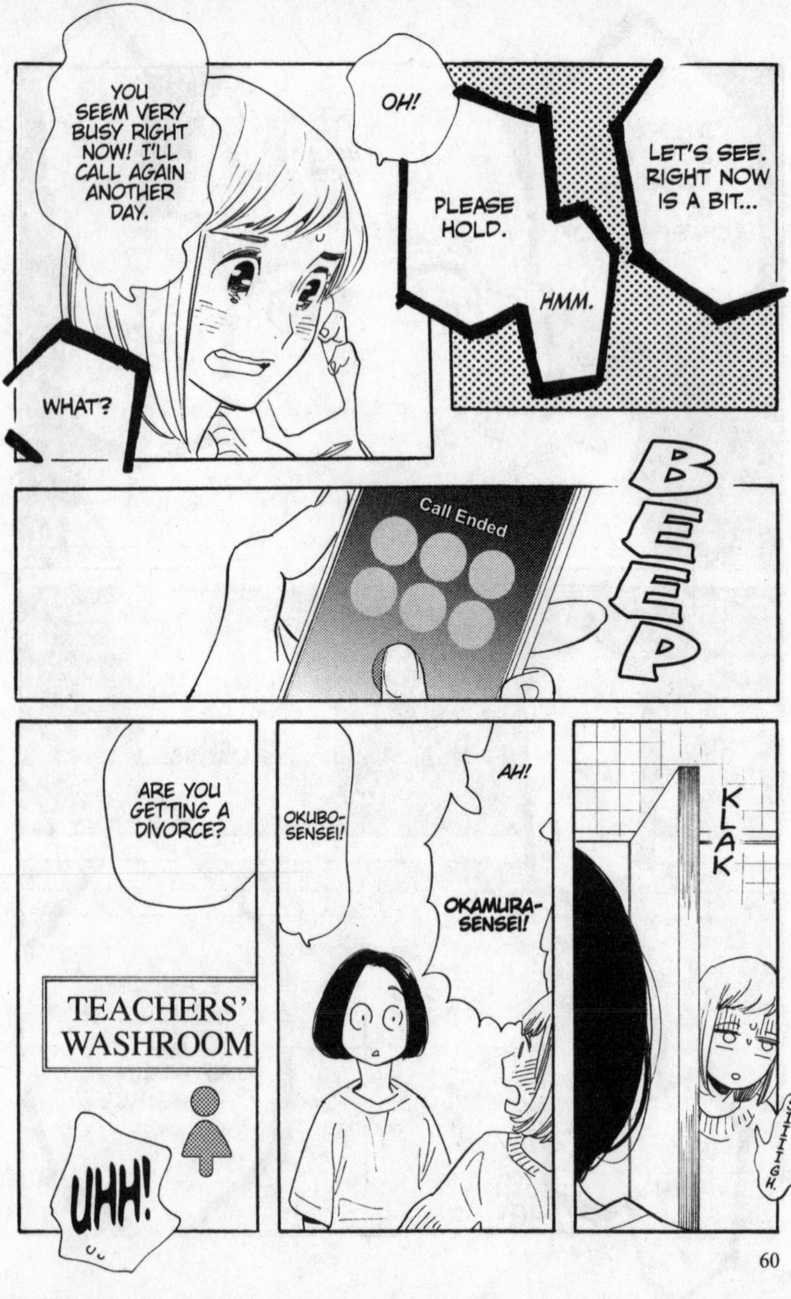

LET'S SEE. RIGHT NOW IS A BIT...
PLEASE HOLD.
HMM.
OH!
YOU SEEM VERY BUSY RIGHT NOW! I'LL CALL AGAIN ANOTHER DAY.
WHAT?
BEEP
Call Ended
KLAK
SIIIIGH.
AH!
OKAMURA-SENSEI!
OKUBO-SENSEI!
ARE YOU GETTING A DIVORCE?
TEACHERS' WASHROOM
UHH!

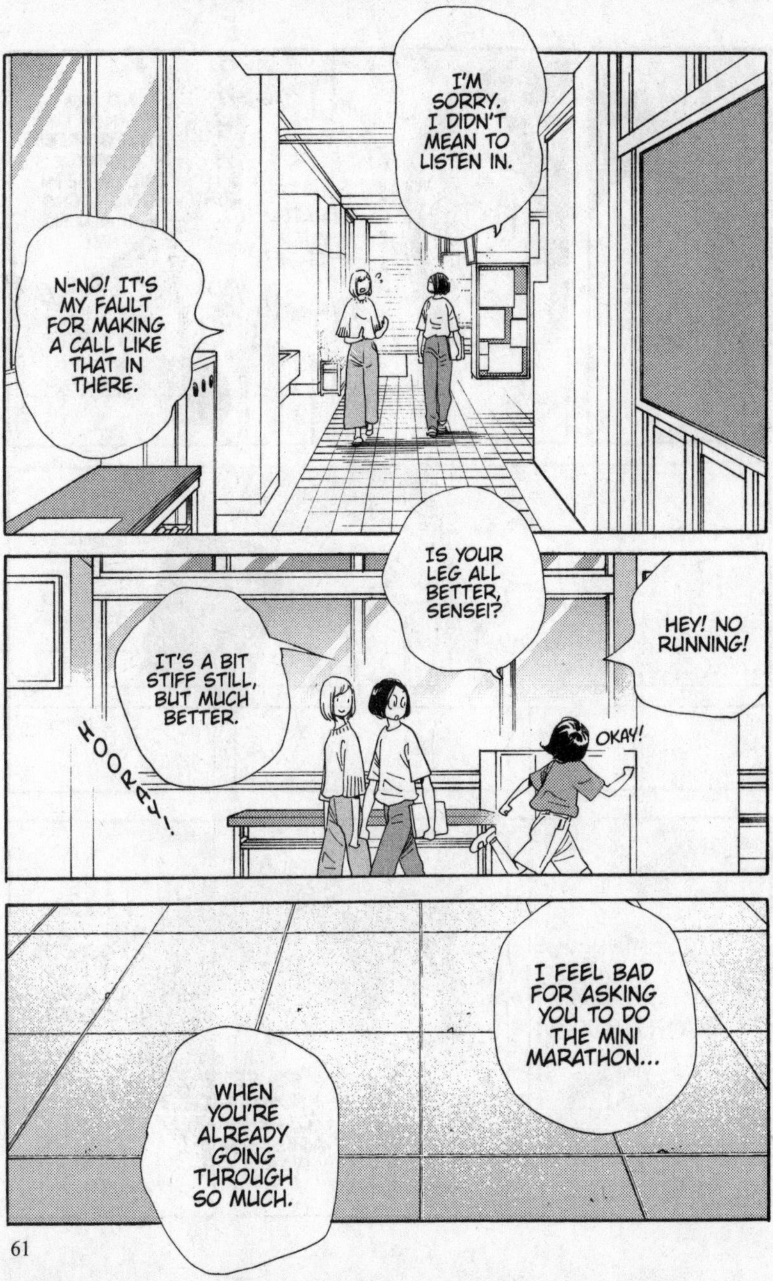
I'M SORRY. I DIDN'T MEAN TO LISTEN IN.
N-NO! IT'S MY FAULT FOR MAKING A CALL LIKE THAT IN THERE.
HEY! NO RUNNING!
OKAY!
IS YOUR LEG ALL BETTER, SENSEI?
IT'S A BIT STIFF STILL, BUT MUCH BETTER.
HOORAY!
I FEEL BAD FOR ASKING YOU TO DO THE MINI MARATHON...
WHEN YOU'RE ALREADY GOING THROUGH SO MUCH.

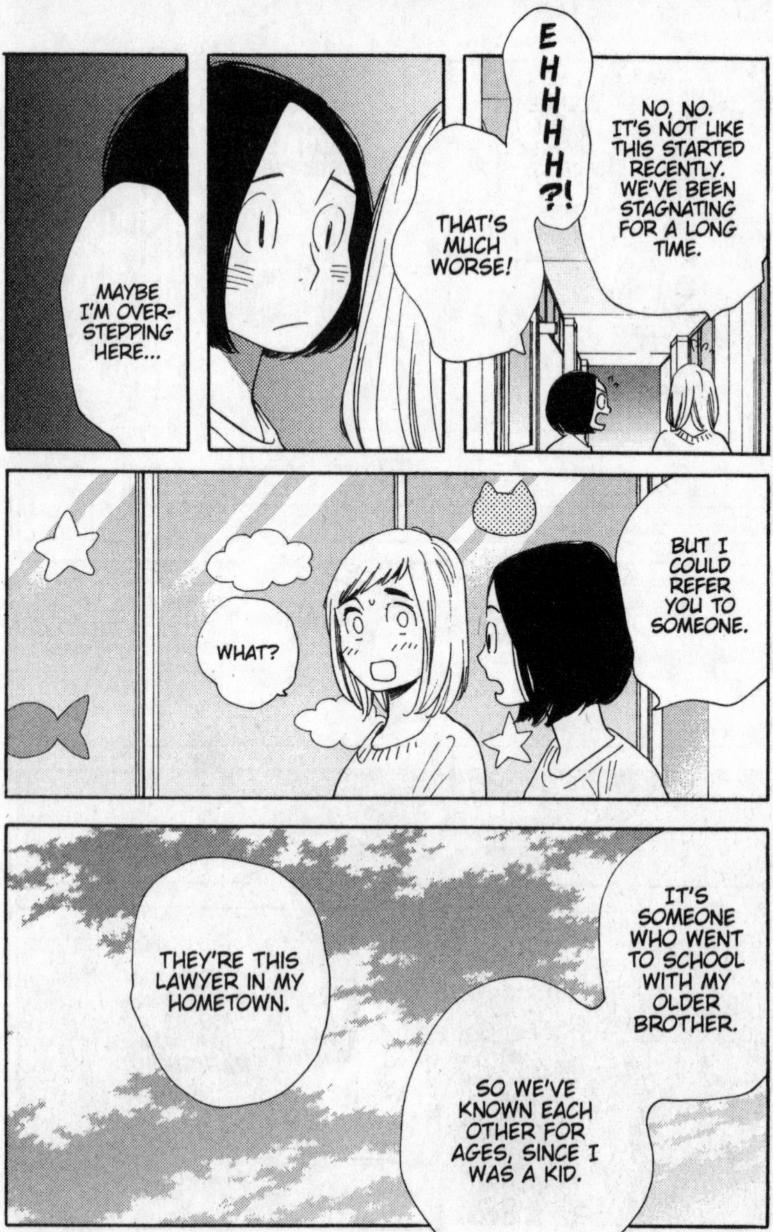
NO, NO. IT'S NOT LIKE THIS STARTED RECENTLY. WE'VE BEEN STAGNATING FOR A LONG TIME.
EHHHH?!
THAT'S MUCH WORSE!
MAYBE I'M OVER-STEPPING HERE...
BUT I COULD REFER YOU TO SOMEONE.
WHAT?
IT'S SOMEONE WHO WENT TO SCHOOL WITH MY OLDER BROTHER.
THEY'RE THIS LAWYER IN MY HOMETOWN.
SO WE'VE KNOWN EACH OTHER FOR AGES, SINCE I WAS A KID.

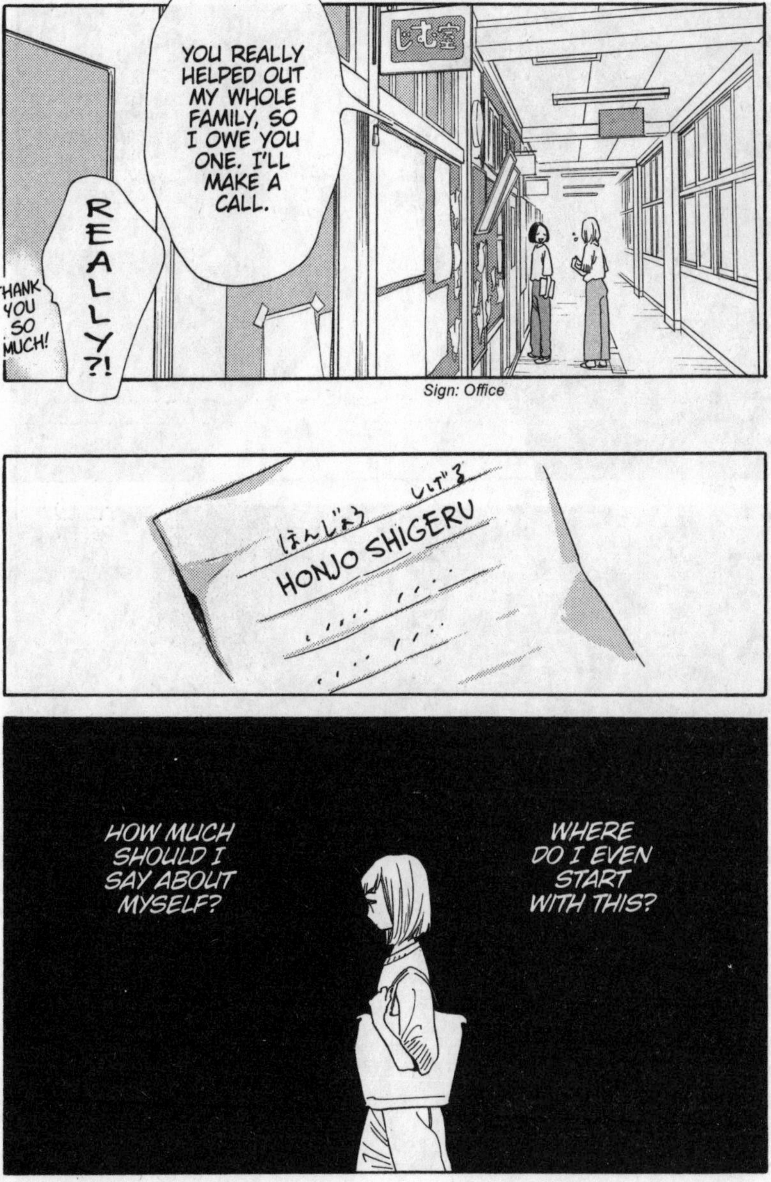
YOU REALLY HELPED OUT MY WHOLE FAMILY, SO I OWE YOU ONE. I'LL MAKE A CALL.
REALLY?!
THANK YOU SO MUCH!
ほんじょう しげる
HONJO SHIGERU
WHERE DO I EVEN START WITH THIS?
HOW MUCH SHOULD I SAY ABOUT MYSELF?
Sign: Office

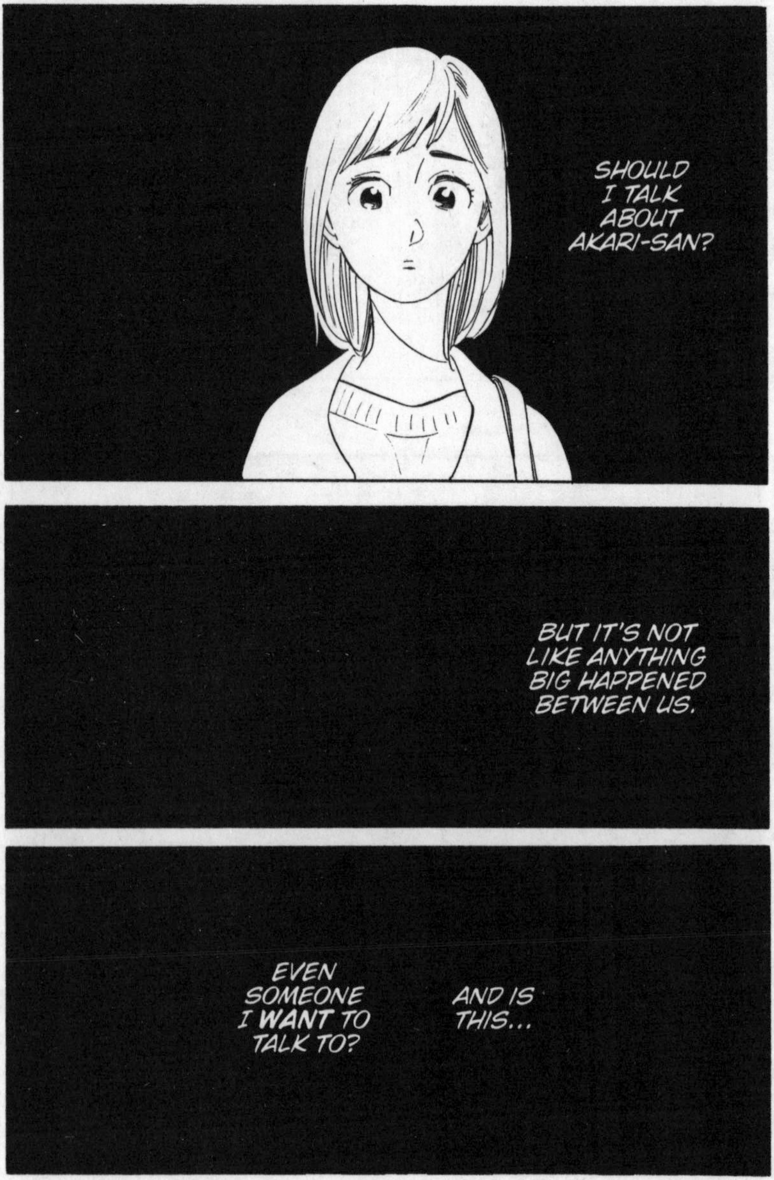
SHOULD I TALK ABOUT AKARI-SAN?
BUT IT'S NOT LIKE ANYTHING BIG HAPPENED BETWEEN US.
AND IS THIS...
EVEN SOMEONE I **WANT** TO TALK TO?

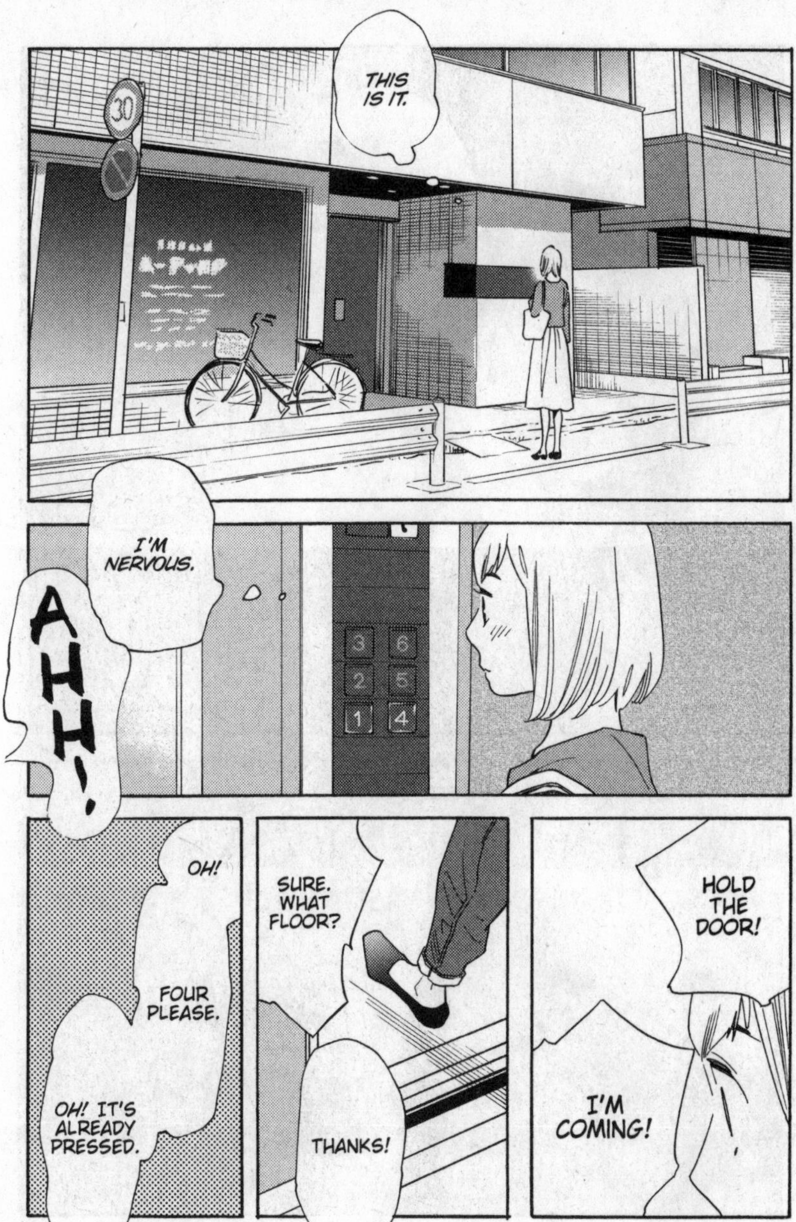
THIS IS IT.
I'M NERVOUS.
AHH!
HOLD THE DOOR!
I'M COMING!
SURE. WHAT FLOOR?
THANKS!
OH!
FOUR PLEASE.
OH! IT'S ALREADY PRESSED.

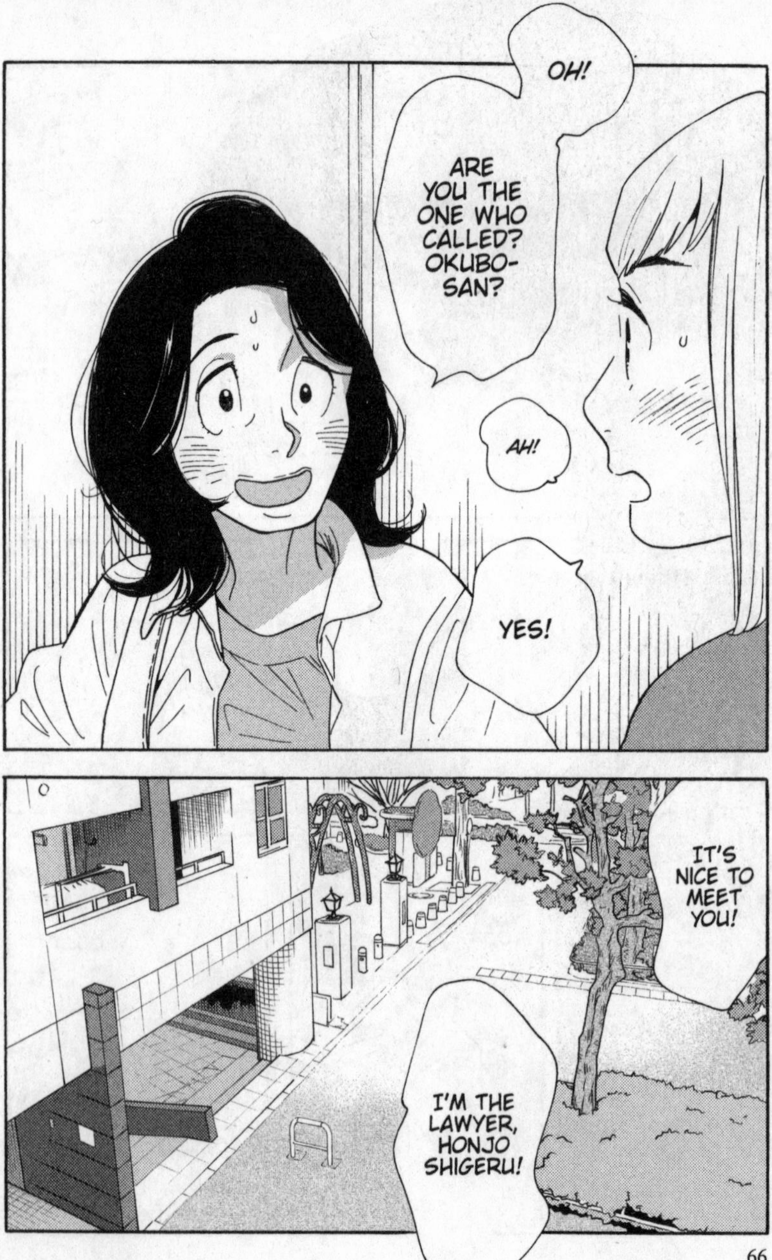
OH!
ARE YOU THE ONE WHO CALLED? OKUBO-SAN?
AH!
YES!
IT'S NICE TO MEET YOU!
I'M THE LAWYER, HONJO SHIGERU!

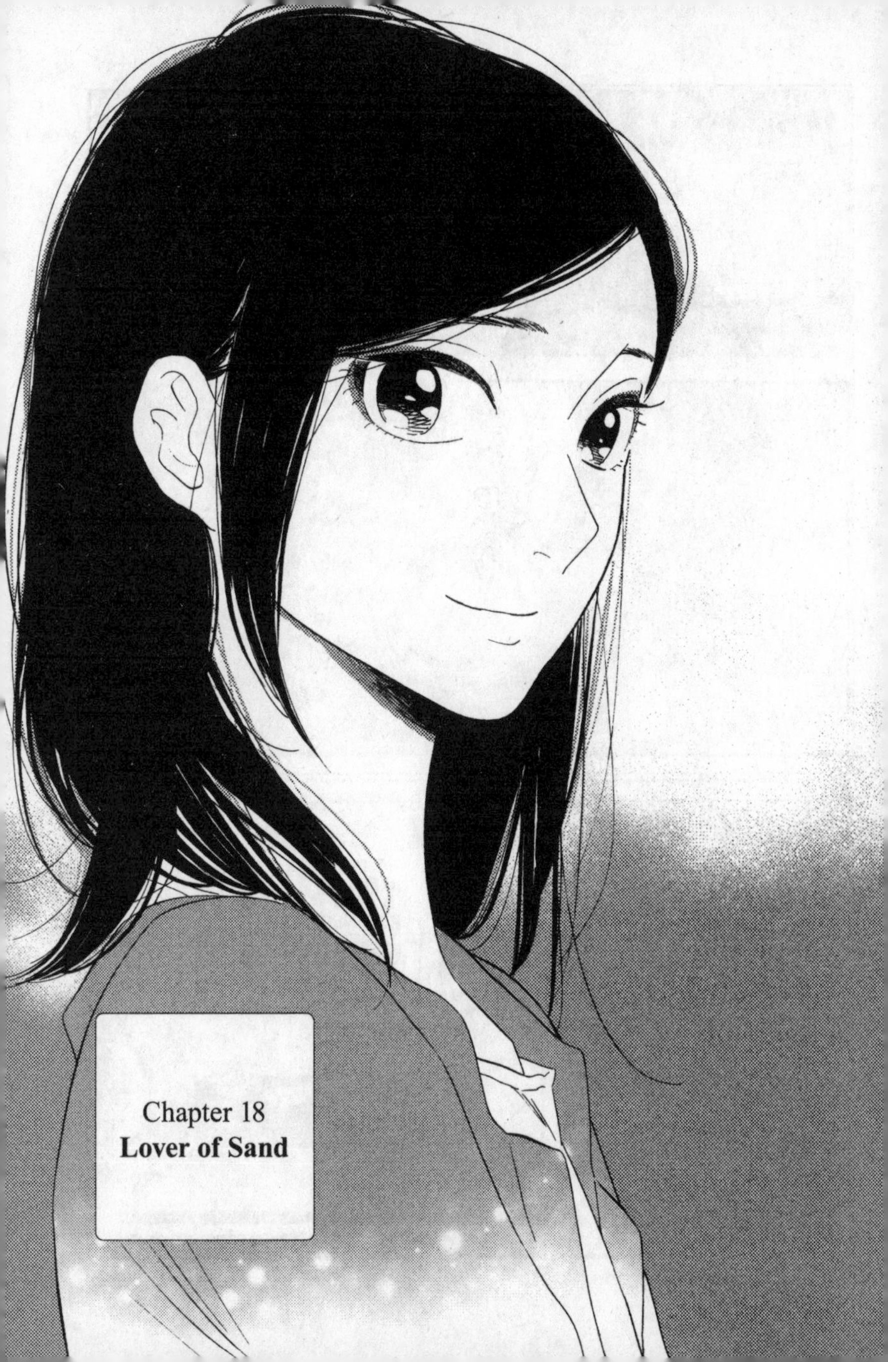
Chapter 18
Lover of Sand

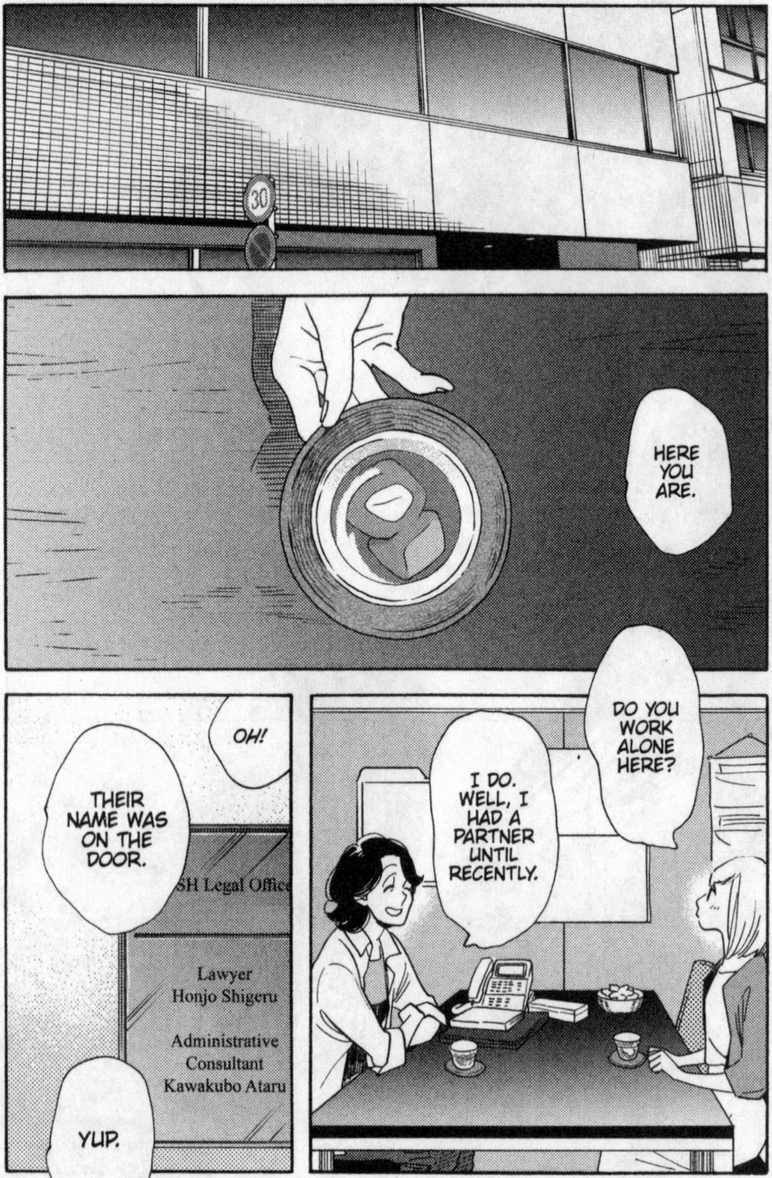
HERE YOU ARE.
DO YOU WORK ALONE HERE?
I DO. WELL, I HAD A PARTNER UNTIL RECENTLY.
OH!
THEIR NAME WAS ON THE DOOR.
SH Legal Office
Lawyer
Honjo Shigeru
Administrative
Consultant
Kawakubo Ataru
YUP.

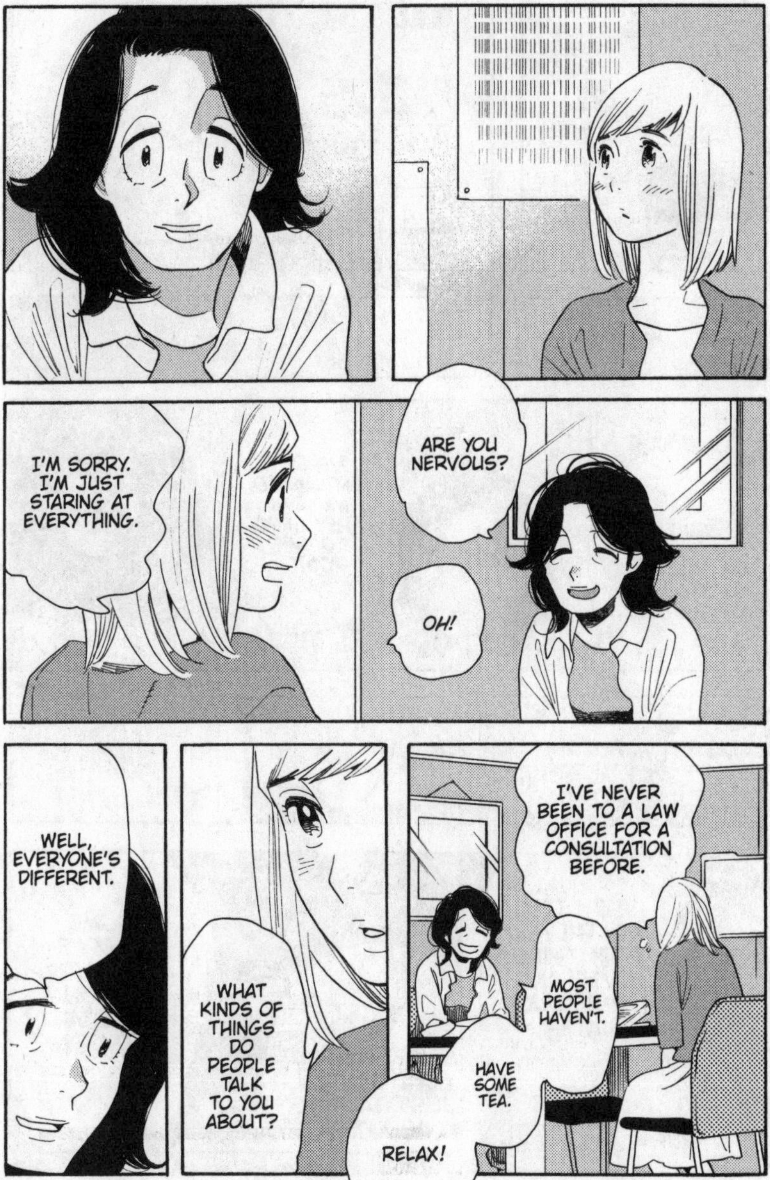
ARE YOU NERVOUS?
OH!
I'M SORRY. I'M JUST STARING AT EVERYTHING.
I'VE NEVER BEEN TO A LAW OFFICE FOR A CONSULTATION BEFORE.
MOST PEOPLE HAVEN'T.
HAVE SOME TEA.
RELAX!
WHAT KINDS OF THINGS DO PEOPLE TALK TO YOU ABOUT?
WELL, EVERYONE'S DIFFERENT.

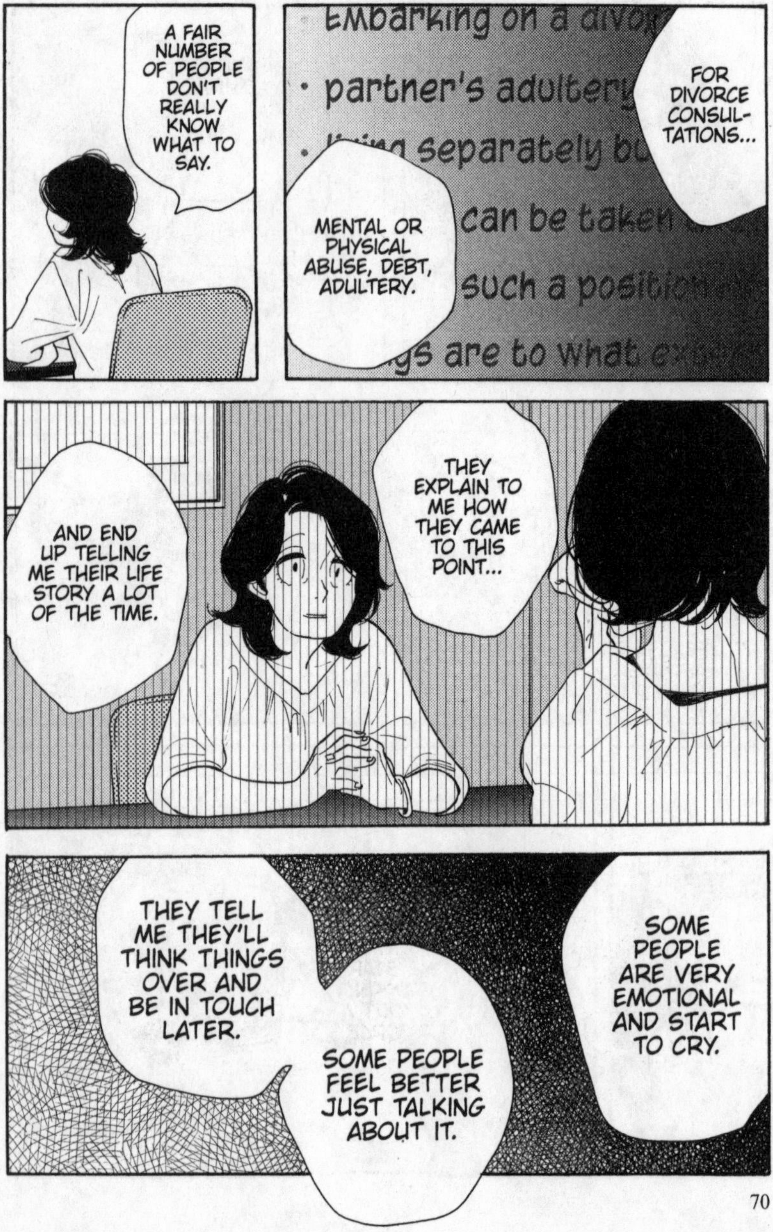
FOR DIVORCE CONSUL-TATIONS...
MENTAL OR PHYSICAL ABUSE, DEBT, ADULTERY.
A FAIR NUMBER OF PEOPLE DON'T REALLY KNOW WHAT TO SAY.
THEY EXPLAIN TO ME HOW THEY CAME TO THIS POINT...
AND END UP TELLING ME THEIR LIFE STORY A LOT OF THE TIME.
SOME PEOPLE ARE VERY EMOTIONAL AND START TO CRY.
SOME PEOPLE FEEL BETTER JUST TALKING ABOUT IT.
THEY TELL ME THEY'LL THINK THINGS OVER AND BE IN TOUCH LATER.

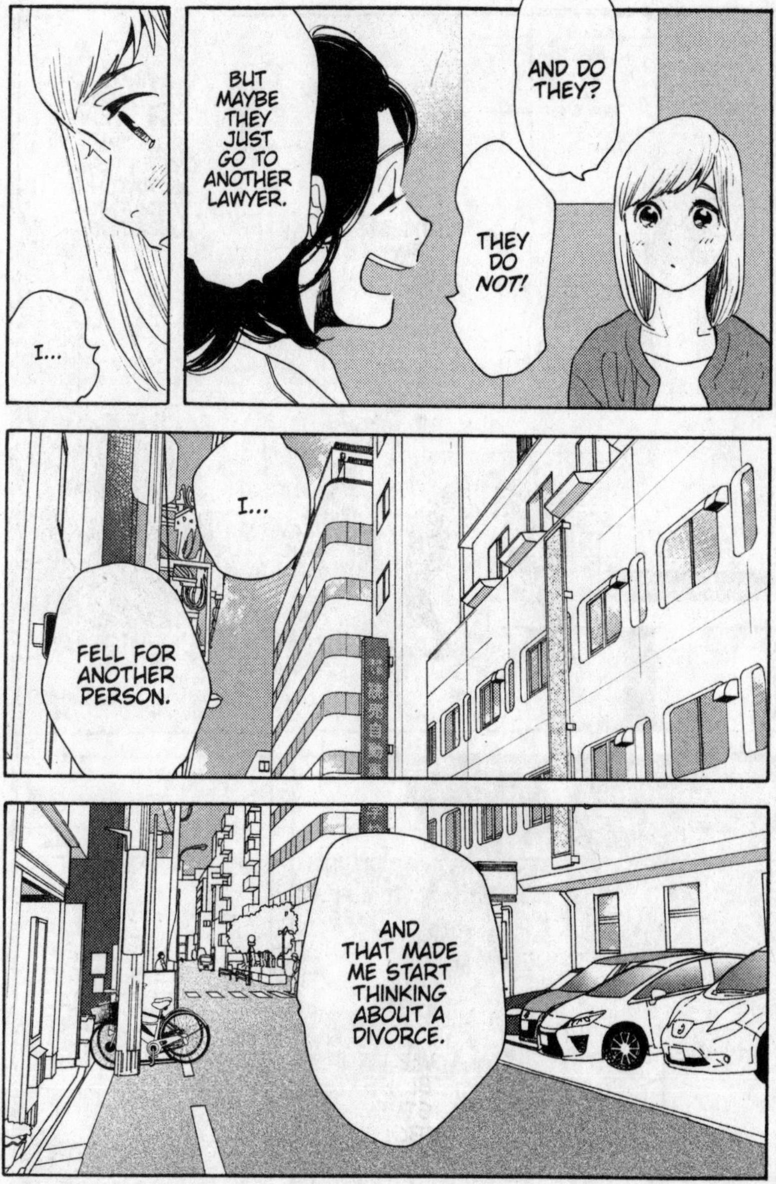
AND DO THEY?
THEY DO NOT!
BUT MAYBE THEY JUST GO TO ANOTHER LAWYER.
I...
I...
FELL FOR ANOTHER PERSON.
AND THAT MADE ME START THINKING ABOUT A DIVORCE.

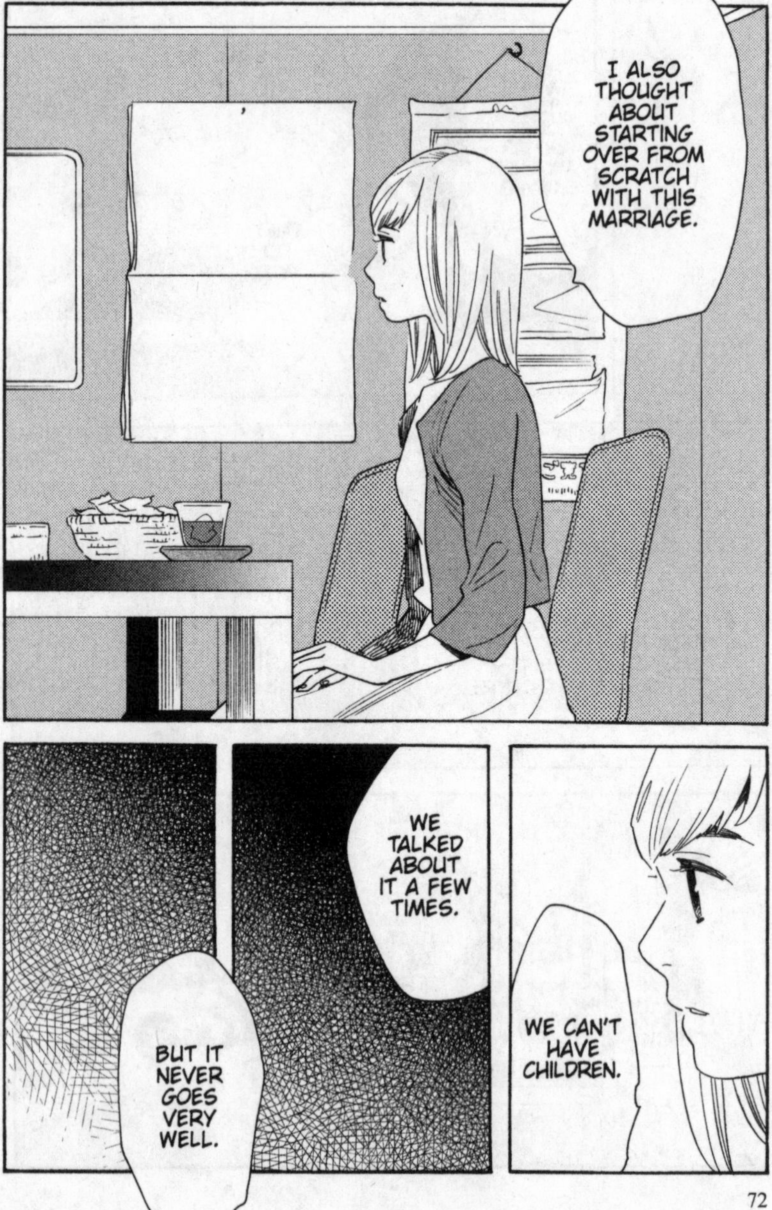
I ALSO THOUGHT ABOUT STARTING OVER FROM SCRATCH WITH THIS MARRIAGE.
WE CAN'T HAVE CHILDREN.
WE TALKED ABOUT IT A FEW TIMES.
BUT IT NEVER GOES VERY WELL.

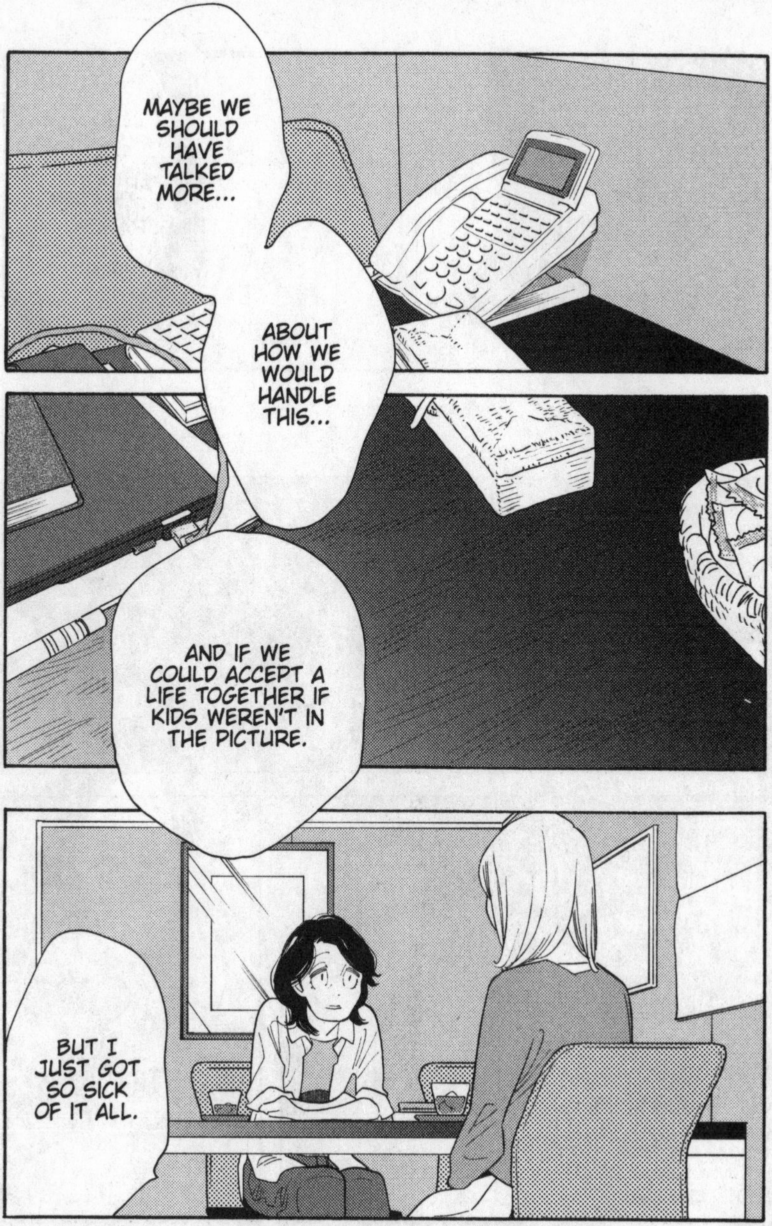
MAYBE WE SHOULD HAVE TALKED MORE...
ABOUT HOW WE WOULD HANDLE THIS...
AND IF WE COULD ACCEPT A LIFE TOGETHER IF KIDS WEREN'T IN THE PICTURE.
BUT I JUST GOT SO SICK OF IT ALL.

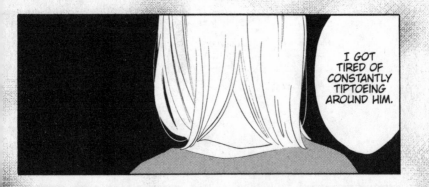

I GOT TIRED OF CONSTANTLY TIPTOEING AROUND HIM.

A business trip?

Yup.

Won't be too long this time, though.

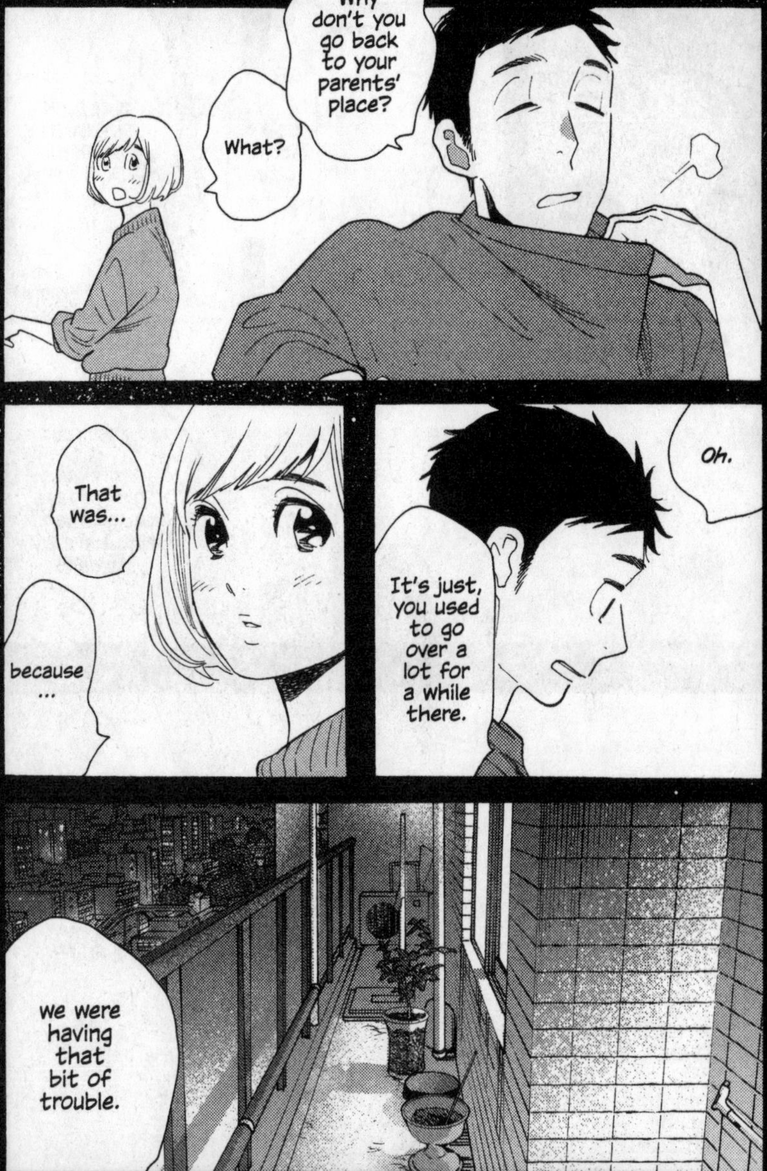
Why don't you go back to your parents' place?
What?
Oh.
It's just, you used to go over a lot for a while there.
That was...
because ...
we were having that bit of trouble.

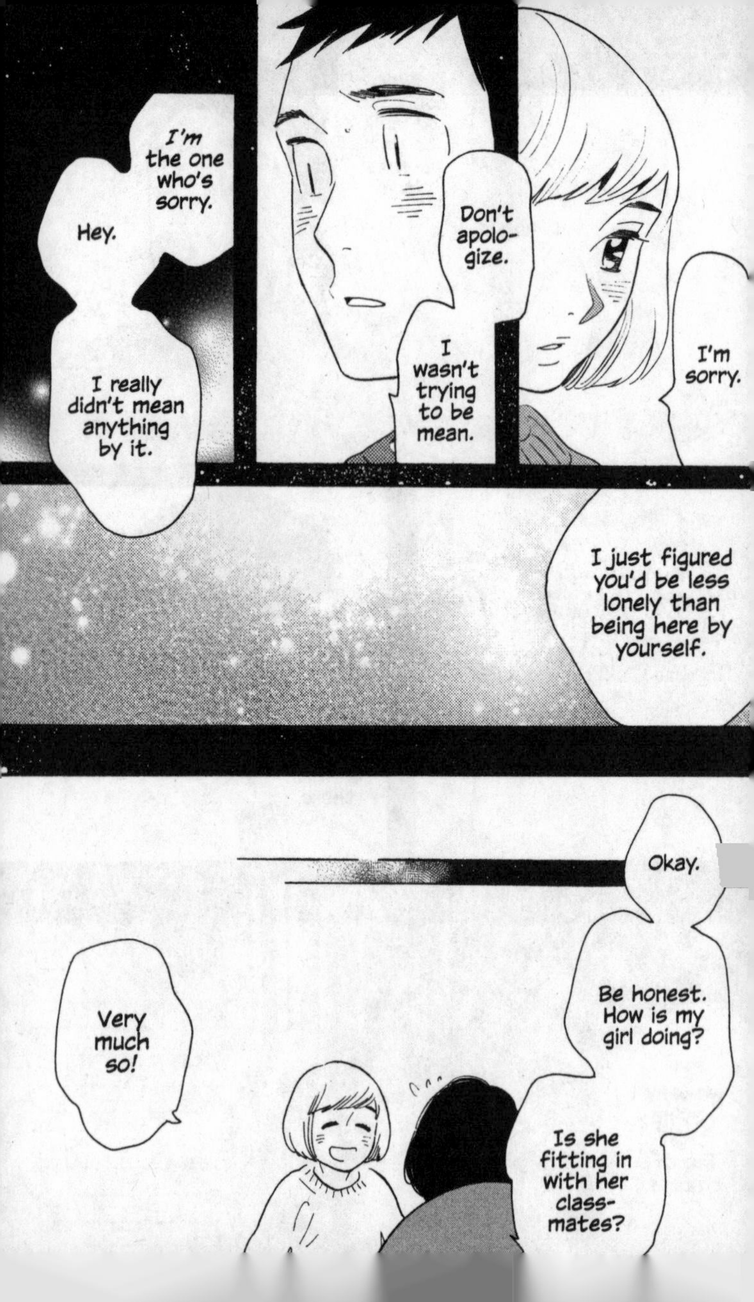
I'm sorry.
Don't apologize.
I wasn't trying to be mean.
I'm the one who's sorry.
Hey.
I really didn't mean anything by it.
I just figured you'd be less lonely than being here by yourself.
Okay.
Be honest. How is my girl doing?
Is she fitting in with her classmates?
Very much so!

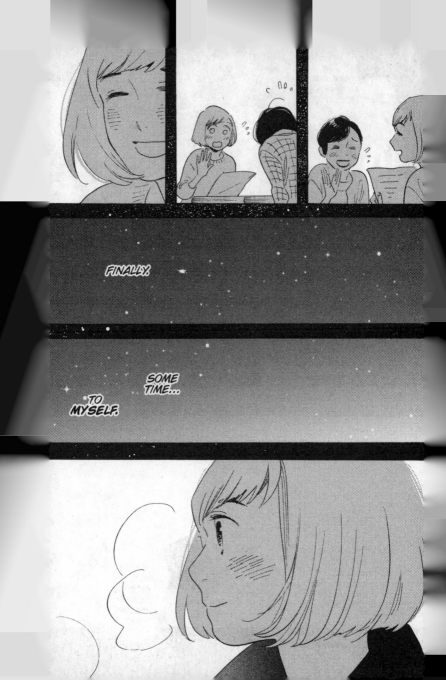

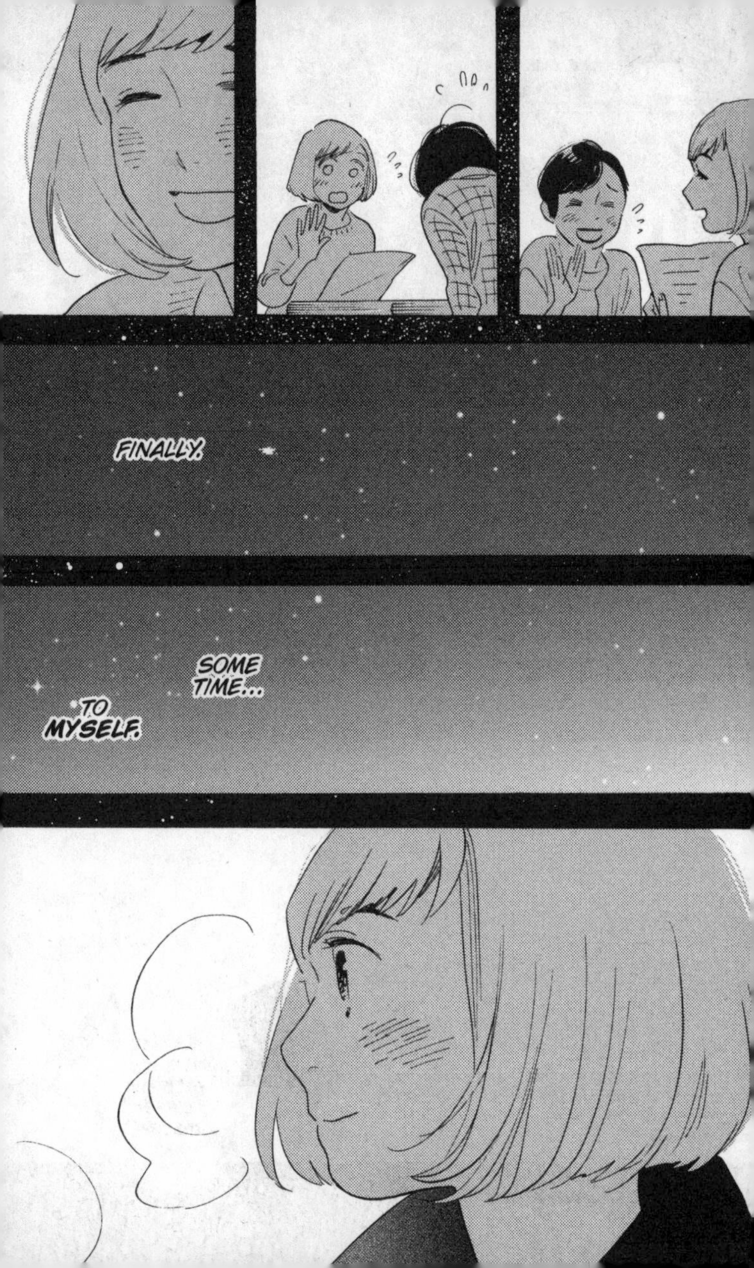
FINALLY.
SOME TIME...
TO MYSELF.

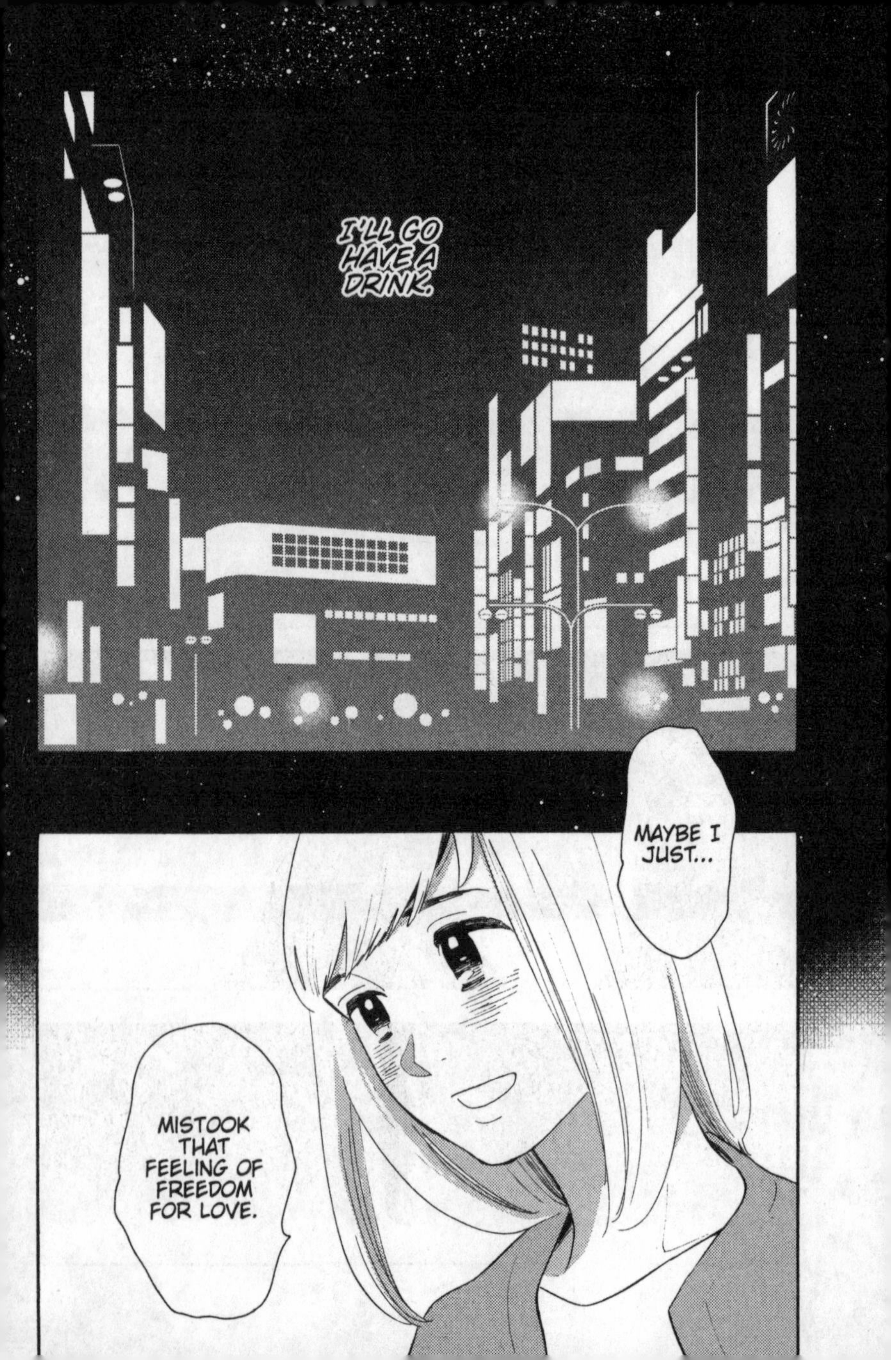
I'LL GO HAVE A DRINK.
MAYBE I JUST...
MISTOOK THAT FEELING OF FREEDOM FOR LOVE.

EITHER WAY...

THAT WAS THE FIRST TIME MY FEELINGS WAVERED LIKE THAT.

AND I THOUGHT THAT MAYBE I COULDN'T KEEP PRETENDING.

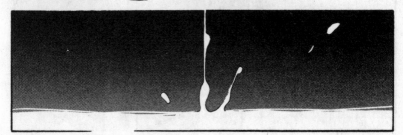

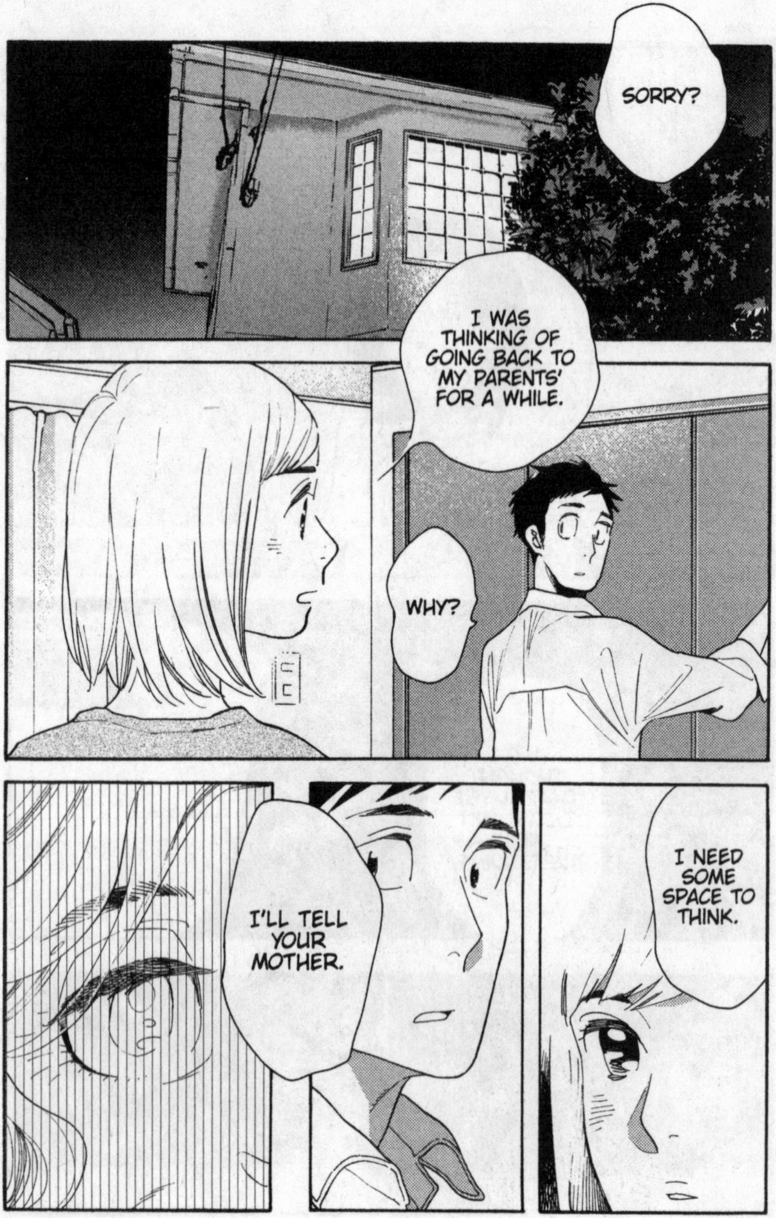
SORRY?
I WAS THINKING OF GOING BACK TO MY PARENTS' FOR A WHILE.
WHY?
I NEED SOME SPACE TO THINK.
I'LL TELL YOUR MOTHER.

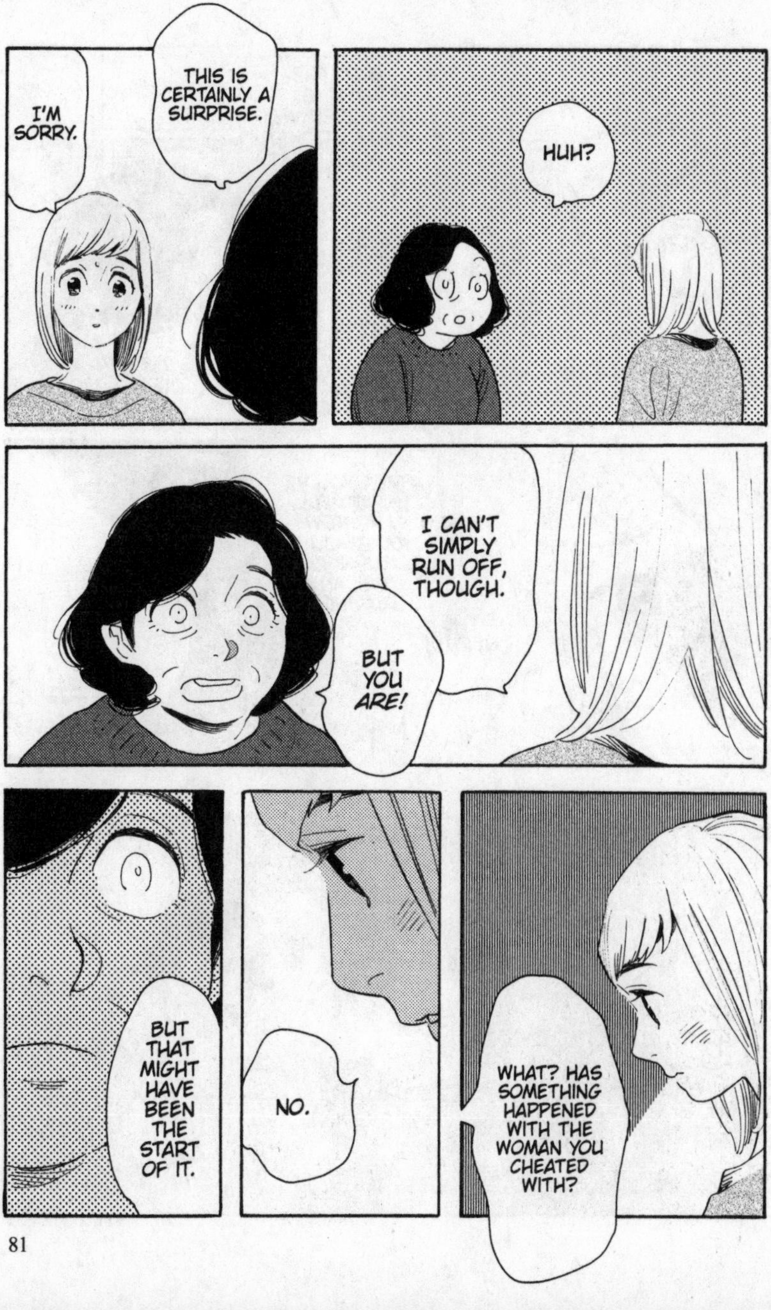
HUH?
THIS IS CERTAINLY A SURPRISE.
I'M SORRY.
I CAN'T SIMPLY RUN OFF, THOUGH.
BUT YOU ARE!
WHAT? HAS SOMETHING HAPPENED WITH THE WOMAN YOU CHEATED WITH?
NO.
BUT THAT MIGHT HAVE BEEN THE START OF IT.

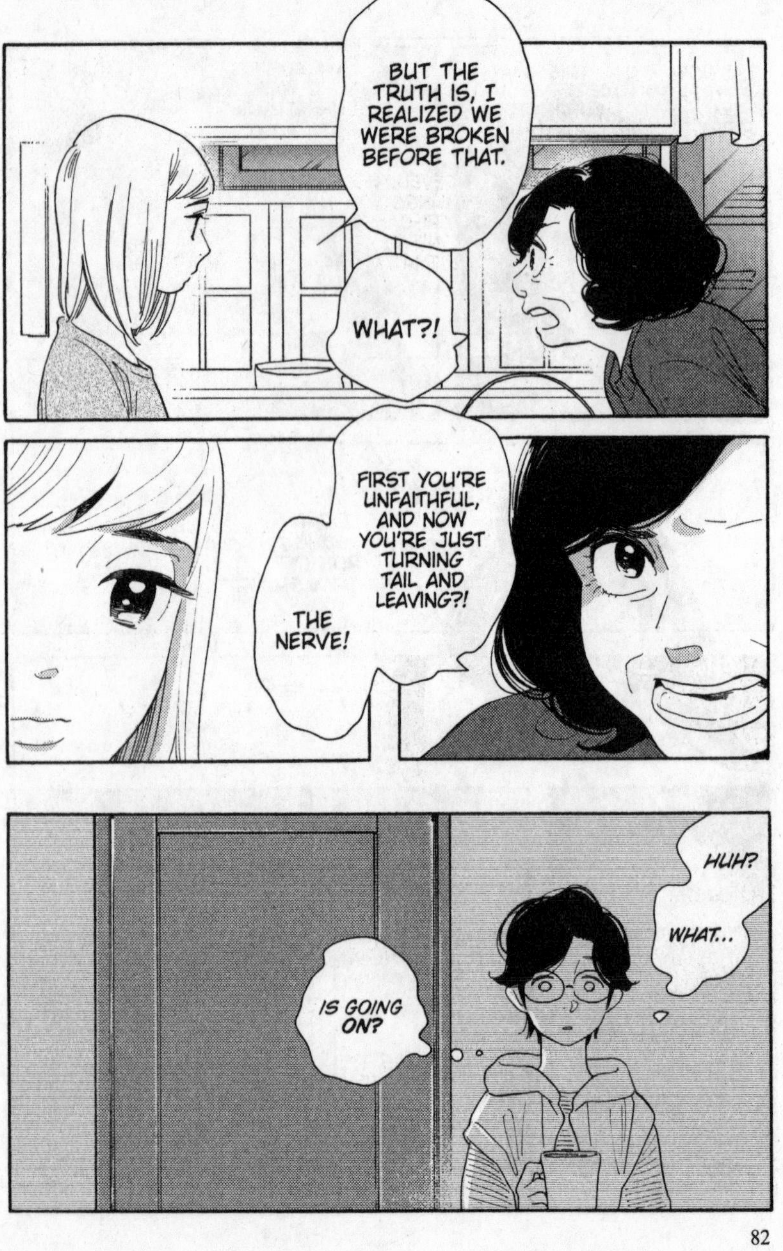
BUT THE TRUTH IS, I REALIZED WE WERE BROKEN BEFORE THAT.
WHAT?!
FIRST YOU'RE UNFAITHFUL, AND NOW YOU'RE JUST TURNING TAIL AND LEAVING?!
THE NERVE!
HUH?
WHAT...
IS GOING ON?

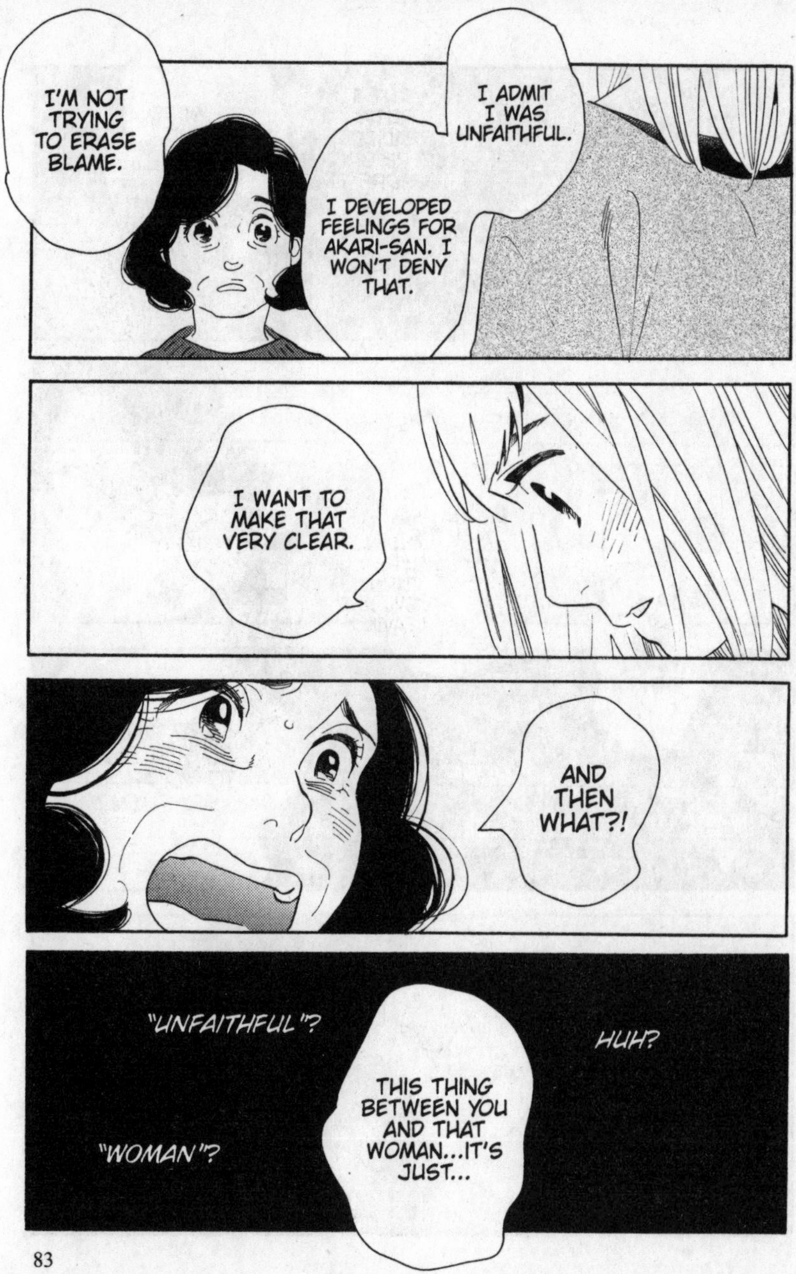
I ADMIT I WAS UNFAITHFUL.
I DEVELOPED FEELINGS FOR AKARI-SAN. I WON'T DENY THAT.
I'M NOT TRYING TO ERASE BLAME.
I WANT TO MAKE THAT VERY CLEAR.
AND THEN WHAT?!
HUH?
"UNFAITHFUL"?
"WOMAN"?
THIS THING BETWEEN YOU AND THAT WOMAN...IT'S JUST...

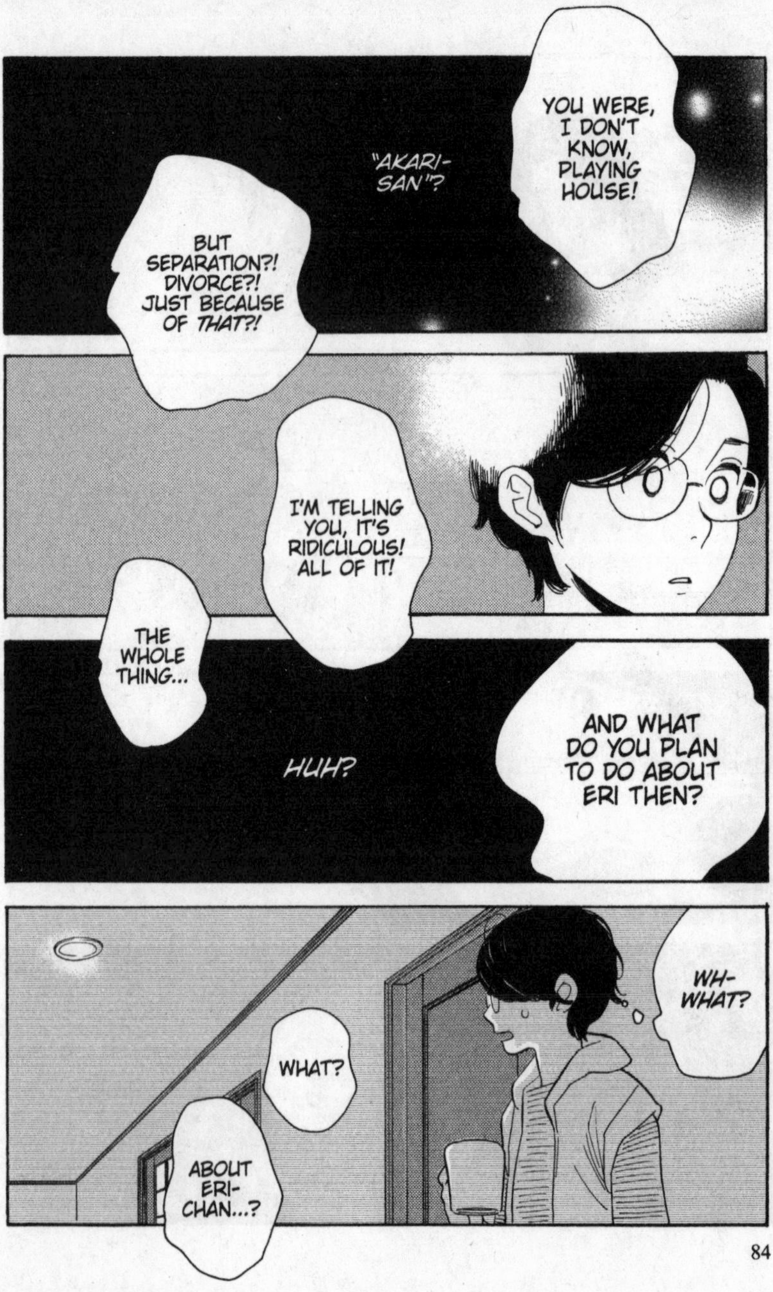
YOU WERE, I DON'T KNOW, PLAYING HOUSE!
"AKARI-SAN"?
BUT SEPARATION?! DIVORCE?! JUST BECAUSE OF *THAT*?!
I'M TELLING YOU, IT'S RIDICULOUS! ALL OF IT!
THE WHOLE THING...
AND WHAT DO YOU PLAN TO DO ABOUT ERI THEN?
HUH?
WH-WHAT?
WHAT?
ABOUT ERI-CHAN...?

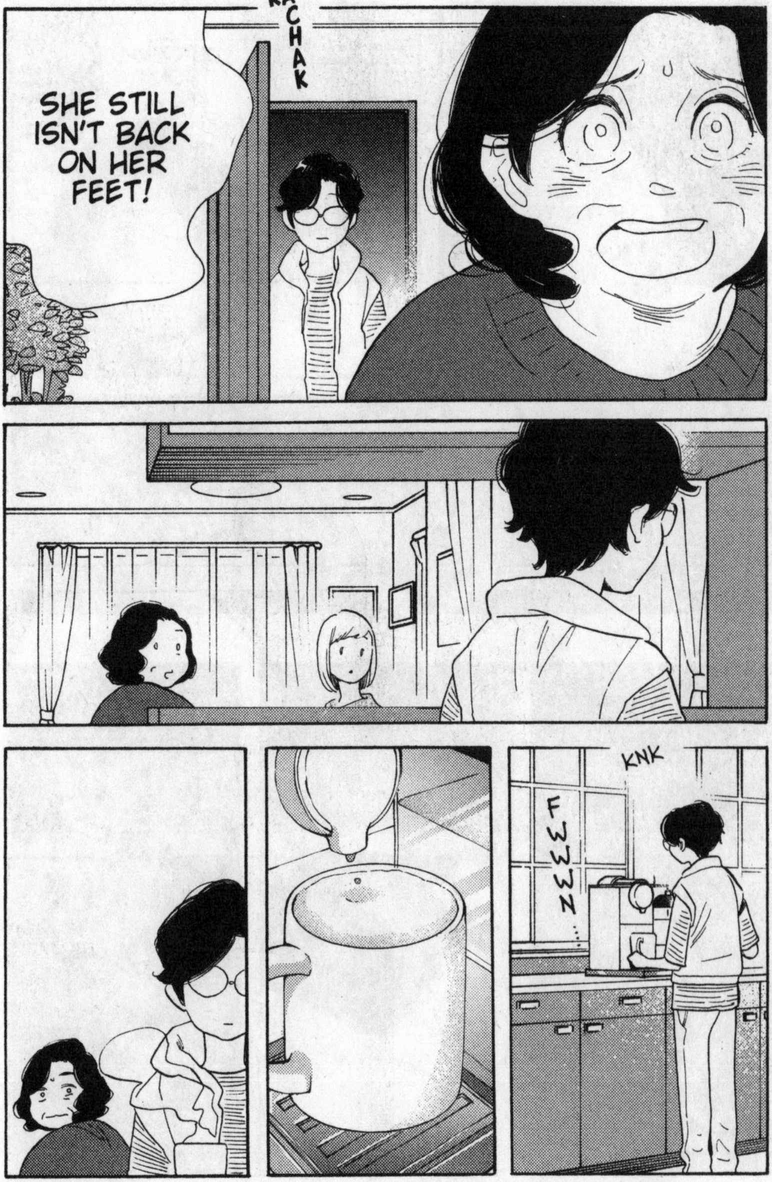
KA-CHAK
SHE STILL ISN'T BACK ON HER FEET!
KNK
FWWWN...

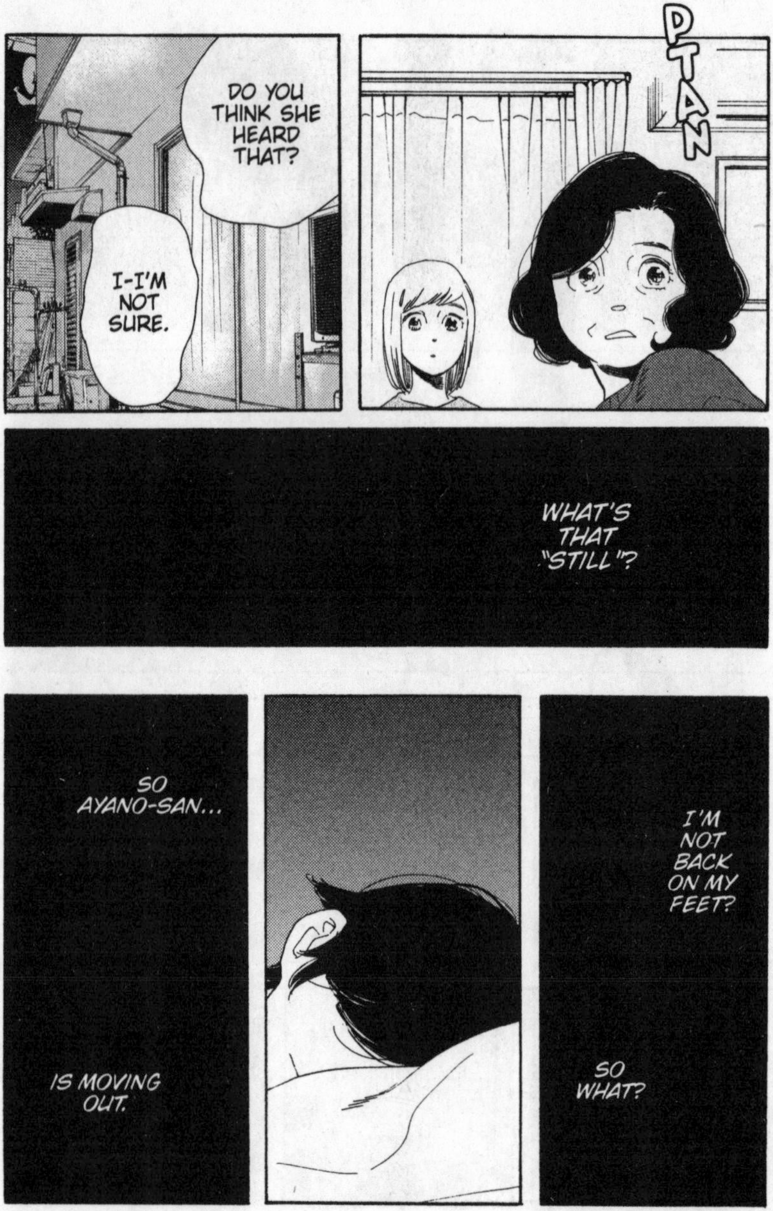
PTAN
DO YOU THINK SHE HEARD THAT?
I-I'M NOT SURE.
WHAT'S THAT "STILL"?
I'M NOT BACK ON MY FEET?
SO WHAT?
SO AYANO-SAN...
IS MOVING OUT.

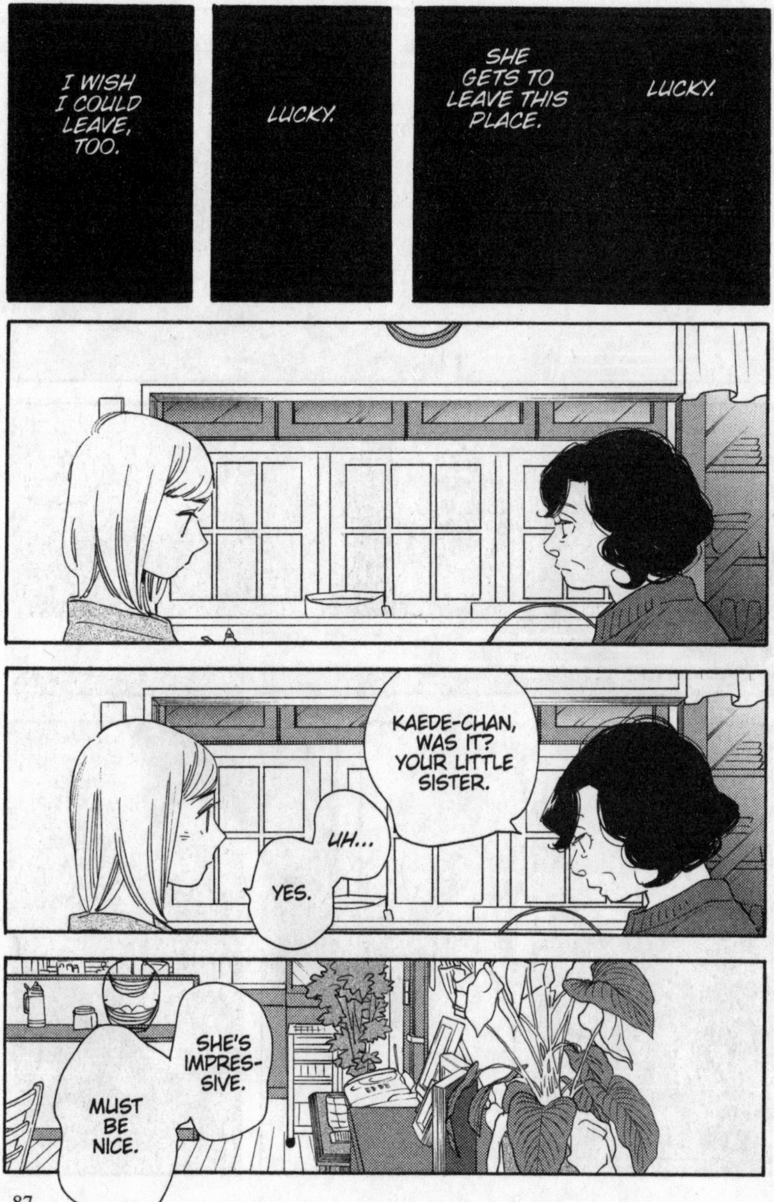
LUCKY.
SHE GETS TO LEAVE THIS PLACE.
LUCKY.
I WISH I COULD LEAVE, TOO.
KAEDE-CHAN, WAS IT? YOUR LITTLE SISTER.
UH... YES.
SHE'S IMPRESSIVE.
MUST BE NICE.

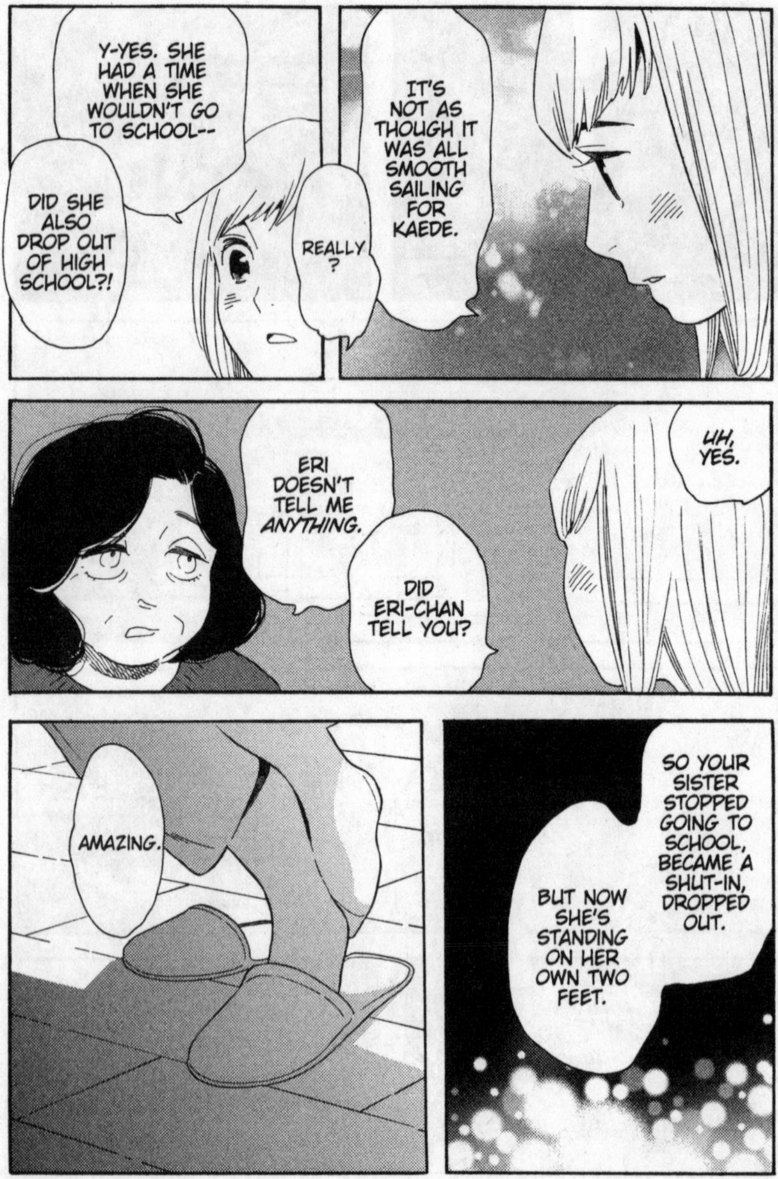
IT'S NOT AS THOUGH IT WAS ALL SMOOTH SAILING FOR KAEDE.
REALLY?
Y-YES. SHE HAD A TIME WHEN SHE WOULDN'T GO TO SCHOOL--
DID SHE ALSO DROP OUT OF HIGH SCHOOL?!
UH, YES.
ERI DOESN'T TELL ME *ANYTHING.*
DID ERI-CHAN TELL YOU?
SO YOUR SISTER STOPPED GOING TO SCHOOL, BECAME A SHUT-IN, DROPPED OUT.
BUT NOW SHE'S STANDING ON HER OWN TWO FEET.
AMAZING.

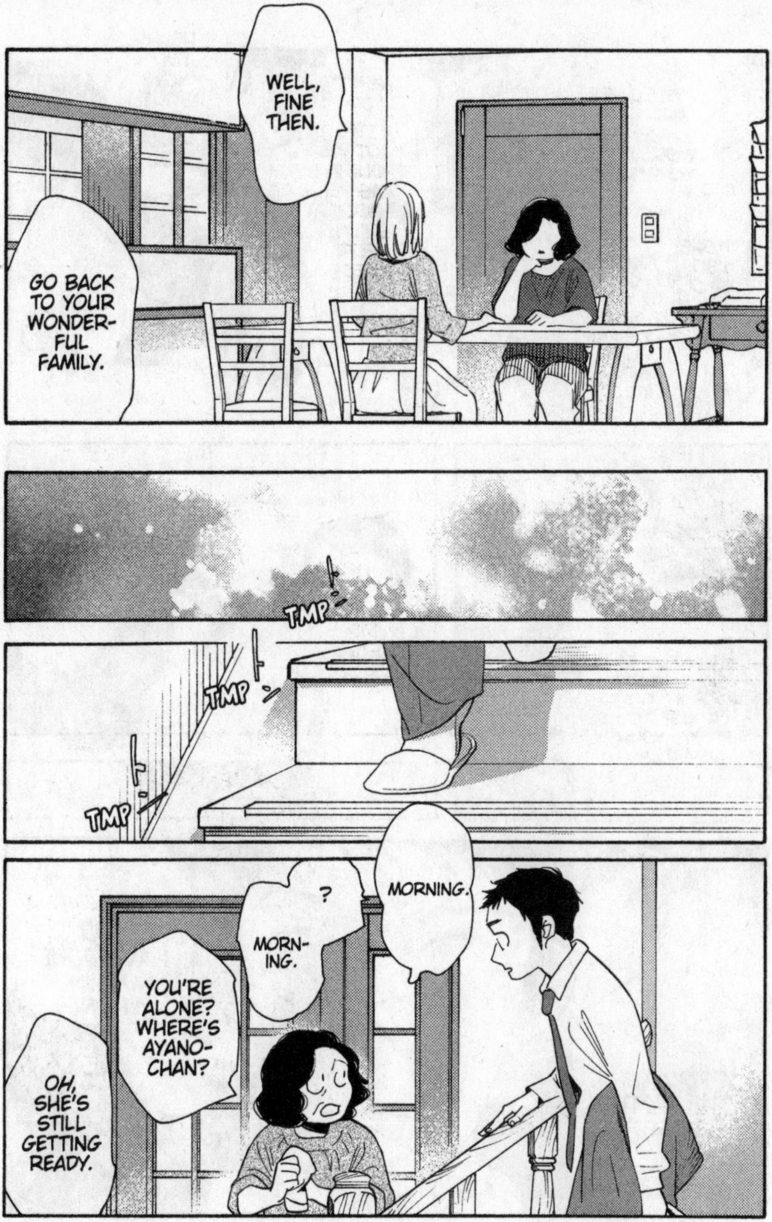
WELL, FINE THEN.
GO BACK TO YOUR WONDERFUL FAMILY.
TMP
TMP
TMP
MORNING.
?
MORNING.
YOU'RE ALONE? WHERE'S AYANO-CHAN?
OH, SHE'S STILL GETTING READY.

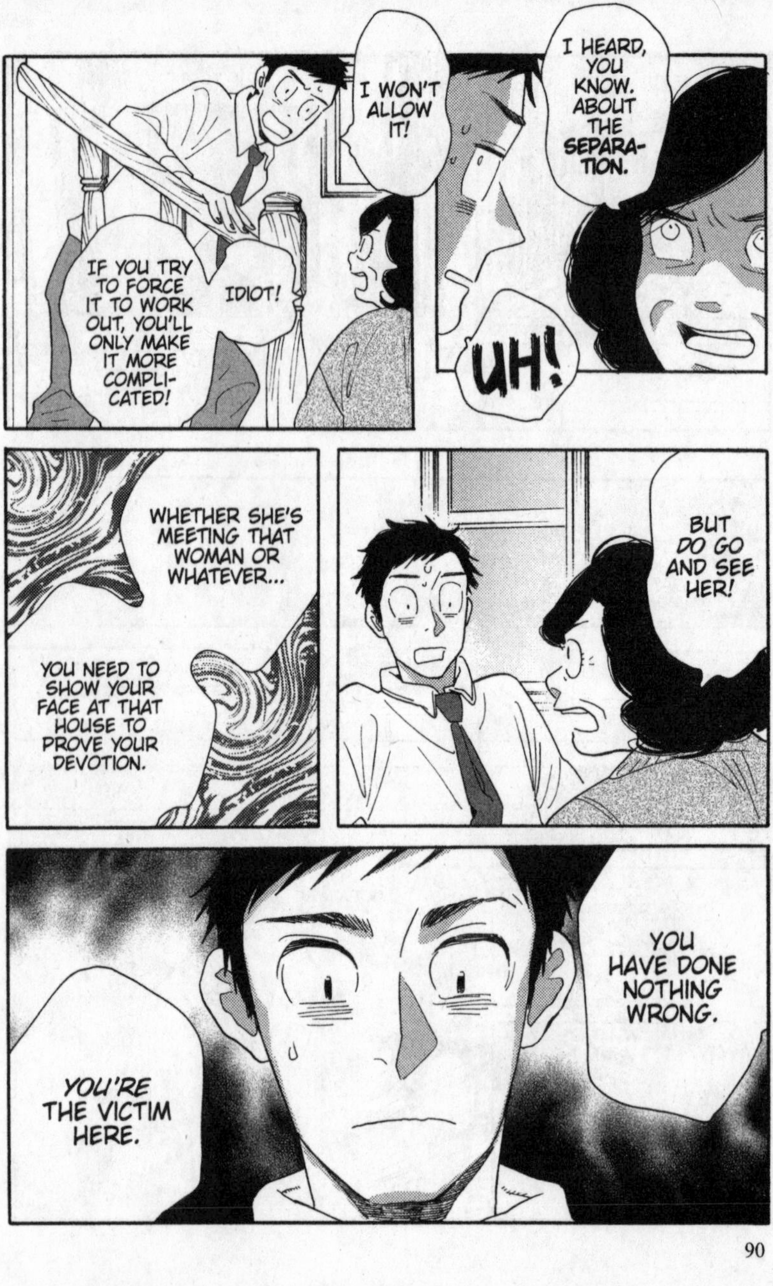
I HEARD, YOU KNOW. ABOUT THE SEPARATION.
UH!
I WON'T ALLOW IT!
IDIOT!
IF YOU TRY TO FORCE IT TO WORK OUT, YOU'LL ONLY MAKE IT MORE COMPLICATED!
BUT *DO GO* AND SEE HER!
WHETHER SHE'S MEETING THAT WOMAN OR WHATEVER...
YOU NEED TO SHOW YOUR FACE AT THAT HOUSE TO PROVE YOUR DEVOTION.
YOU HAVE DONE NOTHING WRONG.
YOU'RE THE VICTIM HERE.

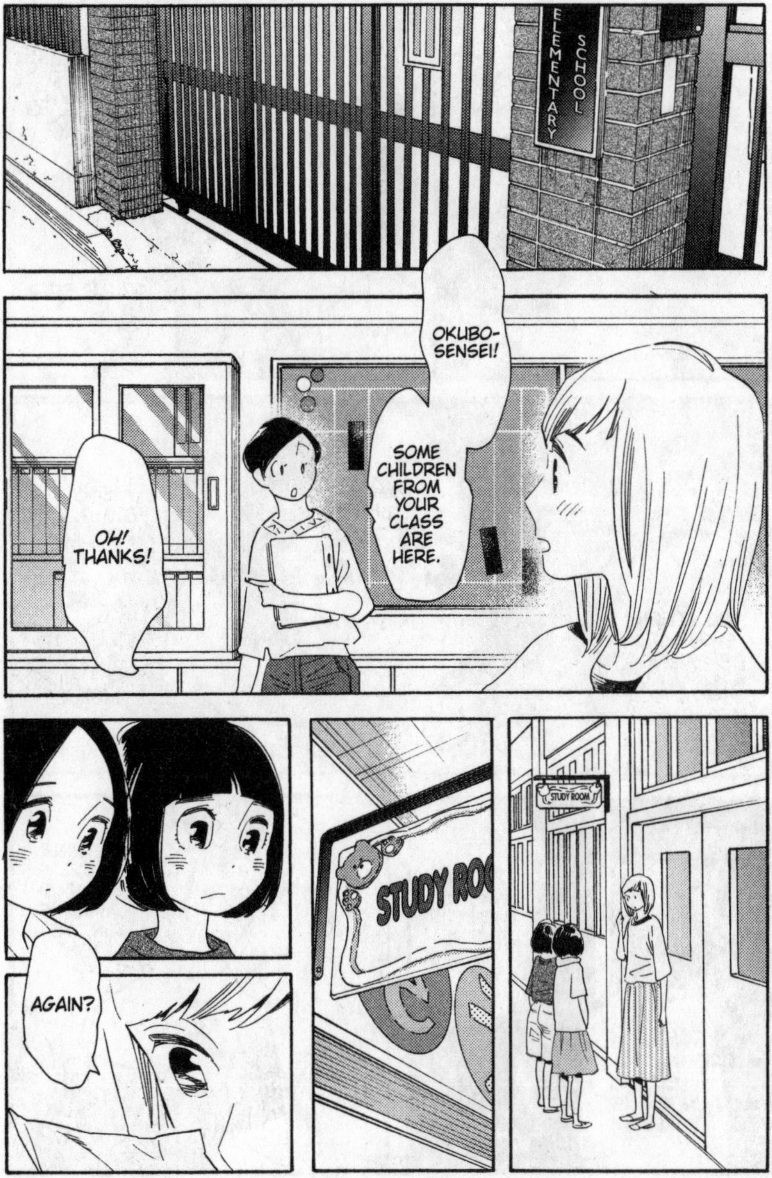
ELEMENTARY SCHOOL
OKUBO-SENSEI!
SOME CHILDREN FROM YOUR CLASS ARE HERE.
OH! THANKS!
STUDY ROOM
AGAIN?

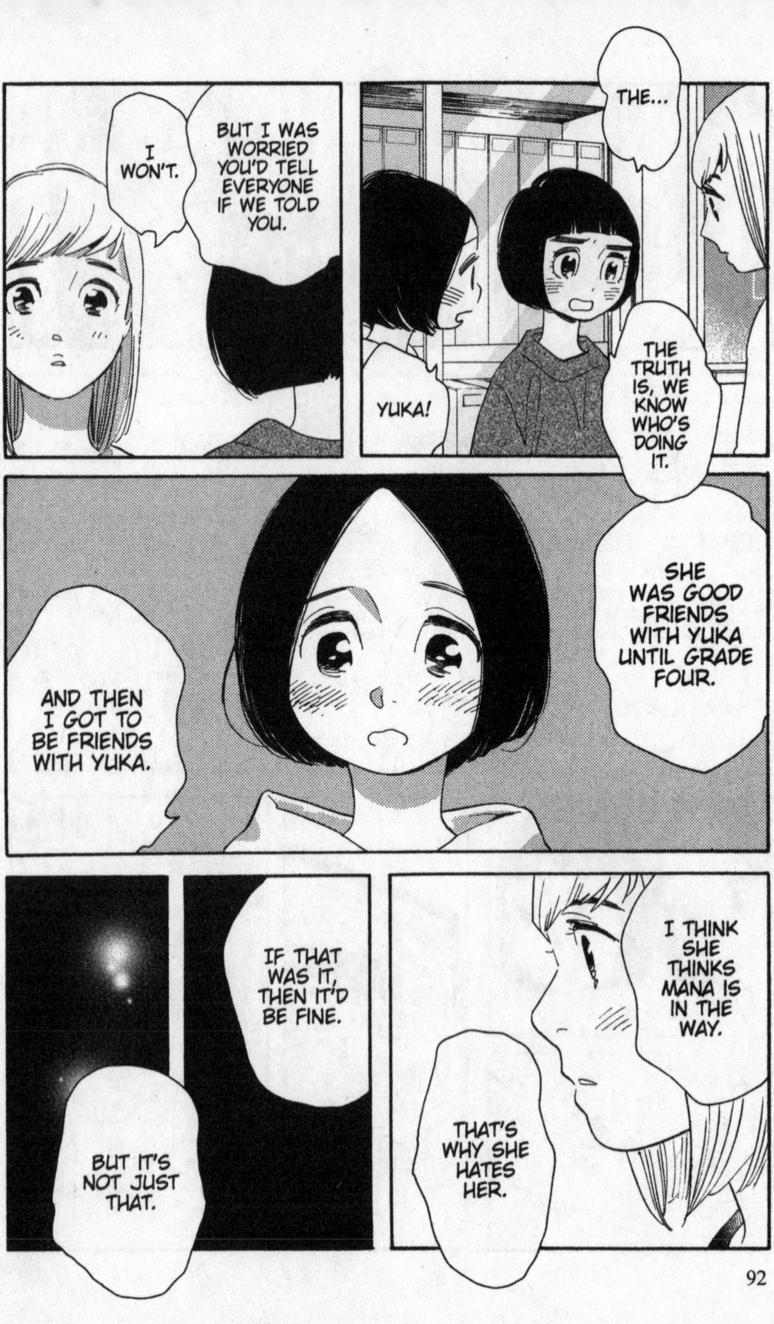
THE...
THE TRUTH IS, WE KNOW WHO'S DOING IT.
YUKA!
BUT I WAS WORRIED YOU'D TELL EVERYONE IF WE TOLD YOU.
I WON'T.
SHE WAS GOOD FRIENDS WITH YUKA UNTIL GRADE FOUR.
AND THEN I GOT TO BE FRIENDS WITH YUKA.
I THINK SHE THINKS MANA IS IN THE WAY.
THAT'S WHY SHE HATES HER.
IF THAT WAS IT, THEN IT'D BE FINE.
BUT IT'S NOT JUST THAT.

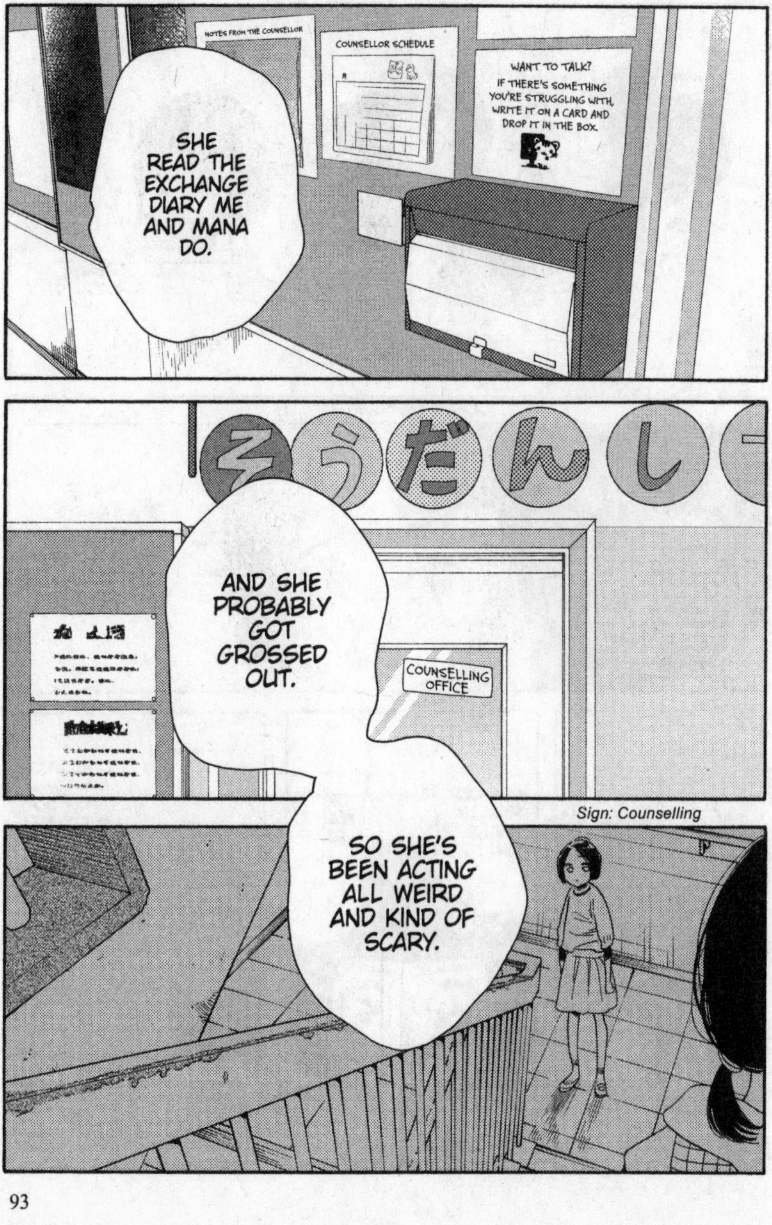
NOTES FROM THE COUNSELLOR
COUNSELLOR SCHEDULE
WANT TO TALK? IF THERE'S SOMETHING YOU'RE STRUGGLING WITH, WRITE IT ON A CARD AND DROP IT IN THE BOX.
SHE READ THE EXCHANGE DIARY ME AND MANA DO.
AND SHE PROBABLY GOT GROSSED OUT.
COUNSELLING OFFICE
Sign: Counselling
SO SHE'S BEEN ACTING ALL WEIRD AND KIND OF SCARY.

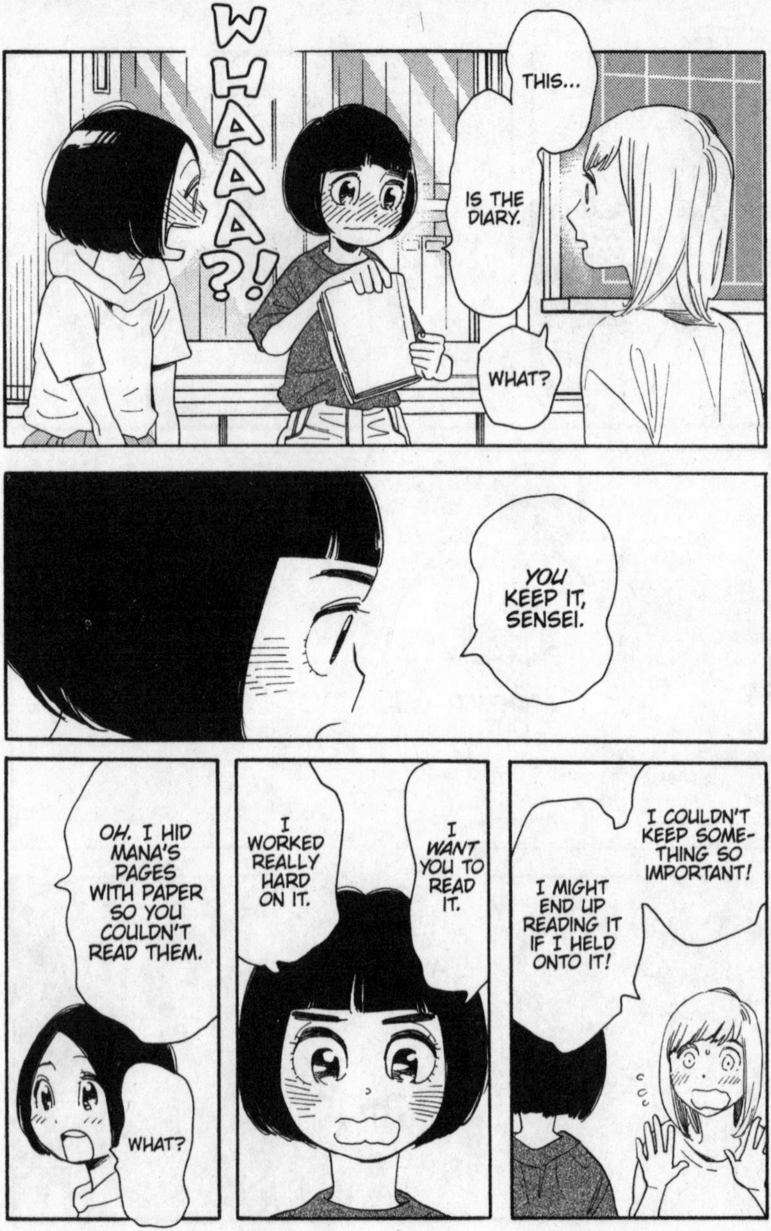
THIS...
IS THE DIARY.
WHAAA?!
WHAT?
YOU KEEP IT, SENSEI.
I COULDN'T KEEP SOMETHING SO IMPORTANT!
I MIGHT END UP READING IT IF I HELD ONTO IT!
I *WANT* YOU TO READ IT.
I WORKED REALLY HARD ON IT.
OH. I HID MANA'S PAGES WITH PAPER SO YOU COULDN'T READ THEM.
WHAT?

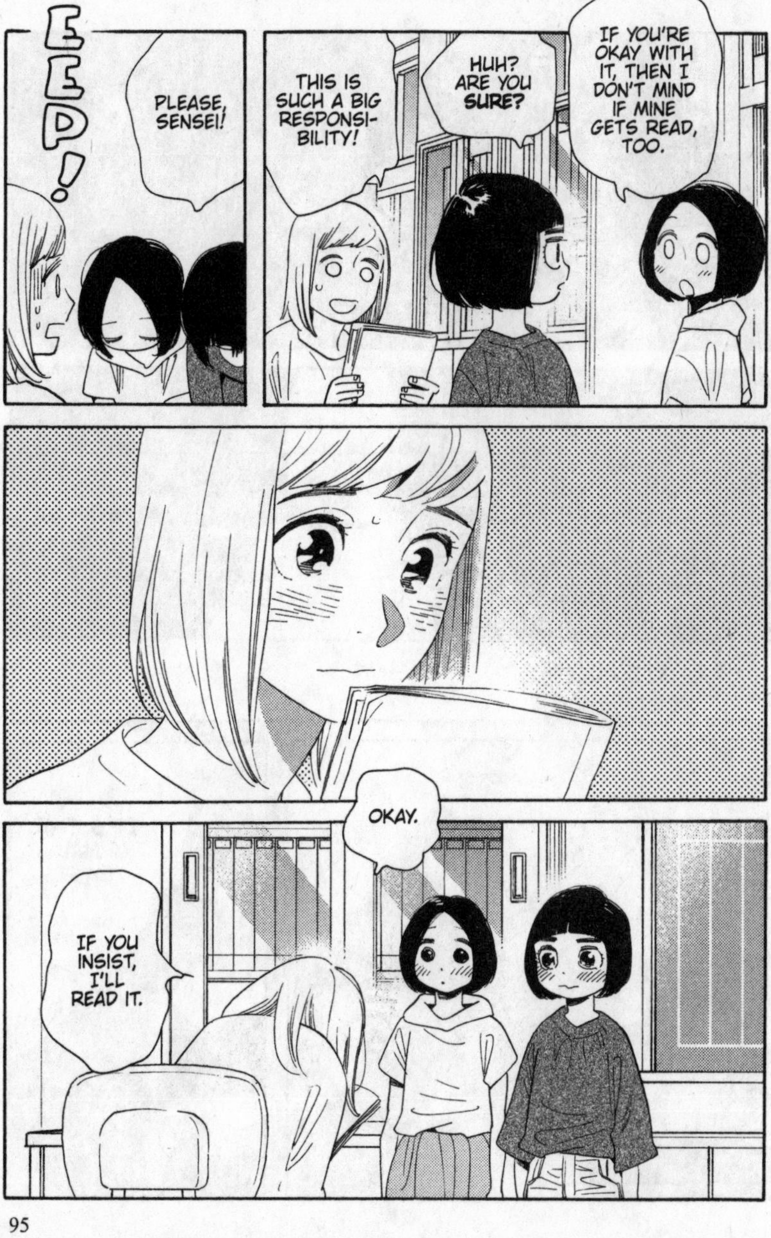
IF YOU'RE OKAY WITH IT, THEN I DON'T MIND IF MINE GETS READ, TOO.
HUH? ARE YOU SURE?
THIS IS SUCH A BIG RESPONSI-BILITY!
PLEASE, SENSEI!
EEP!
OKAY.
IF YOU INSIST, I'LL READ IT.

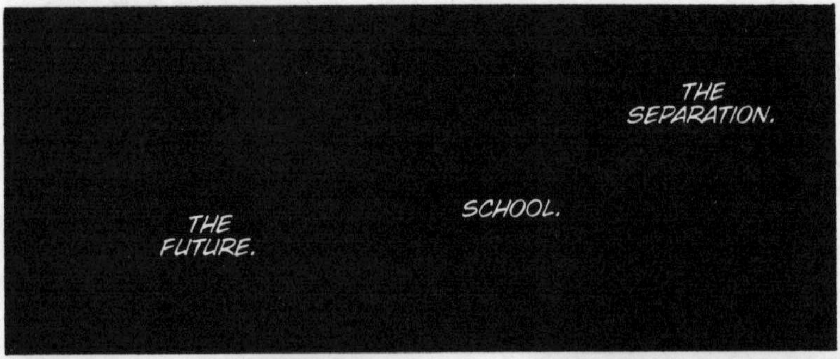
THE SEPARATION.
SCHOOL.
THE FUTURE.

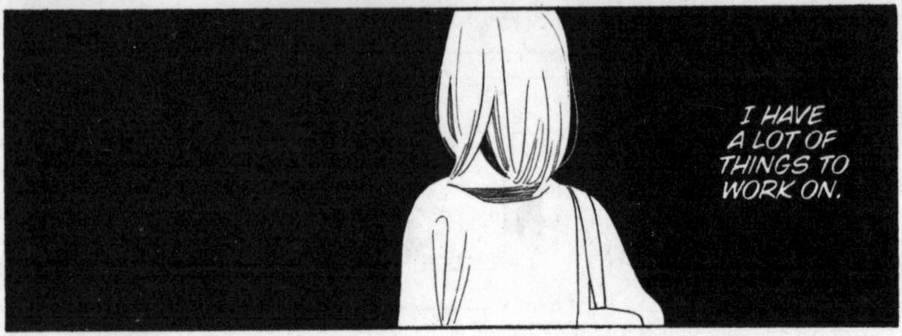
I HAVE A LOT OF THINGS TO WORK ON.

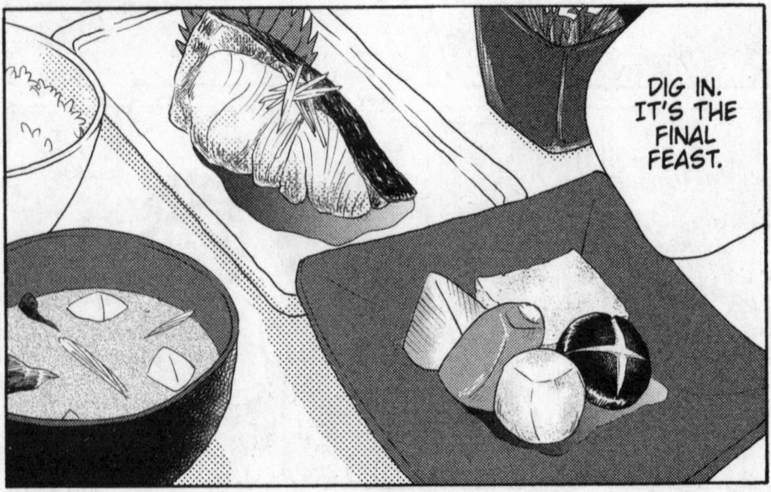
DIG IN. IT'S THE FINAL FEAST.

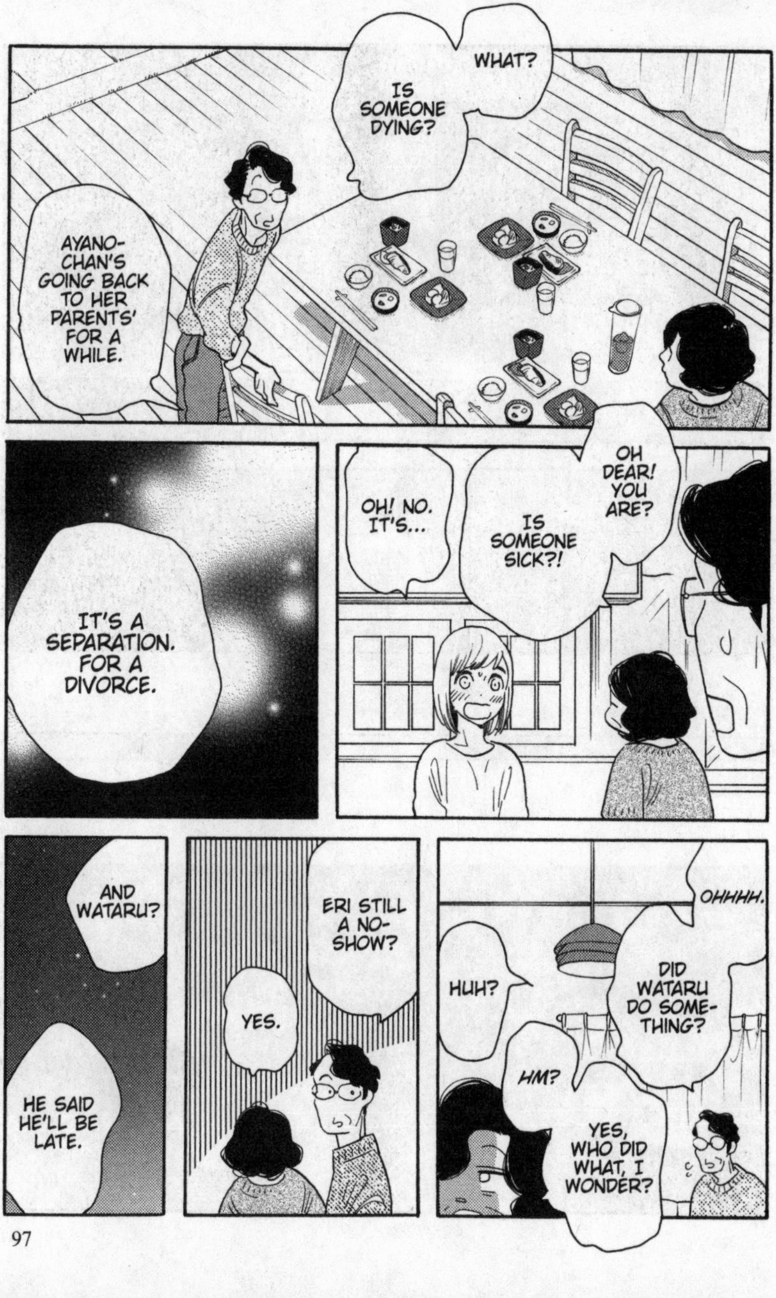
WHAT?
IS SOMEONE DYING?
AYANO-CHAN'S GOING BACK TO HER PARENTS' FOR A WHILE.
OH DEAR! YOU ARE?
IS SOMEONE SICK?!
OH! NO. IT'S...
IT'S A SEPARATION. FOR A DIVORCE.
OHHHH.
DID WATARU DO SOME-THING?
HUH?
HM?
YES, WHO DID WHAT, I WONDER?
ERI STILL A NO-SHOW?
YES.
AND WATARU?
HE SAID HE'LL BE LATE.

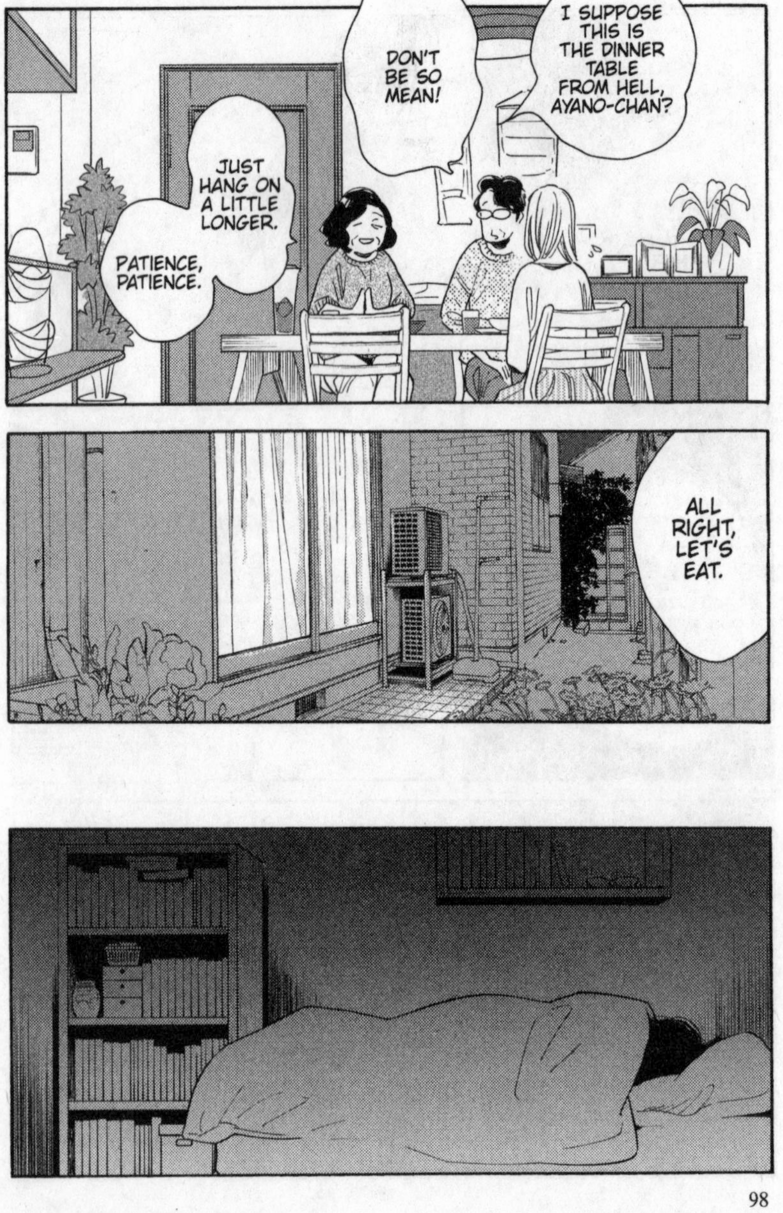
I SUPPOSE THIS IS THE DINNER TABLE FROM HELL, AYANO-CHAN?
DON'T BE SO MEAN!
JUST HANG ON A LITTLE LONGER.
PATIENCE, PATIENCE.
ALL RIGHT, LET'S EAT.

Chapter 19

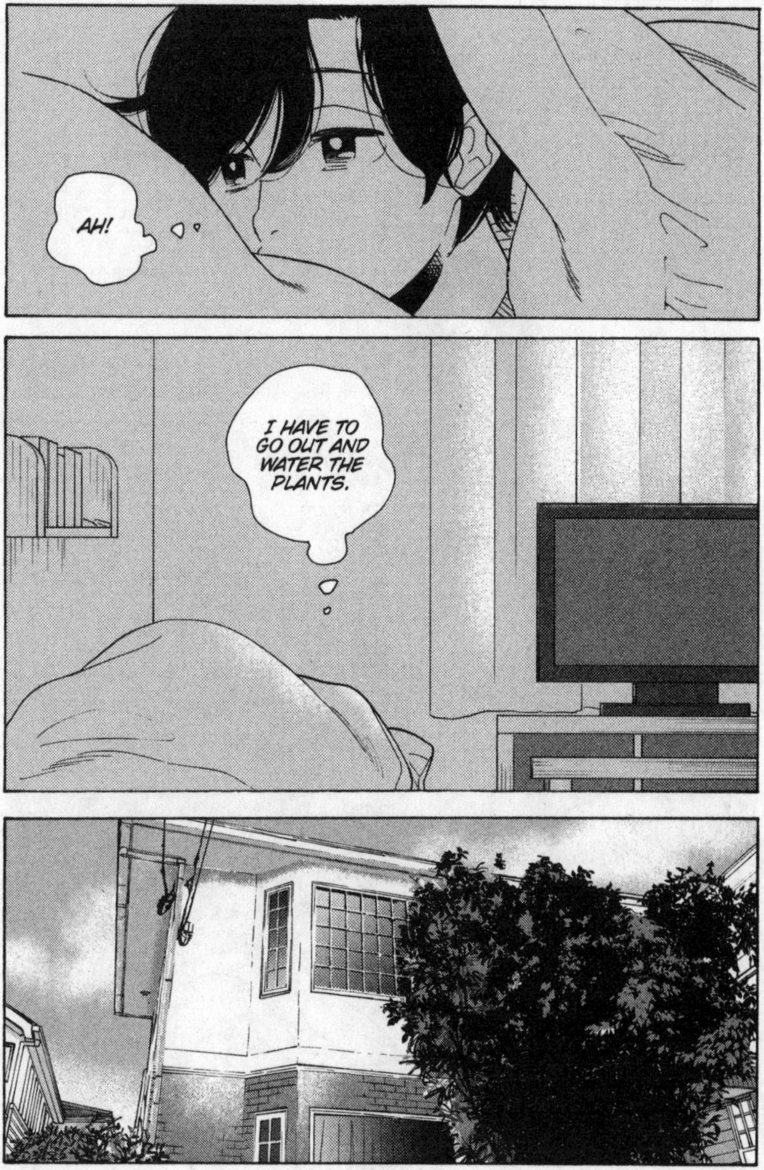
AH!
I HAVE TO GO OUT AND WATER THE PLANTS.

Chapter 19
Give Me a Slow Boogie

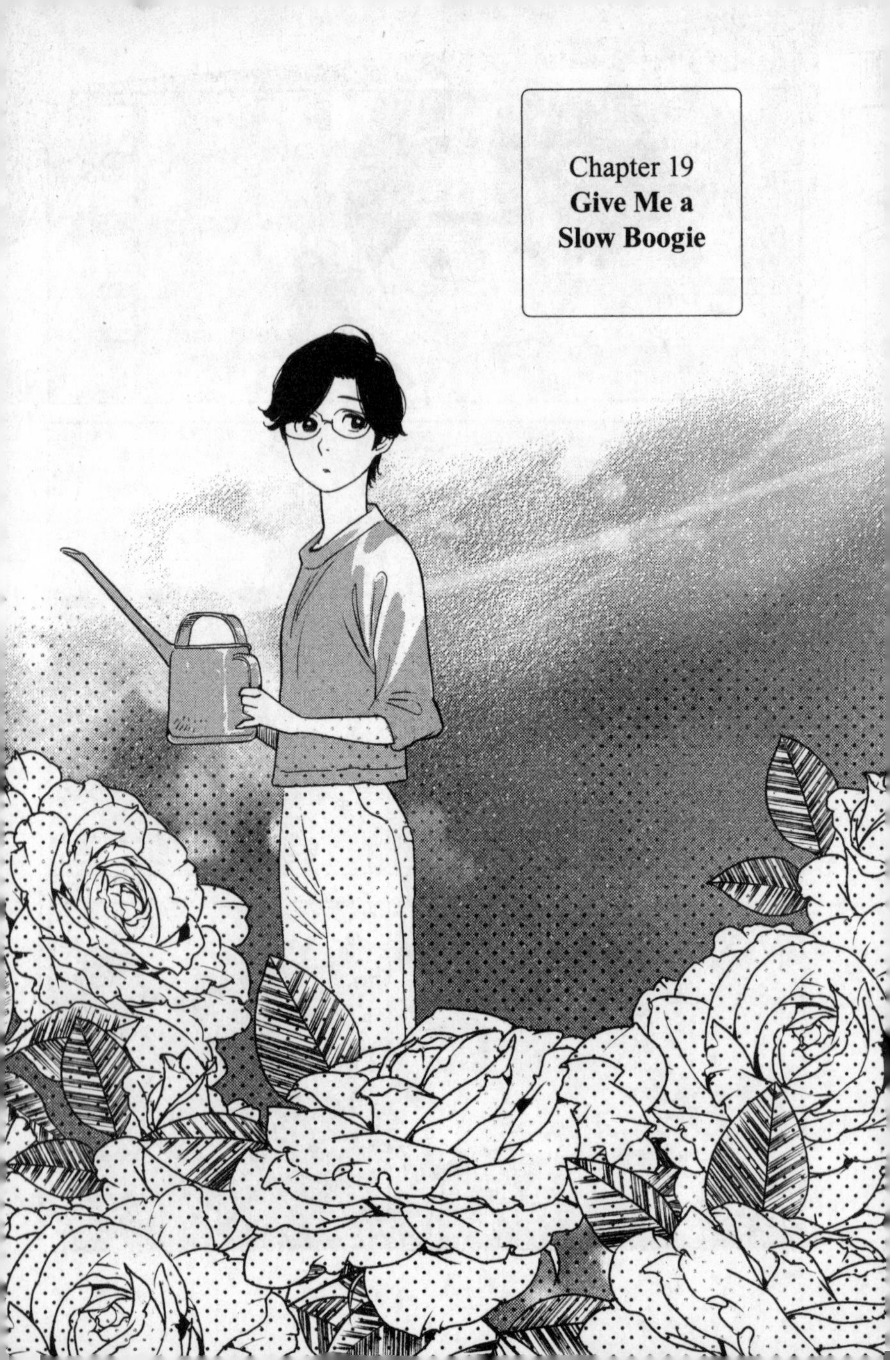

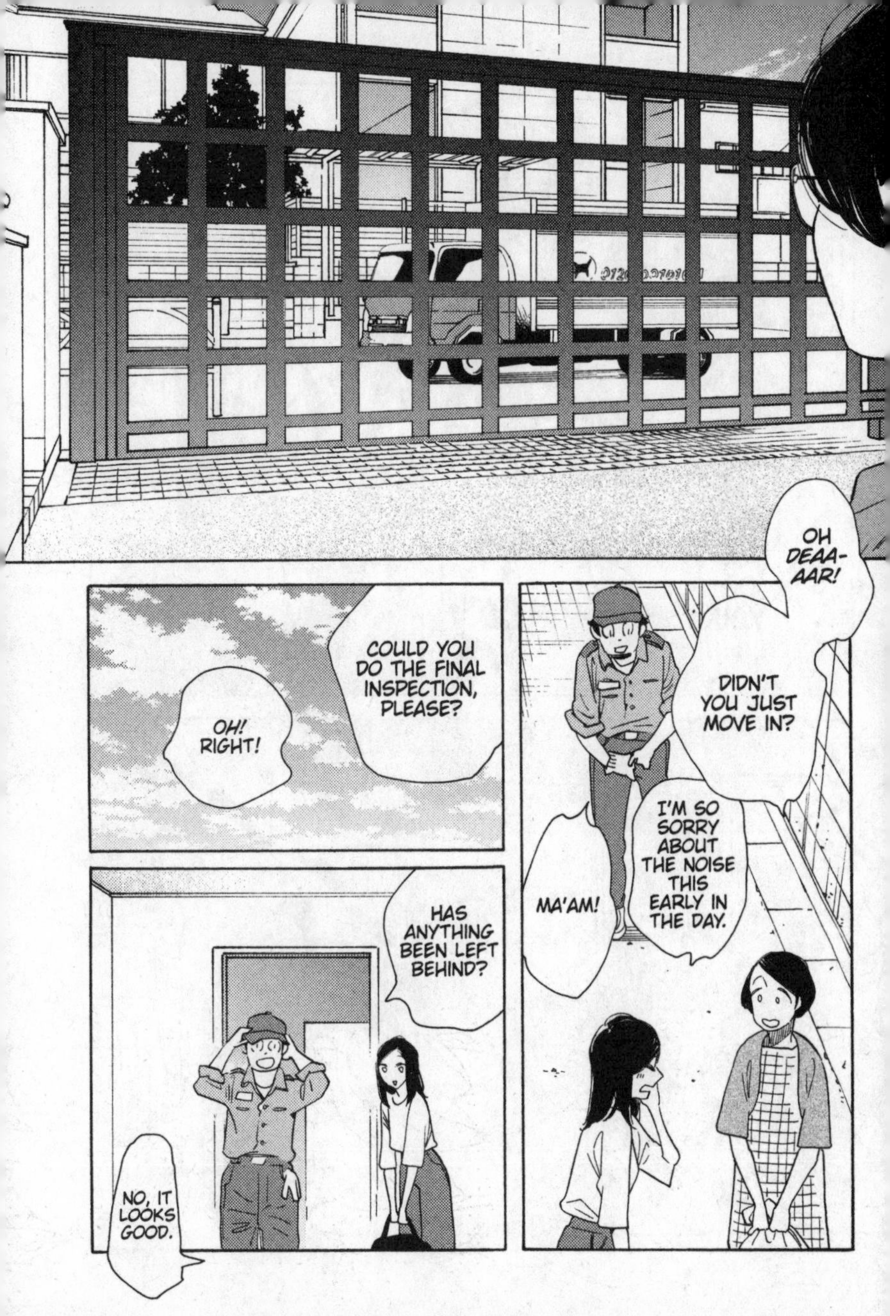
OH DEAAA-AAR!
DIDN'T YOU JUST MOVE IN?
I'M SO SORRY ABOUT THE NOISE THIS EARLY IN THE DAY.
MA'AM!
COULD YOU DO THE FINAL INSPECTION, PLEASE?
OH! RIGHT!
HAS ANYTHING BEEN LEFT BEHIND?
NO, IT LOOKS GOOD.

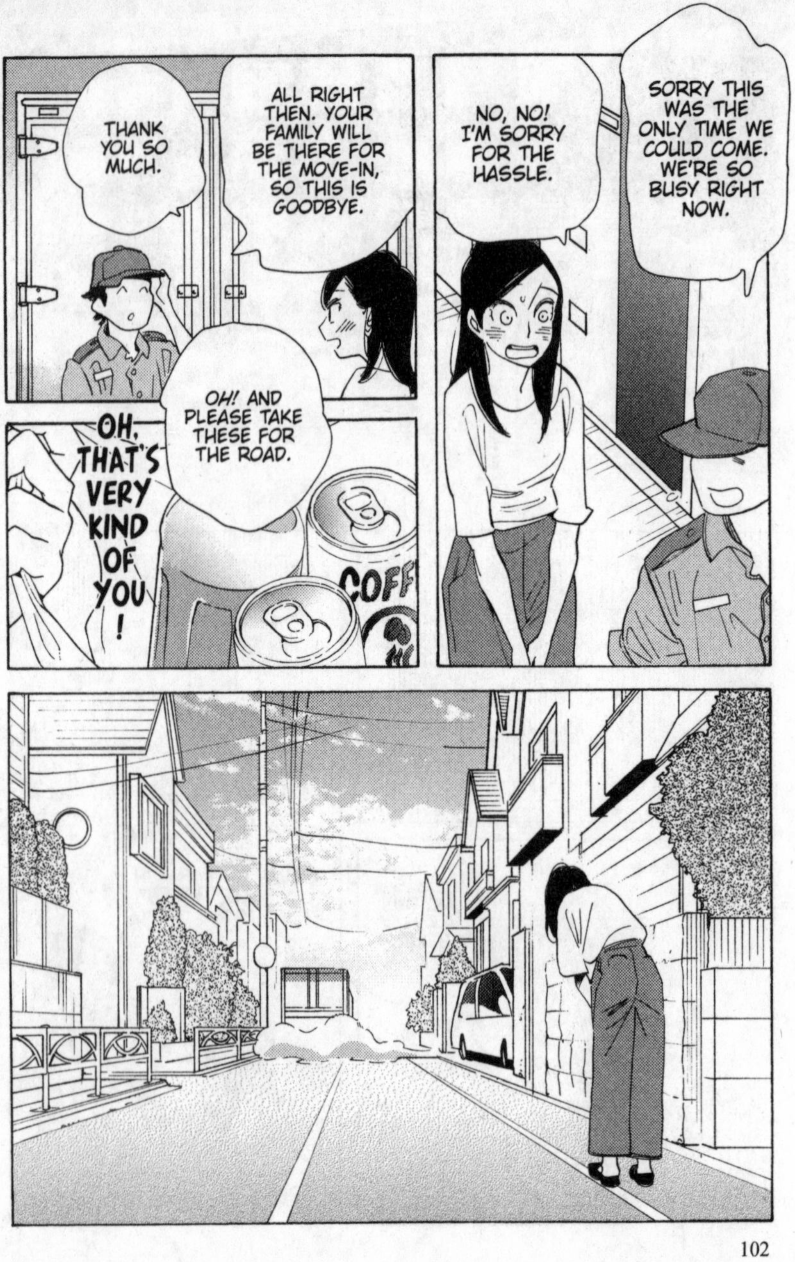
SORRY THIS WAS THE ONLY TIME WE COULD COME. WE'RE SO BUSY RIGHT NOW.
NO, NO! I'M SORRY FOR THE HASSLE.
ALL RIGHT THEN. YOUR FAMILY WILL BE THERE FOR THE MOVE-IN, SO THIS IS GOODBYE.
THANK YOU SO MUCH.
OH! AND PLEASE TAKE THESE FOR THE ROAD.
OH, THAT'S VERY KIND OF YOU!
COFF

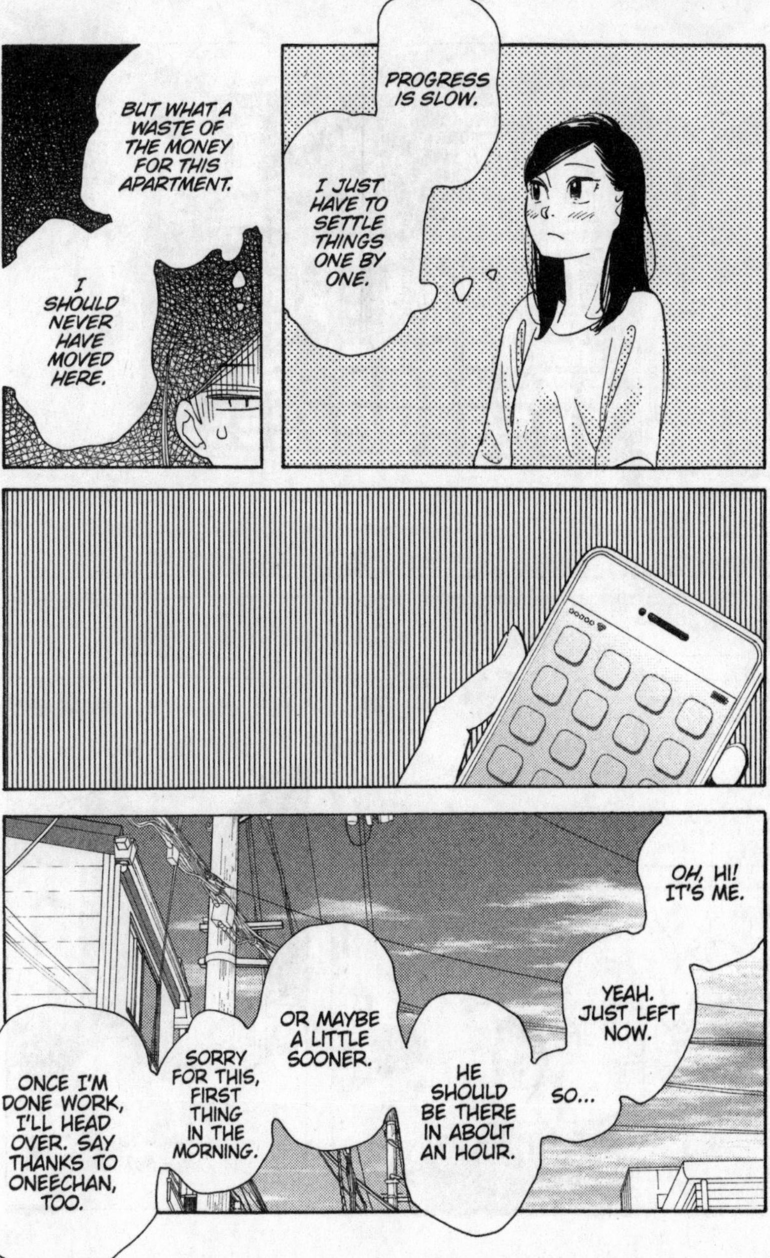
PROGRESS IS SLOW.
I JUST HAVE TO SETTLE THINGS ONE BY ONE.
BUT WHAT A WASTE OF THE MONEY FOR THIS APARTMENT.
I SHOULD NEVER HAVE MOVED HERE.
OH, HI! IT'S ME.
YEAH. JUST LEFT NOW.
SO...
HE SHOULD BE THERE IN ABOUT AN HOUR.
OR MAYBE A LITTLE SOONER.
SORRY FOR THIS, FIRST THING IN THE MORNING.
ONCE I'M DONE WORK, I'LL HEAD OVER. SAY THANKS TO ONEECHAN, TOO.

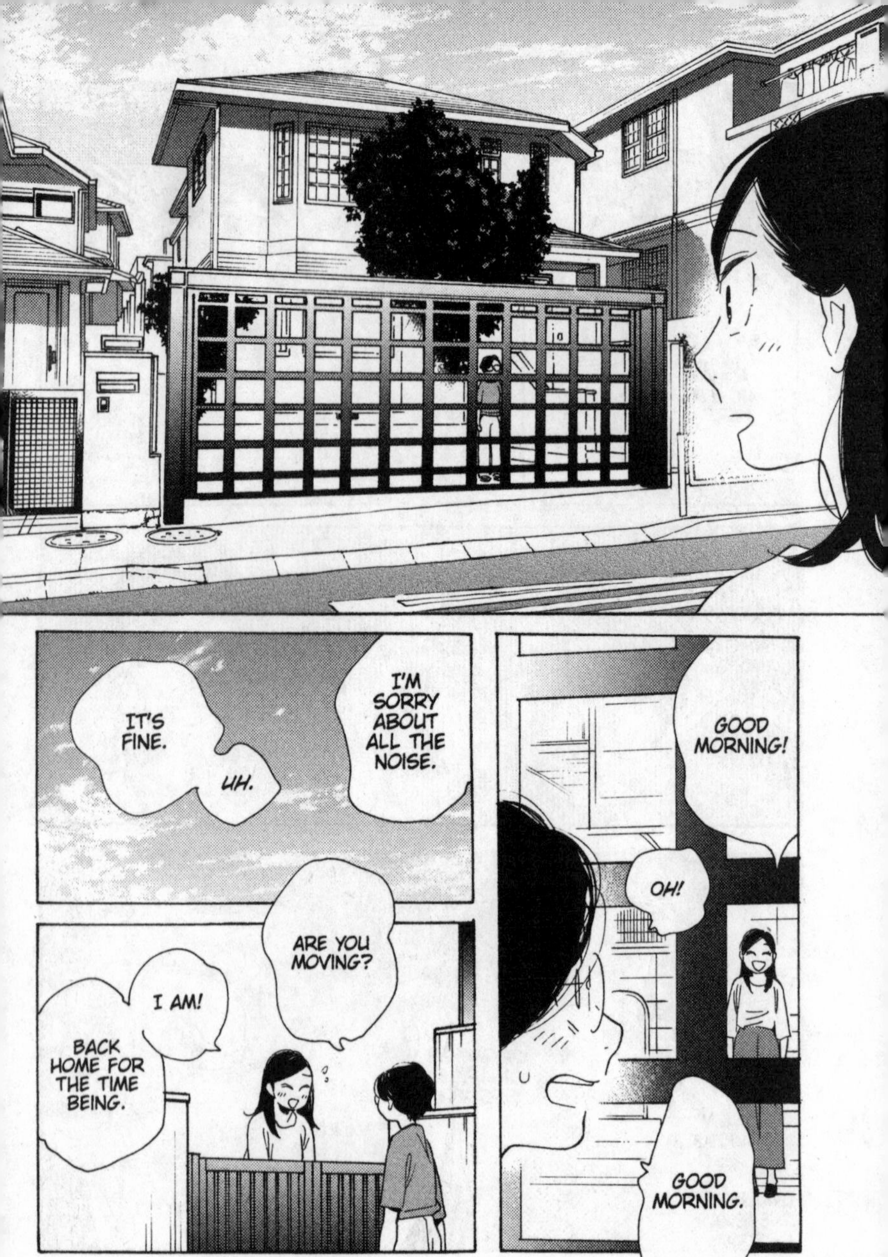
GOOD MORNING!
OH!
GOOD MORNING.
I'M SORRY ABOUT ALL THE NOISE.
UH.
IT'S FINE.
ARE YOU MOVING?
I AM!
BACK HOME FOR THE TIME BEING.

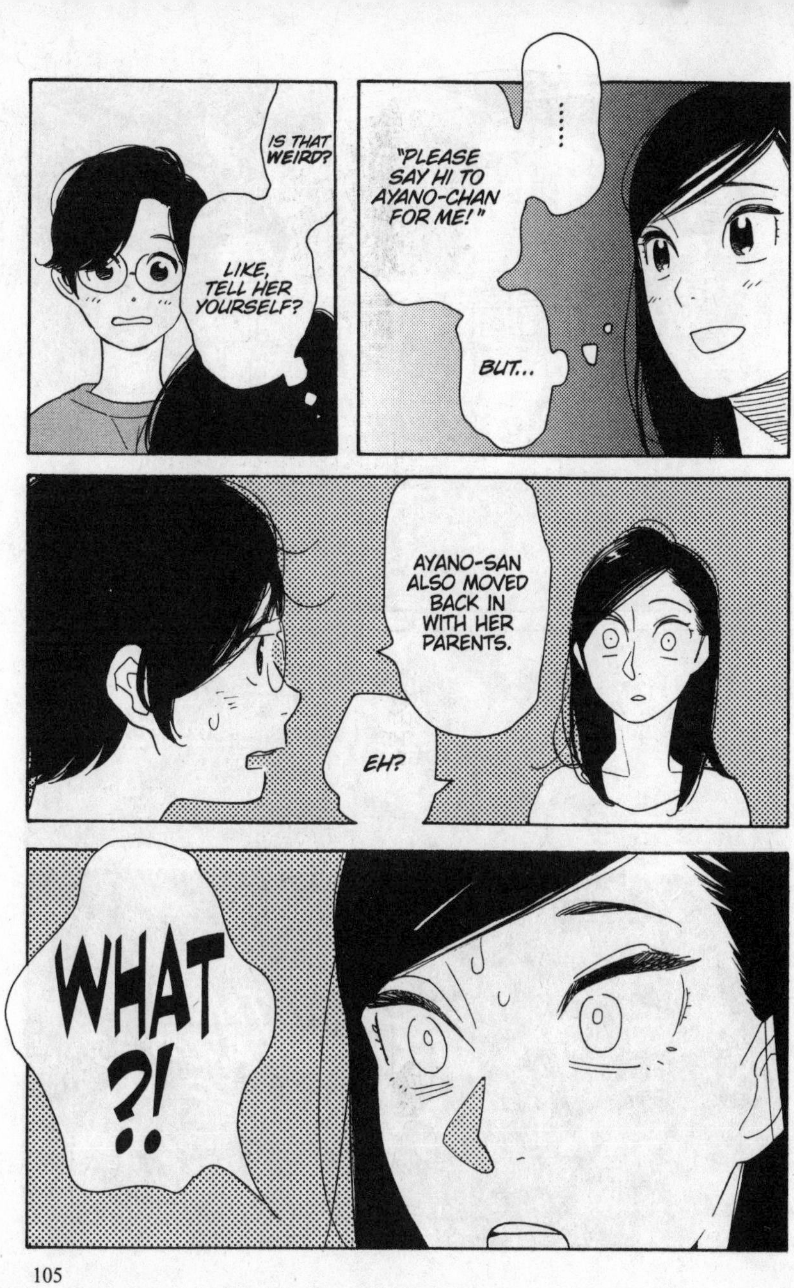
......
"PLEASE SAY HI TO AYANO-CHAN FOR ME!"
BUT...
IS THAT WEIRD?
LIKE, TELL HER YOURSELF?
AYANO-SAN ALSO MOVED BACK IN WITH HER PARENTS.
EH?
WHAT ?!

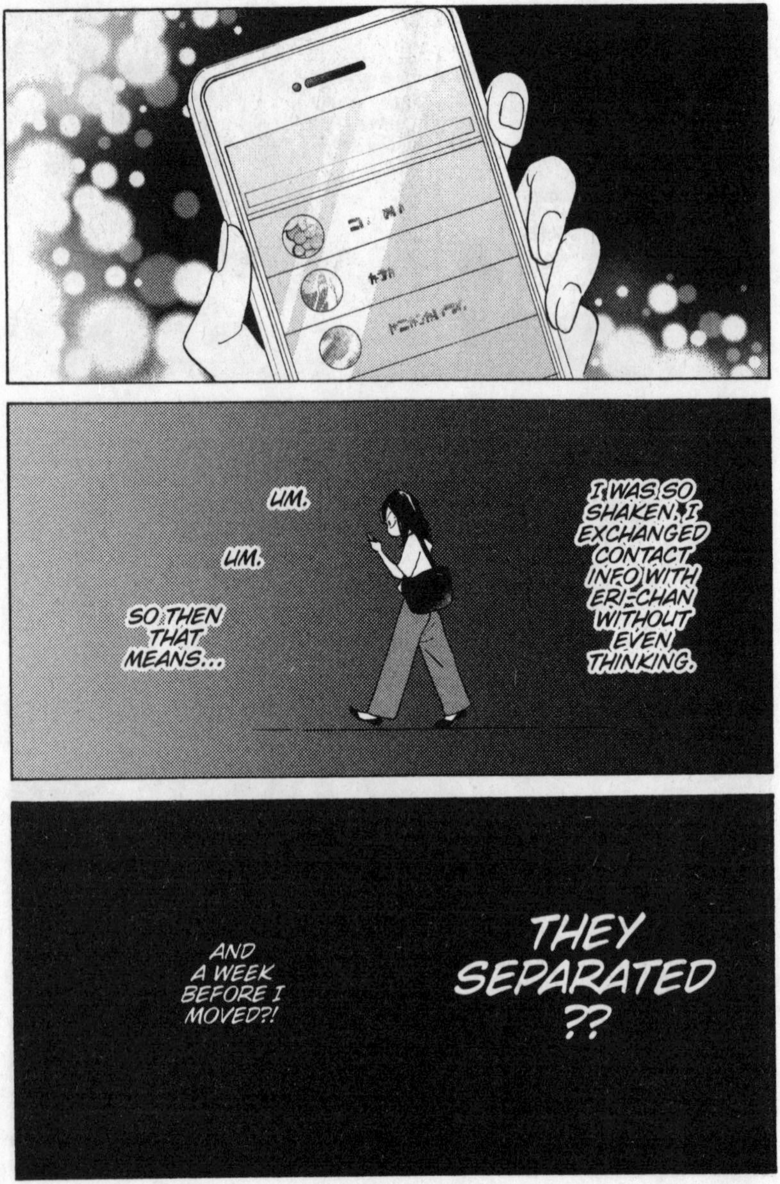
I WAS SO SHAKEN, I EXCHANGED CONTACT INFO WITH ERI-CHAN WITHOUT EVEN THINKING.
UM.
UM.
SO THEN THAT MEANS...
THEY SEPARATED??
AND A WEEK BEFORE I MOVED?!

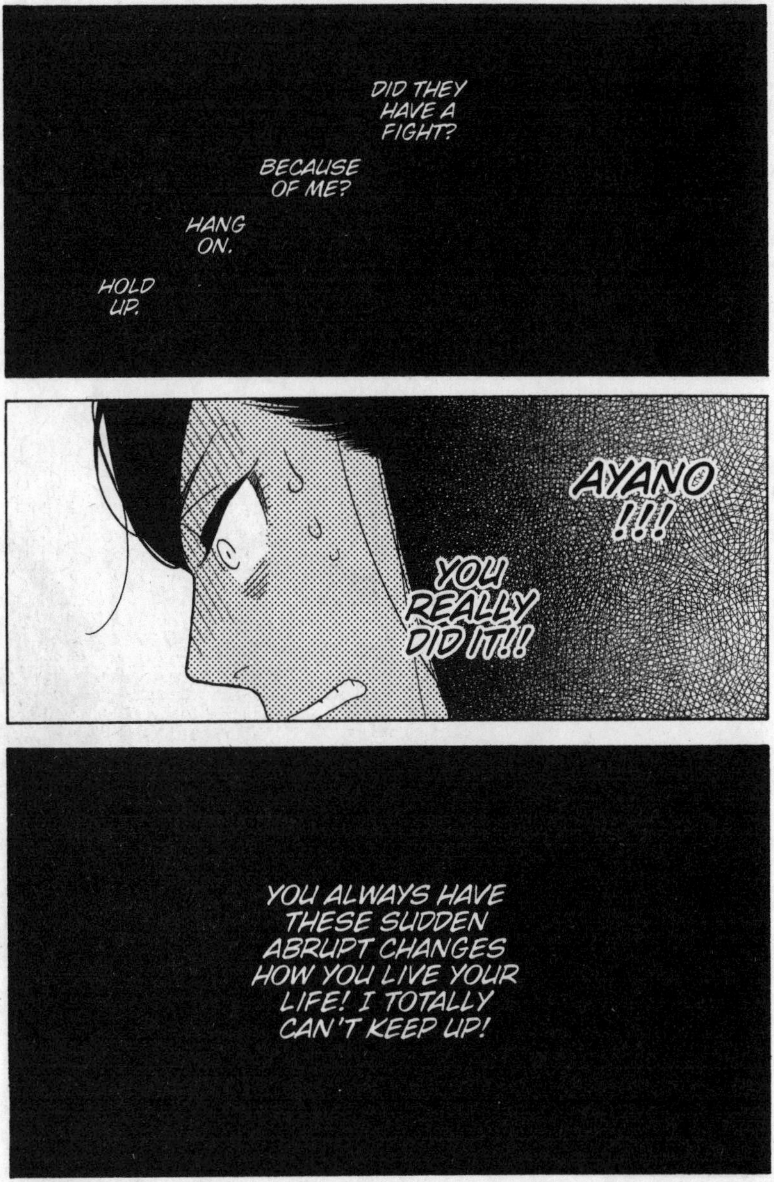
DID THEY HAVE A FIGHT?
BECAUSE OF ME?
HANG ON.
HOLD UP.
AYANO!!!
YOU REALLY DID IT!!
YOU ALWAYS HAVE THESE SUDDEN ABRUPT CHANGES HOW YOU LIVE YOUR LIFE! I TOTALLY CAN'T KEEP UP!

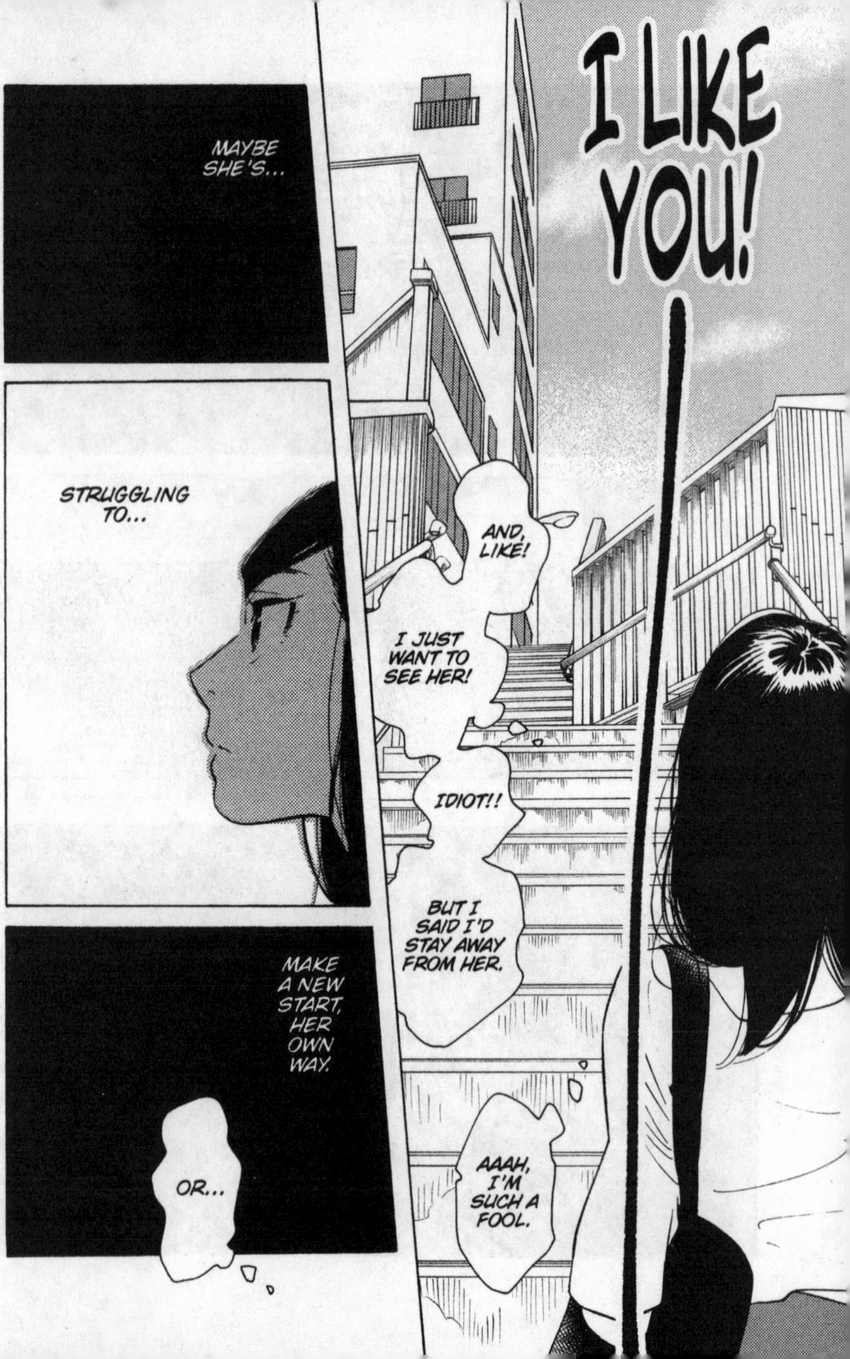
I LIKE YOU!
AND, LIKE!
I JUST WANT TO SEE HER!
IDIOT!!
BUT I SAID I'D STAY AWAY FROM HER.
AAAH, I'M SUCH A FOOL.
MAYBE SHE'S...
STRUGGLING TO...
MAKE A NEW START, HER OWN WAY.
OR...

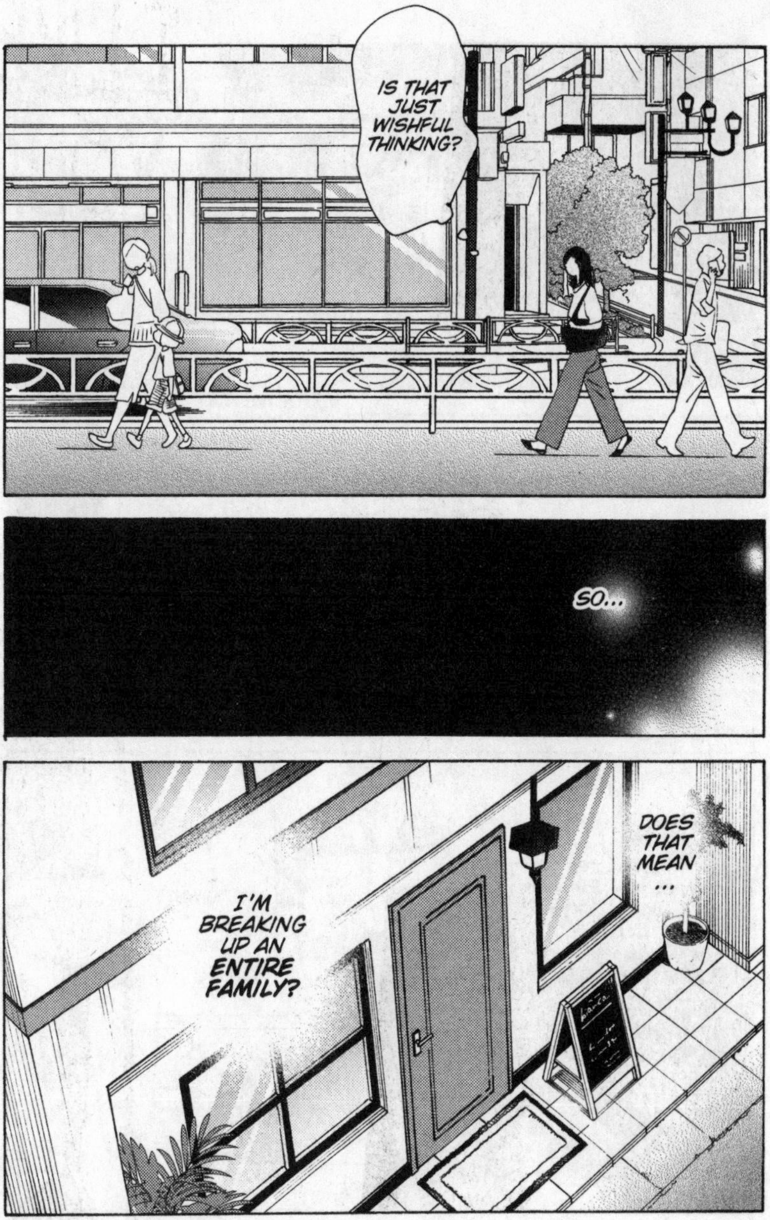
IS THAT JUST WISHFUL THINKING?
SO...
DOES THAT MEAN...
I'M BREAKING UP AN ENTIRE FAMILY?

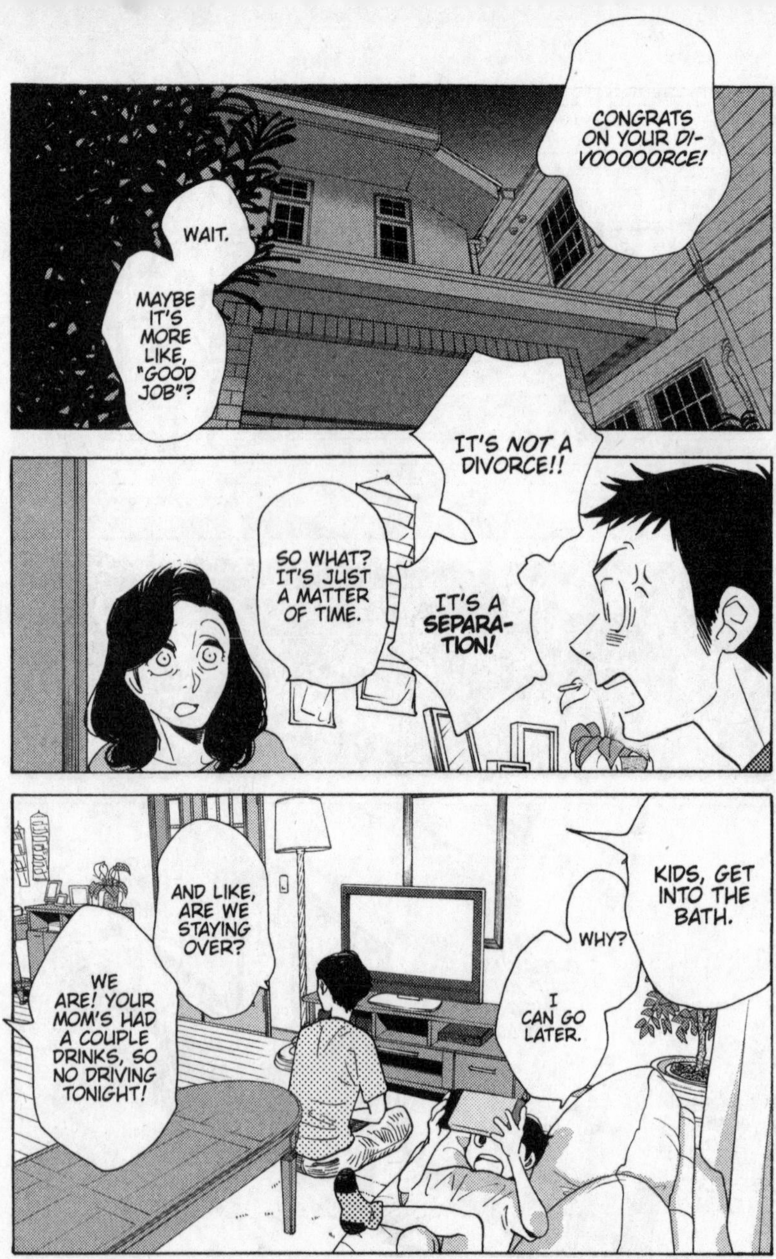
CONGRATS ON YOUR DI-VOOOOORCE!
WAIT.
MAYBE IT'S MORE LIKE, "GOOD JOB"?
IT'S *NOT* A DIVORCE!!
IT'S A SEPARATION!
SO WHAT? IT'S JUST A MATTER OF TIME.
KIDS, GET INTO THE BATH.
WHY?
I CAN GO LATER.
AND LIKE, ARE WE STAYING OVER?
WE ARE! YOUR MOM'S HAD A COUPLE DRINKS, SO NO DRIVING TONIGHT!

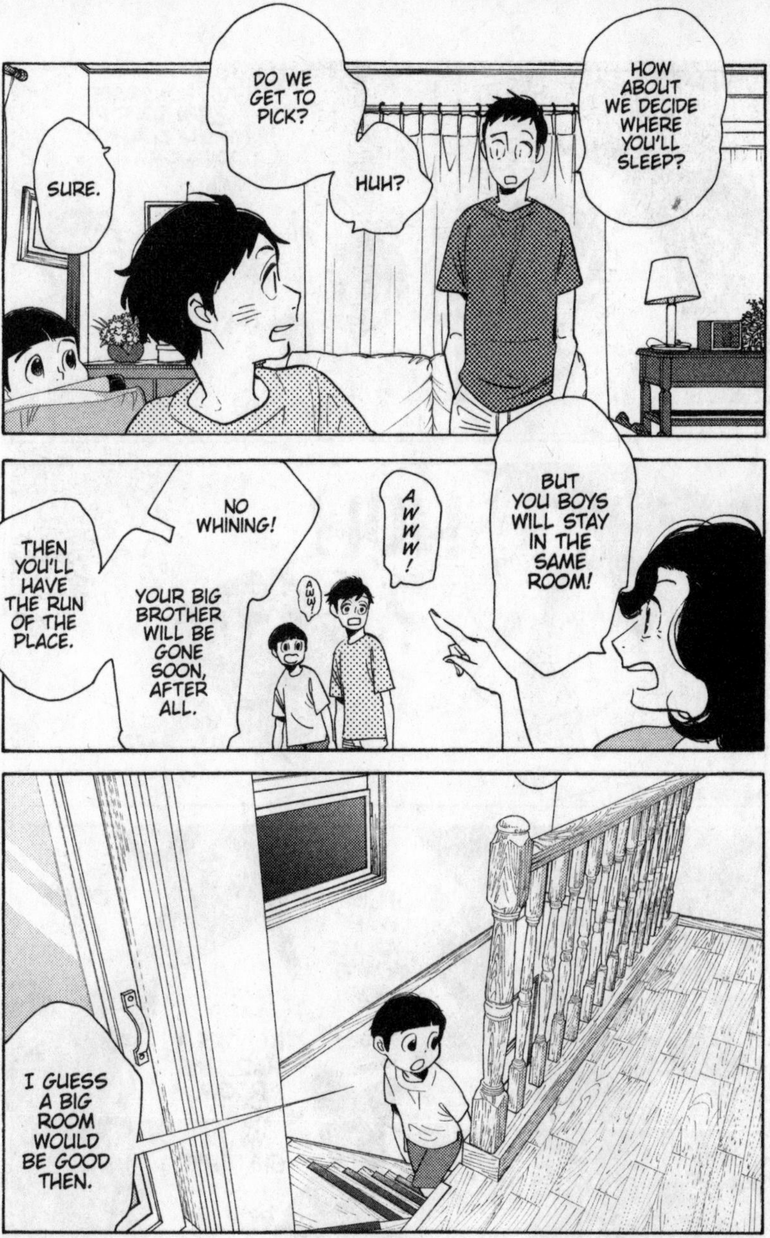
HOW ABOUT WE DECIDE WHERE YOU'LL SLEEP?
HUH?
DO WE GET TO PICK?
SURE.
BUT YOU BOYS WILL STAY IN THE SAME ROOM!
AWWW!
AWW!
NO WHINING!
YOUR BIG BROTHER WILL BE GONE SOON, AFTER ALL.
THEN YOU'LL HAVE THE RUN OF THE PLACE.
I GUESS A BIG ROOM WOULD BE GOOD THEN.

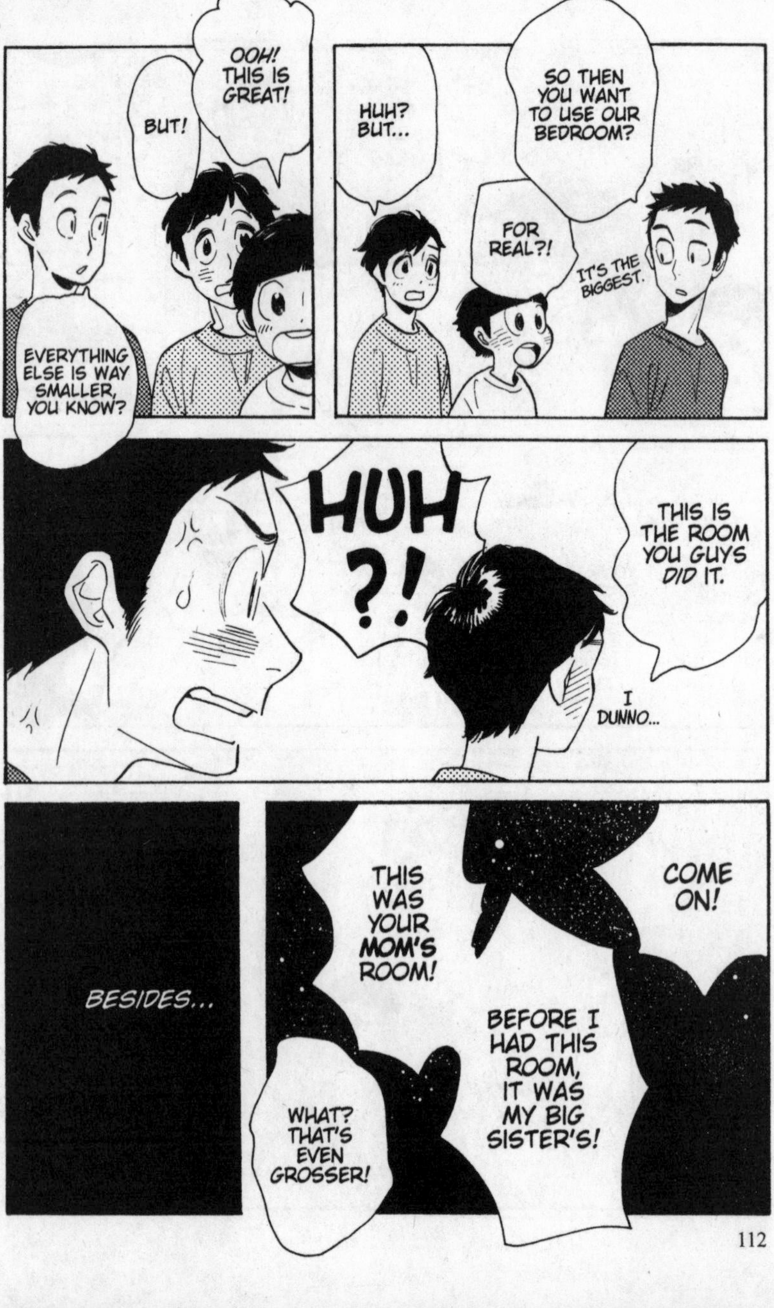
SO THEN YOU WANT TO USE OUR BEDROOM?
IT'S THE BIGGEST.
FOR REAL?!
HUH? BUT...
OOH! THIS IS GREAT!
BUT!
EVERYTHING ELSE IS WAY SMALLER, YOU KNOW?
THIS IS THE ROOM YOU GUYS *DID* IT.
HUH ?!
I DUNNO...
COME ON!
THIS WAS YOUR MOM'S ROOM!
BEFORE I HAD THIS ROOM, IT WAS MY BIG SISTER'S!
WHAT? THAT'S EVEN GROSSER!
BESIDES...

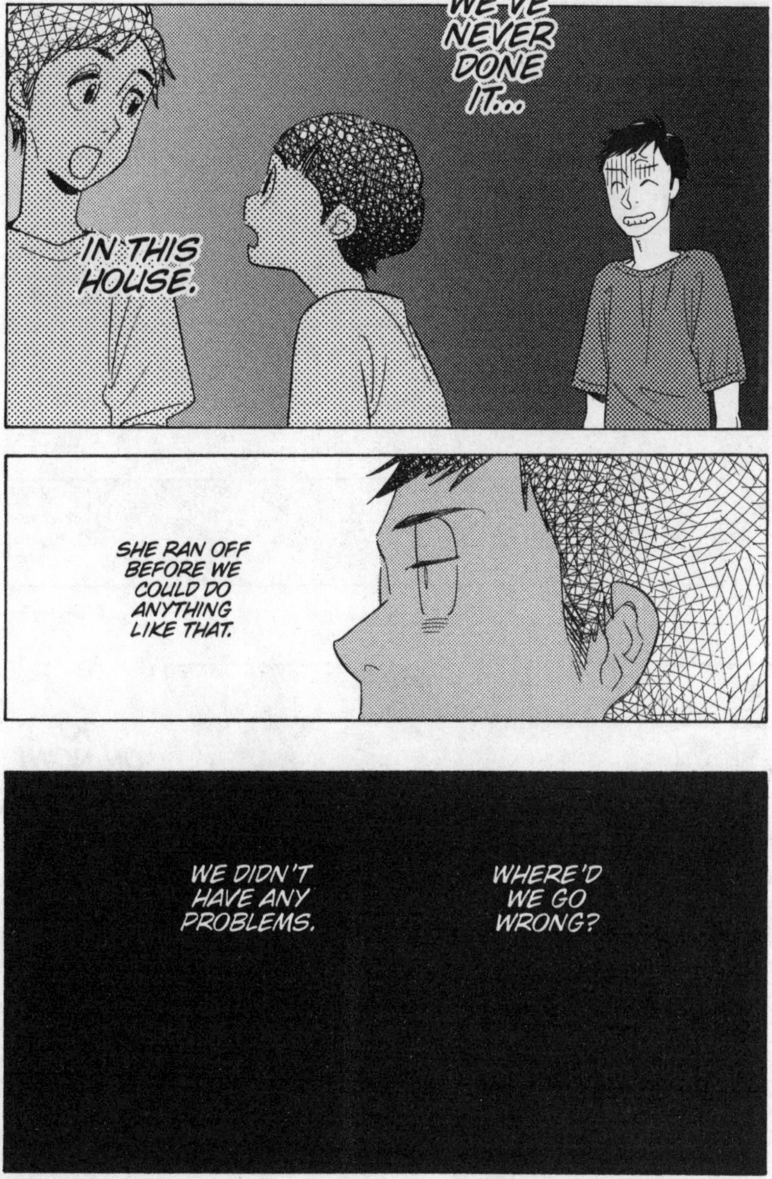
WE'VE NEVER DONE IT...
IN THIS HOUSE.
SHE RAN OFF BEFORE WE COULD DO ANYTHING LIKE THAT.
WHERE'D WE GO WRONG?
WE DIDN'T HAVE ANY PROBLEMS.

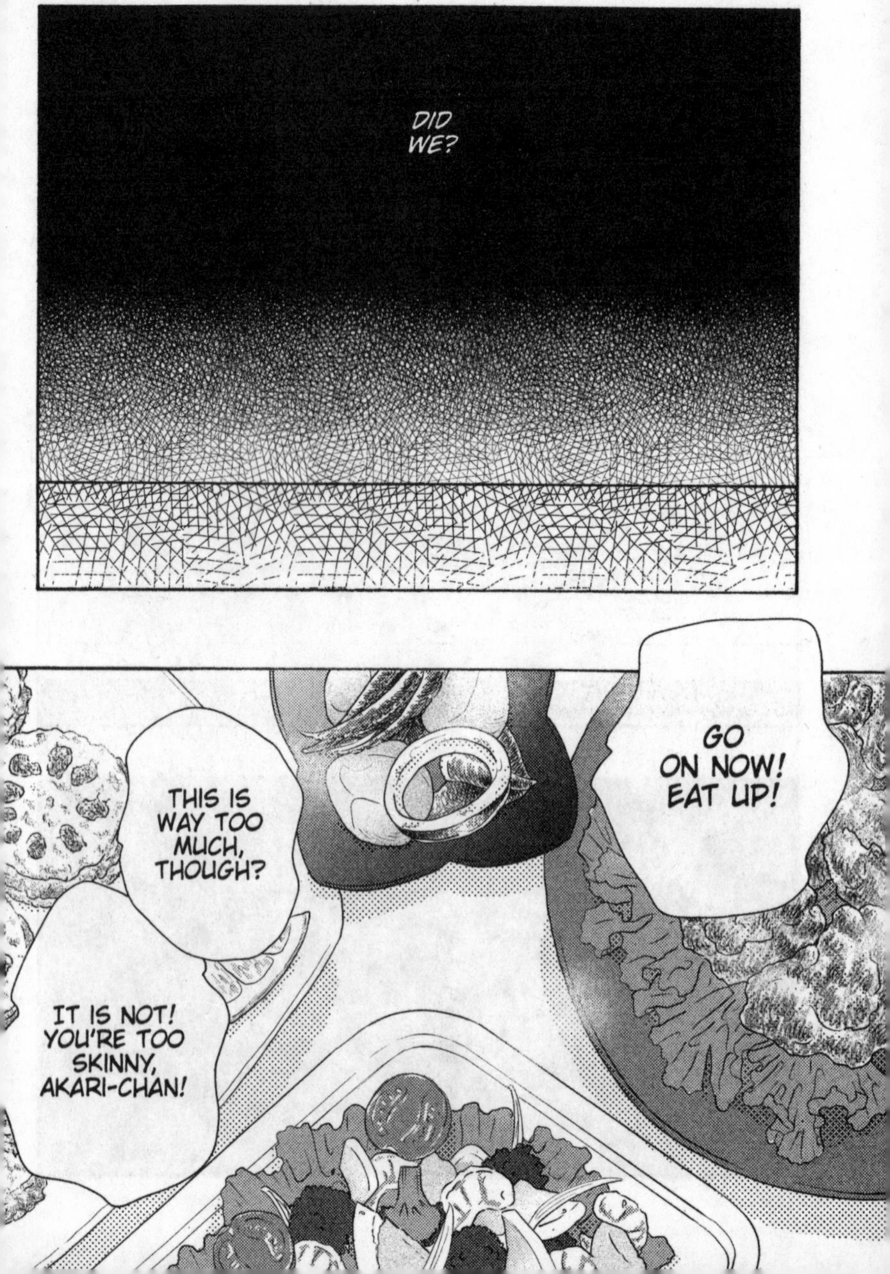
DID WE?
GO ON NOW! EAT UP!
THIS IS WAY TOO MUCH, THOUGH?
IT IS NOT! YOU'RE TOO SKINNY, AKARI-CHAN!

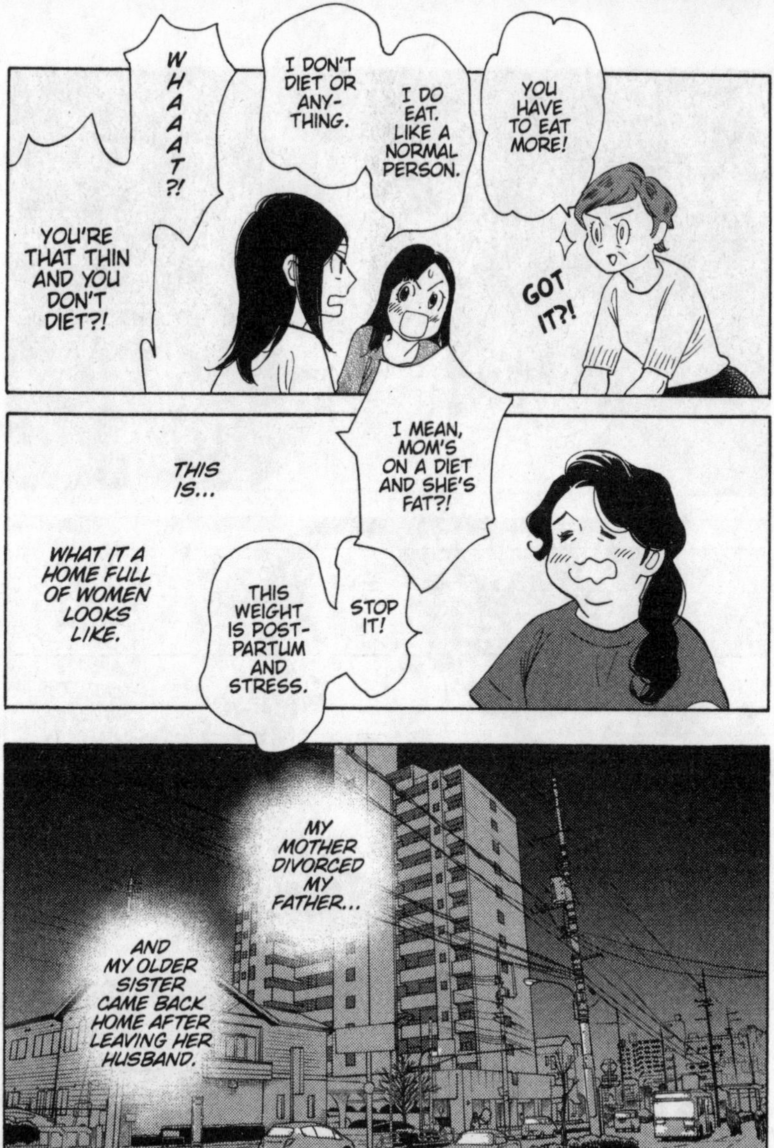
YOU HAVE TO EAT MORE!
GOT IT?!
I DO EAT. LIKE A NORMAL PERSON.
I DON'T DIET OR ANY-THING.
WHAAAAT?!
YOU'RE THAT THIN AND YOU DON'T DIET?!
I MEAN, MOM'S ON A DIET AND SHE'S FAT?!
STOP IT!
THIS WEIGHT IS POST-PARTUM AND STRESS.
THIS IS...
WHAT IT A HOME FULL OF WOMEN LOOKS LIKE.
MY MOTHER DIVORCED MY FATHER...
AND MY OLDER SISTER CAME BACK HOME AFTER LEAVING HER HUSBAND.

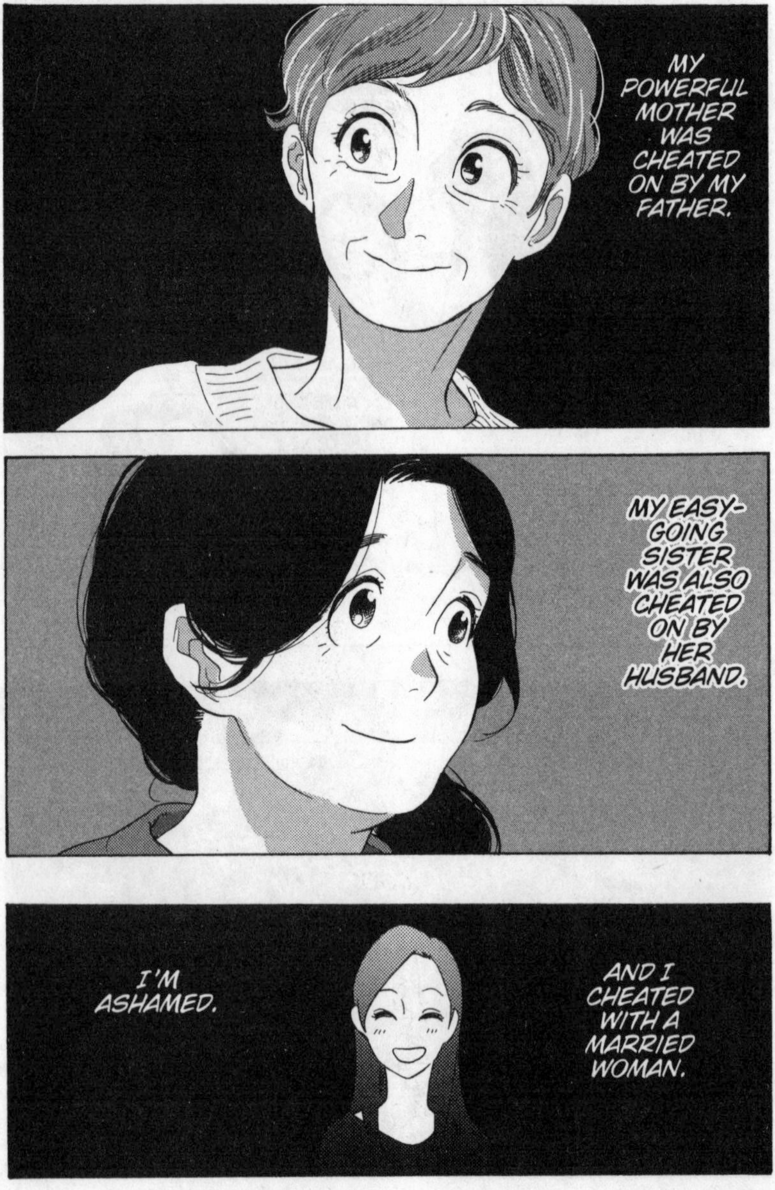
MY POWERFUL MOTHER WAS CHEATED ON BY MY FATHER.
MY EASY-GOING SISTER WAS ALSO CHEATED ON BY HER HUSBAND.
AND I CHEATED WITH A MARRIED WOMAN.
I'M ASHAMED.

I DON'T DESERVE TO LIVE HERE WITH THESE PEOPLE.

AND EVEN NOW, I'M HEAD OVER HEELS IN LOVE WITH HER.

HERE. EAT THIS, TOO.

I DON'T DESERVE TO EAT THE FRIED LOTUS ROOT THAT MY MOTHER MADE ME.

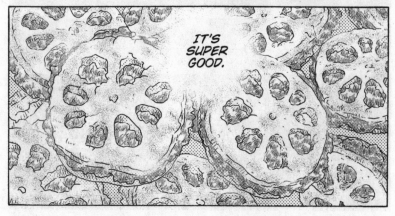

IT'S SUPER GOOD.

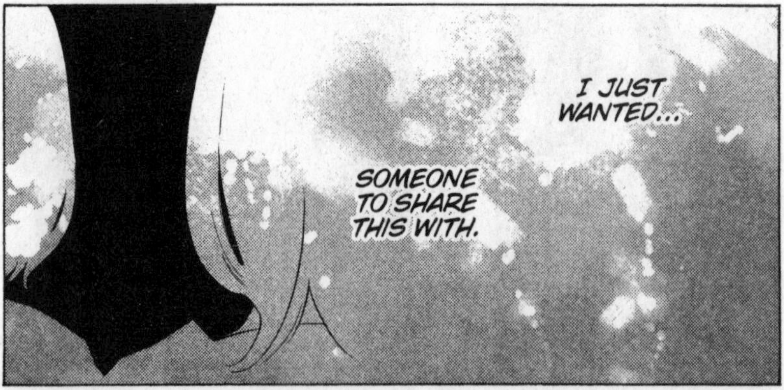
I JUST WANTED...
SOMEONE TO SHARE THIS WITH.
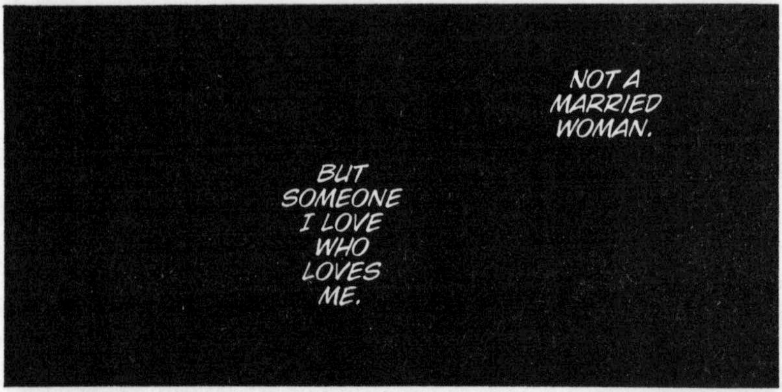
NOT A MARRIED WOMAN.
BUT SOMEONE I LOVE WHO LOVES ME.
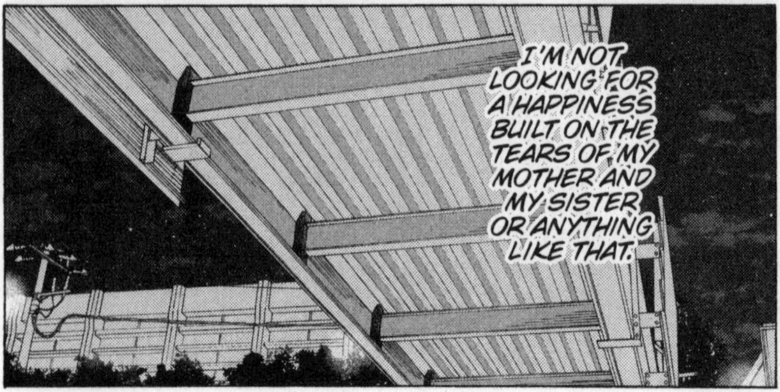
I'M NOT LOOKING FOR A HAPPINESS BUILT ON THE TEARS OF MY MOTHER AND MY SISTER OR ANYTHING LIKE THAT.

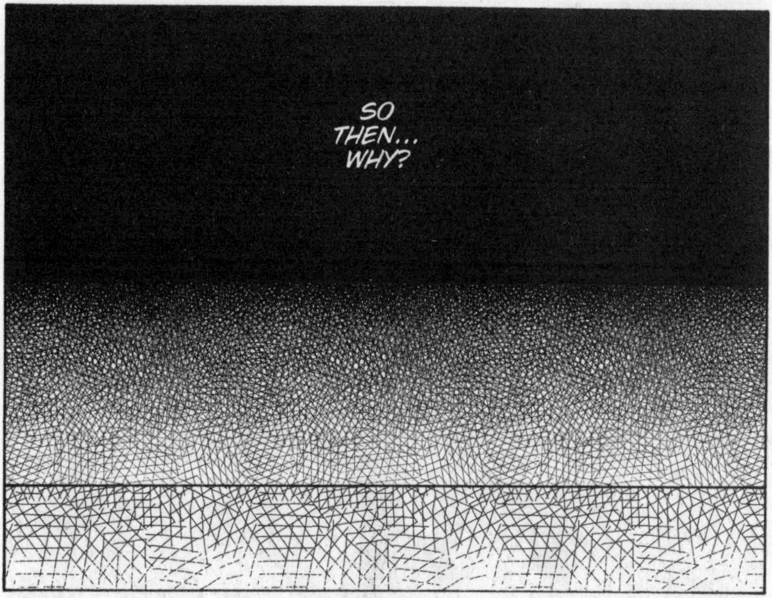
SO THEN... WHY?

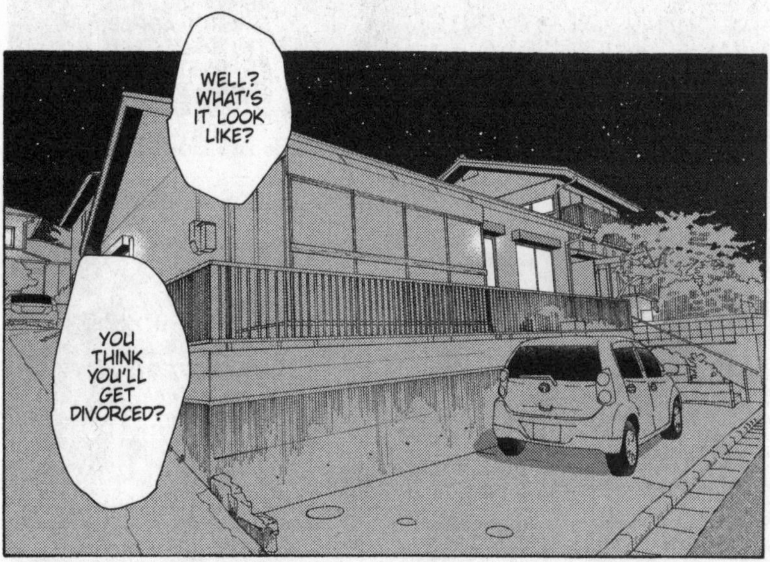
WELL? WHAT'S IT LOOK LIKE?
YOU THINK YOU'LL GET DIVORCED?

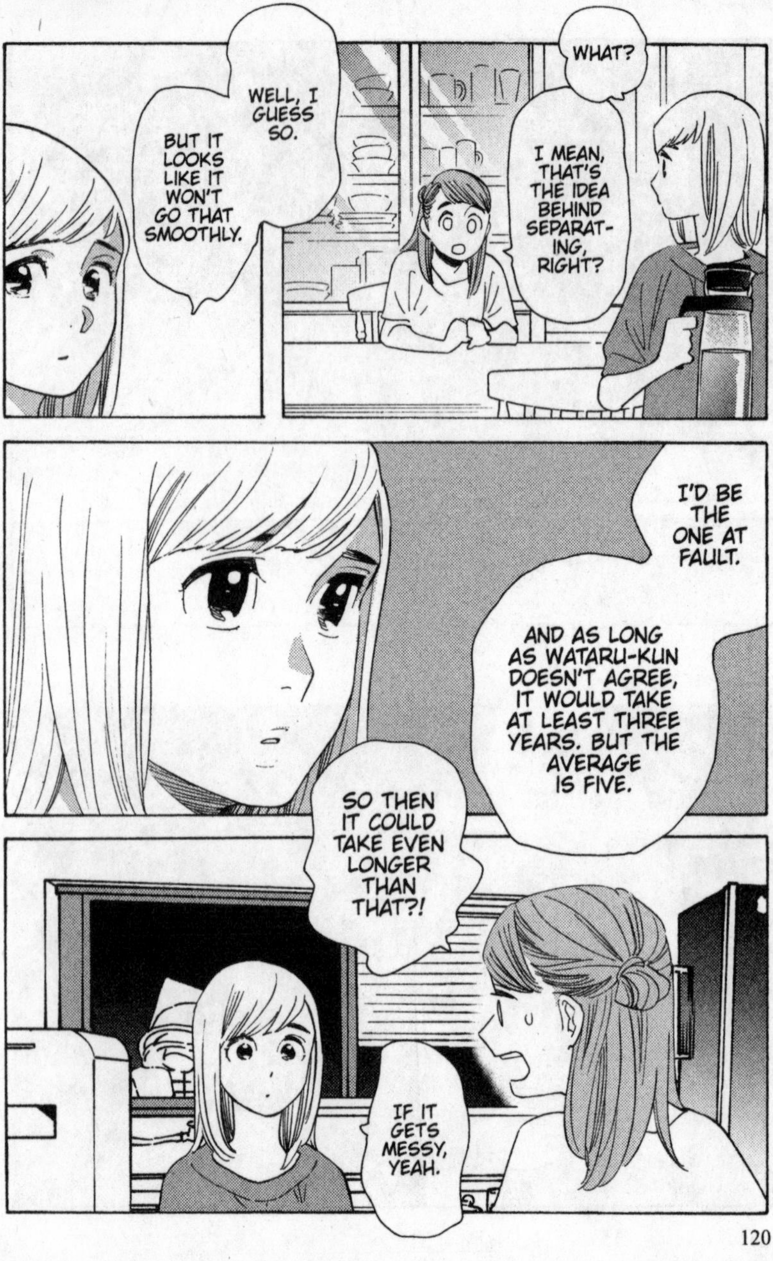
WHAT?
I MEAN, THAT'S THE IDEA BEHIND SEPARAT-ING, RIGHT?
WELL, I GUESS SO.
BUT IT LOOKS LIKE IT WON'T GO THAT SMOOTHLY.
I'D BE THE ONE AT FAULT.
AND AS LONG AS WATARU-KUN DOESN'T AGREE, IT WOULD TAKE AT LEAST THREE YEARS. BUT THE AVERAGE IS FIVE.
SO THEN IT COULD TAKE EVEN LONGER THAN THAT?!
IF IT GETS MESSY, YEAH.

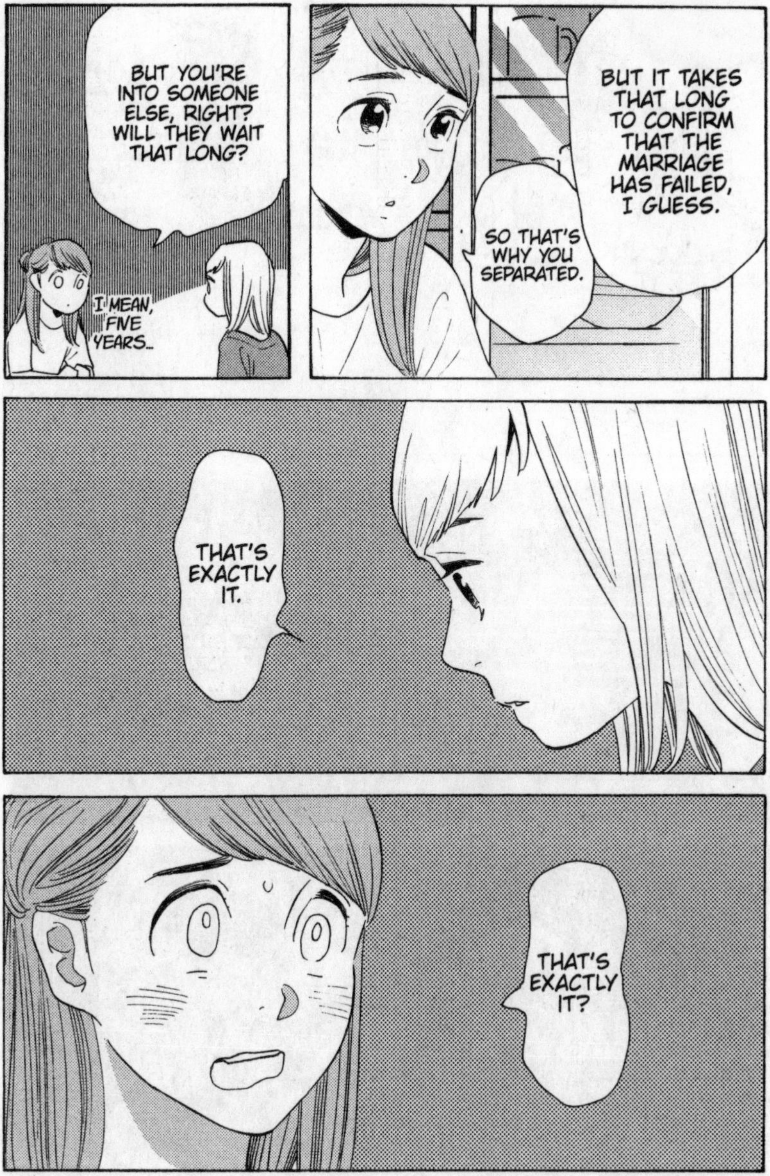
BUT IT TAKES THAT LONG TO CONFIRM THAT THE MARRIAGE HAS FAILED, I GUESS.
SO THAT'S WHY YOU SEPARATED.
BUT YOU'RE INTO SOMEONE ELSE, RIGHT? WILL THEY WAIT THAT LONG?
I MEAN, FIVE YEARS...
THAT'S EXACTLY IT.
THAT'S EXACTLY IT?

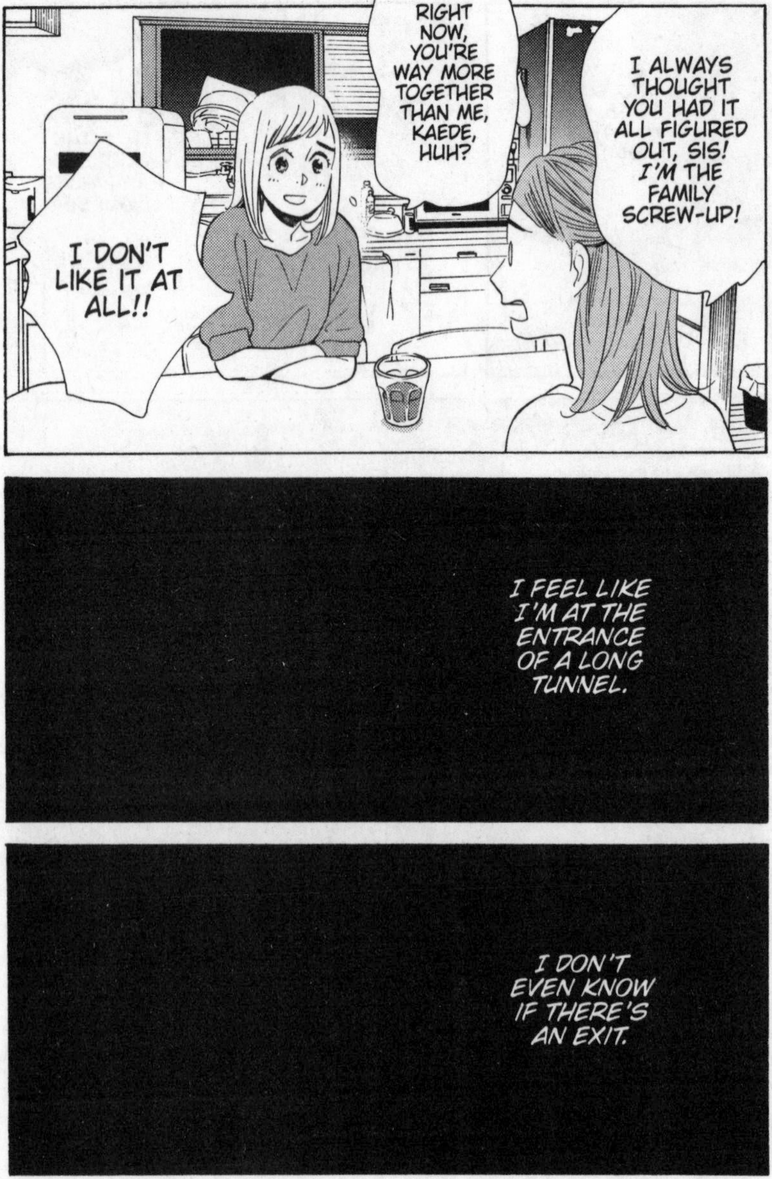
I ALWAYS THOUGHT YOU HAD IT ALL FIGURED OUT, SIS! I'M THE FAMILY SCREW-UP!
RIGHT NOW, YOU'RE WAY MORE TOGETHER THAN ME, KAEDE, HUH?
I DON'T LIKE IT AT ALL!!
I FEEL LIKE I'M AT THE ENTRANCE OF A LONG TUNNEL.
I DON'T EVEN KNOW IF THERE'S AN EXIT.

Chapter 20

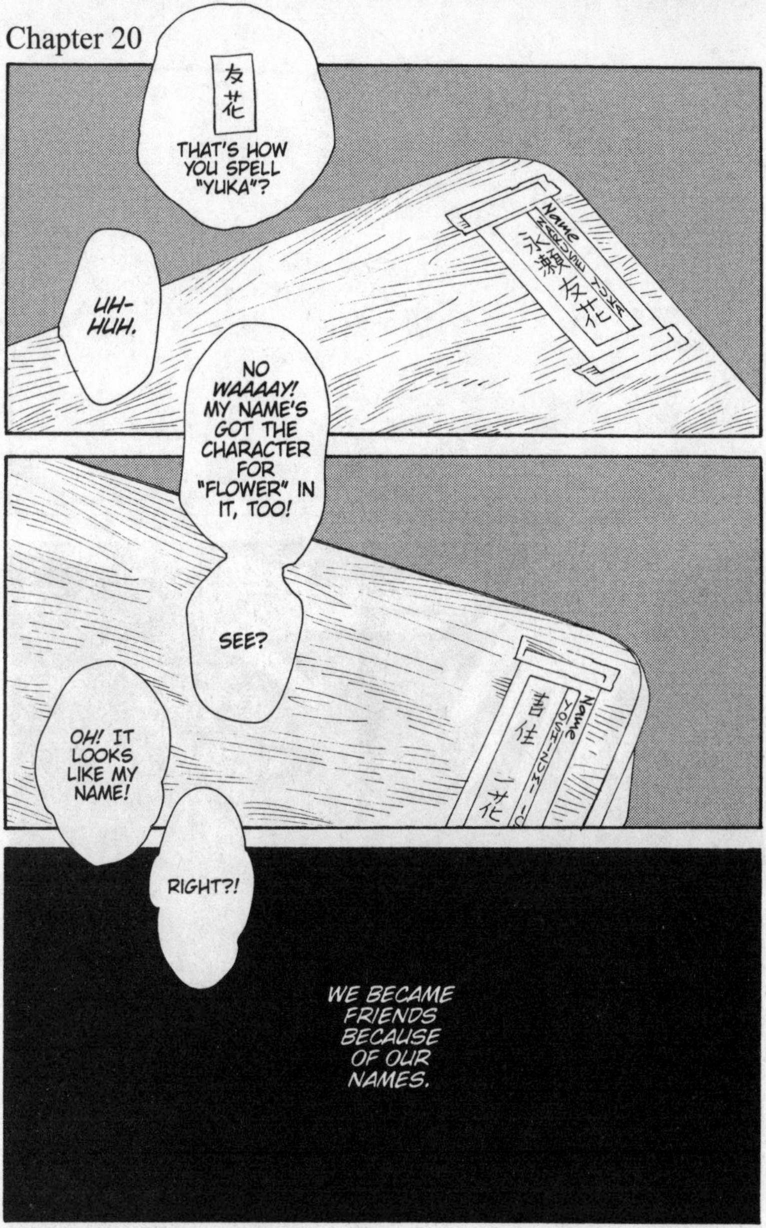
友花
THAT'S HOW YOU SPELL "YUKA"?
Name
永瀬友花
UH-HUH.
NO WAAAAY! MY NAME'S GOT THE CHARACTER FOR "FLOWER" IN IT, TOO!
SEE?
Name
吉住
OH! IT LOOKS LIKE MY NAME!
RIGHT?!
WE BECAME FRIENDS BECAUSE OF OUR NAMES.

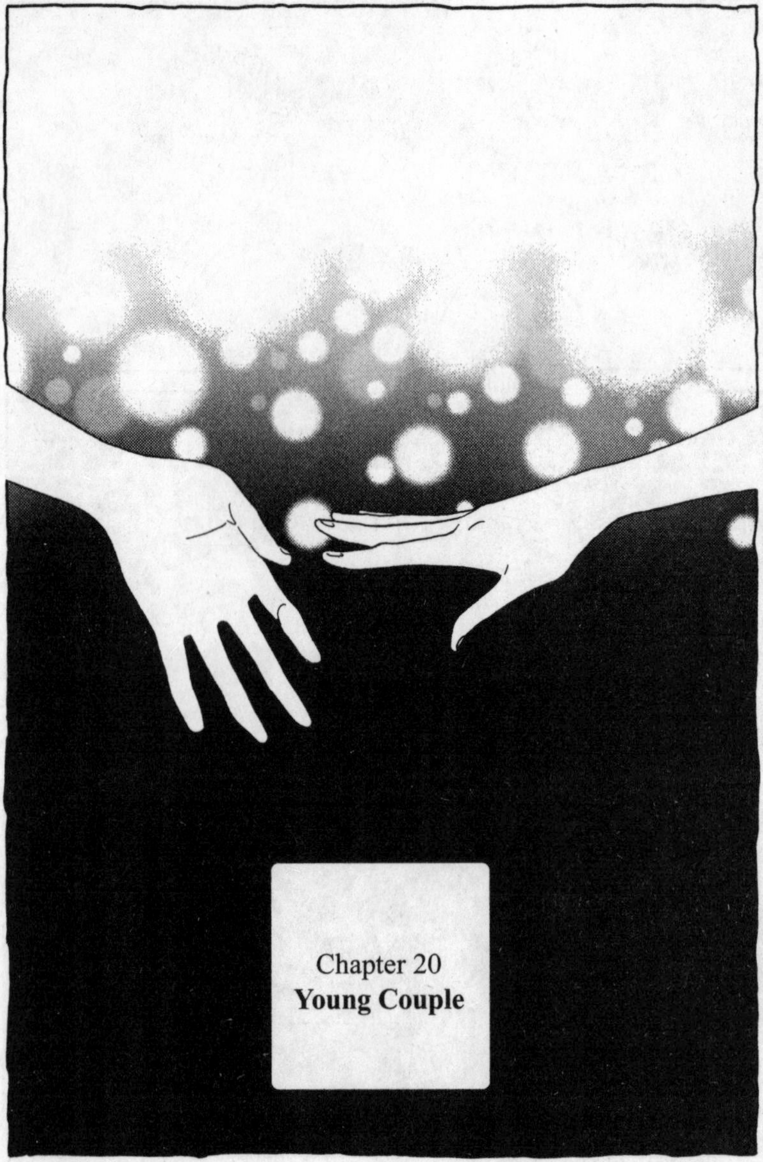

Chapter 20
Young Couple

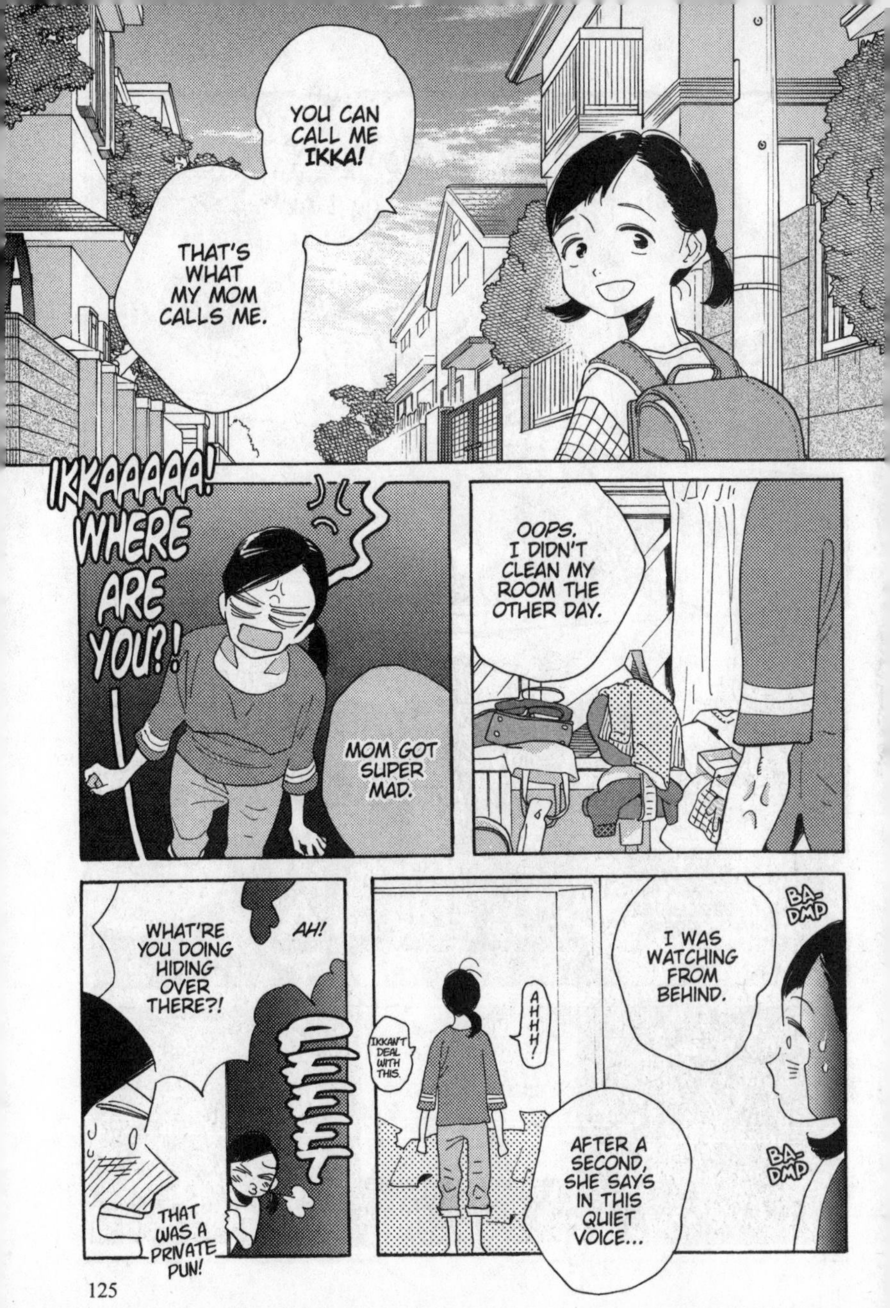
YOU CAN CALL ME IKKA!
THAT'S WHAT MY MOM CALLS ME.
OOPS. I DIDN'T CLEAN MY ROOM THE OTHER DAY.
IKKAAAAA! WHERE ARE YOU?!
MOM GOT SUPER MAD.
BA-DMP
I WAS WATCHING FROM BEHIND.
BA-DMP
AFTER A SECOND, SHE SAYS IN THIS QUIET VOICE...
AHHH!
IKKAN'T DEAL WITH THIS.
AH!
WHAT'RE YOU DOING HIDING OVER THERE?!
PFFFT
THAT WAS A PRIVATE PUN!

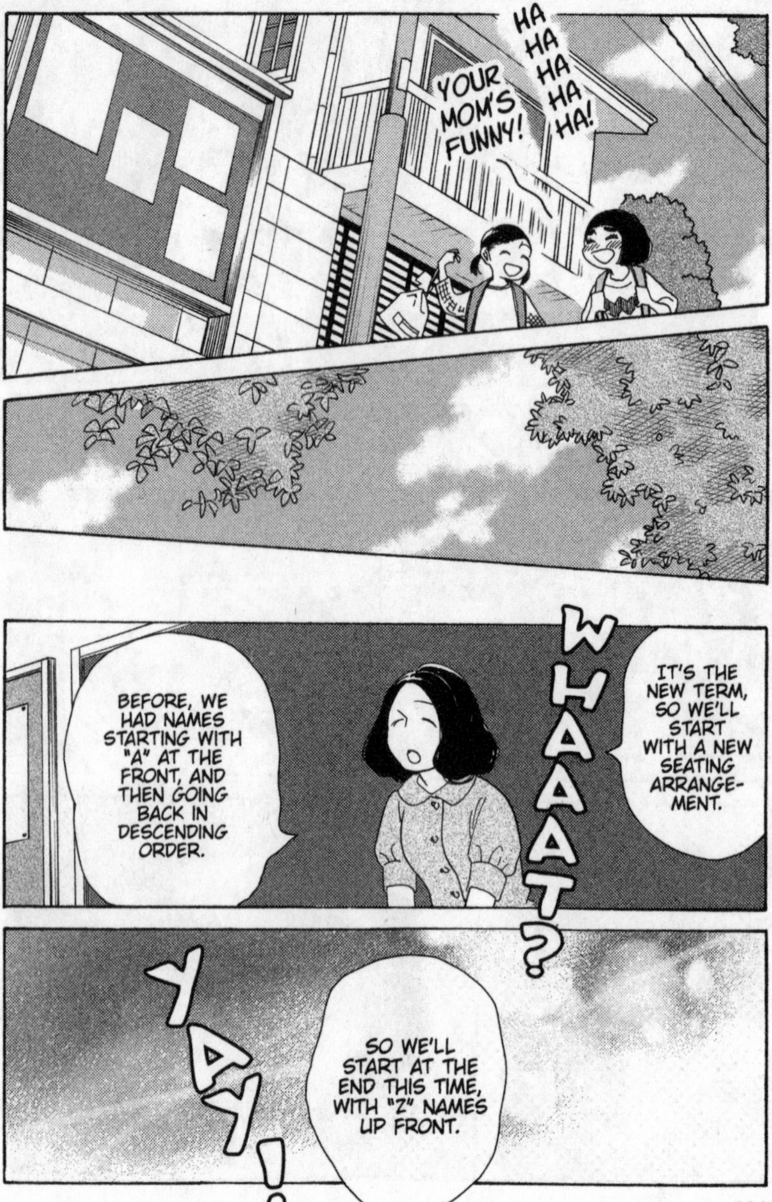
HA HA HA HA HA!
YOUR MOM'S FUNNY!
IT'S THE NEW TERM, SO WE'LL START WITH A NEW SEATING ARRANGE-MENT.
WHAAAT?
BEFORE, WE HAD NAMES STARTING WITH "A" AT THE FRONT, AND THEN GOING BACK IN DESCENDING ORDER.
SO WE'LL START AT THE END THIS TIME, WITH "Z" NAMES UP FRONT.
YAY!

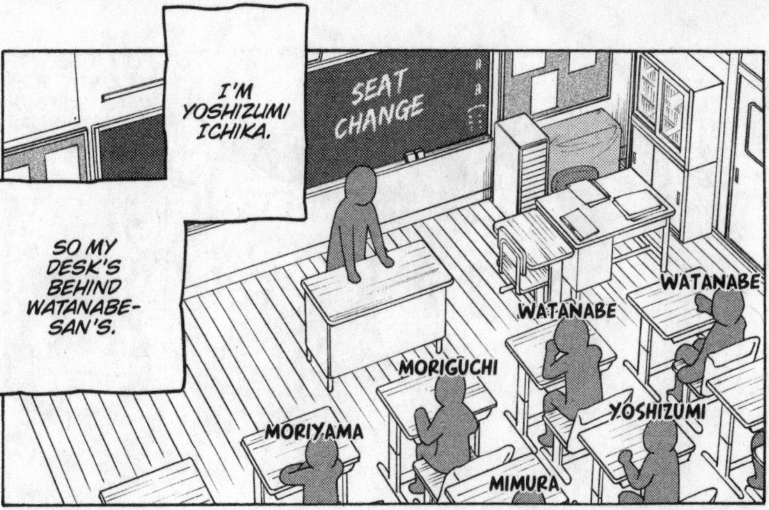
I'M YOSHIZUMI ICHIKA.
SO MY DESK'S BEHIND WATANABE-SAN'S.
SEAT CHANGE
WATANABE
WATANABE
MORIGUCHI
YOSHIZUMI
MORIYAMA
MIMURA

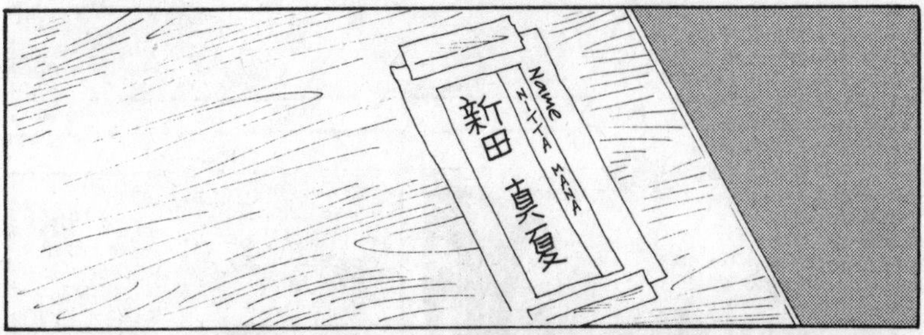
Name
NIITA MANA
新田 真夏

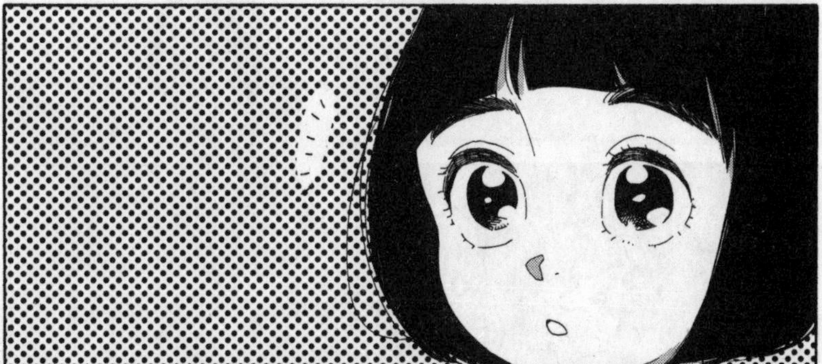

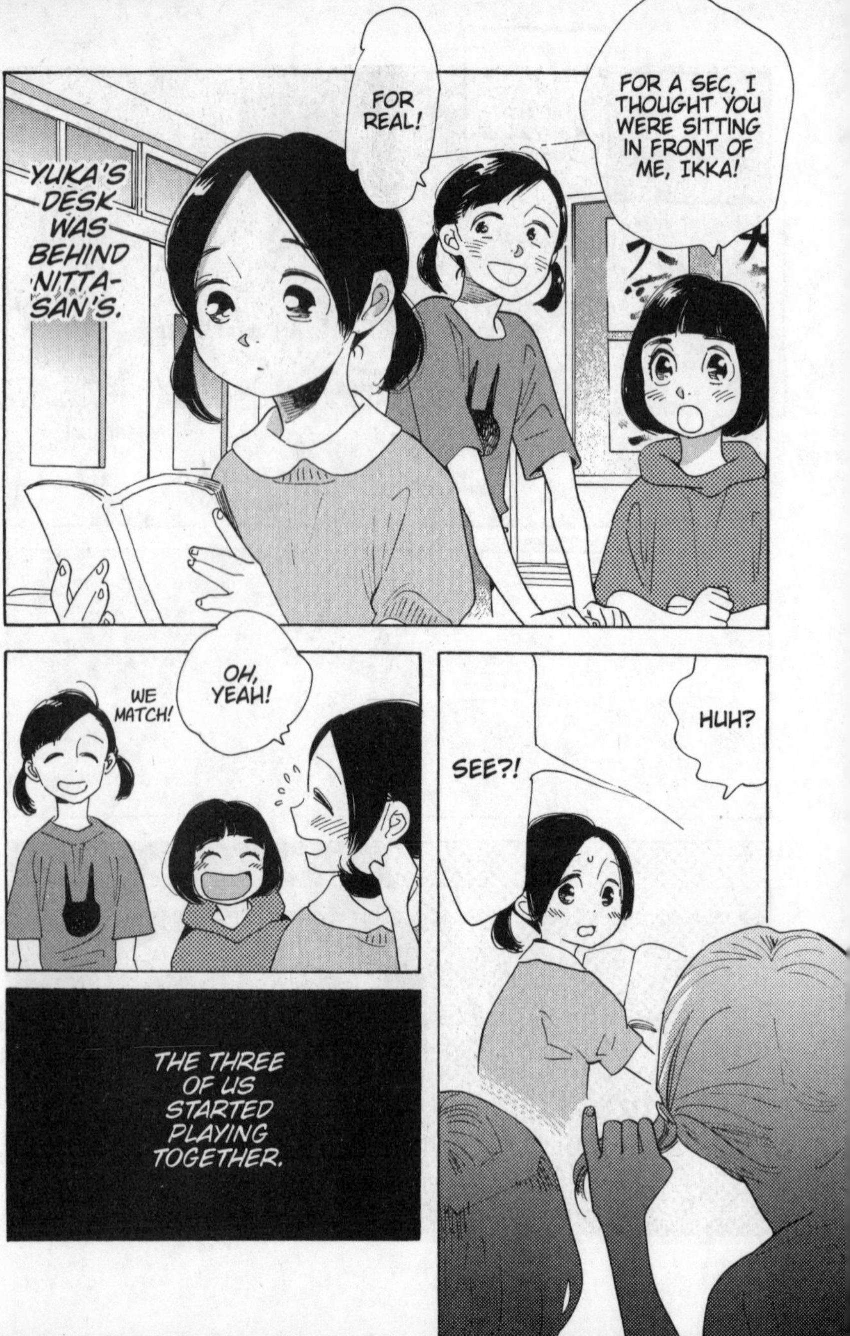
FOR A SEC, I THOUGHT YOU WERE SITTING IN FRONT OF ME, IKKA!
FOR REAL!
YUKA'S DESK WAS BEHIND NITTA-SAN'S.
HUH?
SEE?!
OH, YEAH!
WE MATCH!
THE THREE OF US STARTED PLAYING TOGETHER.

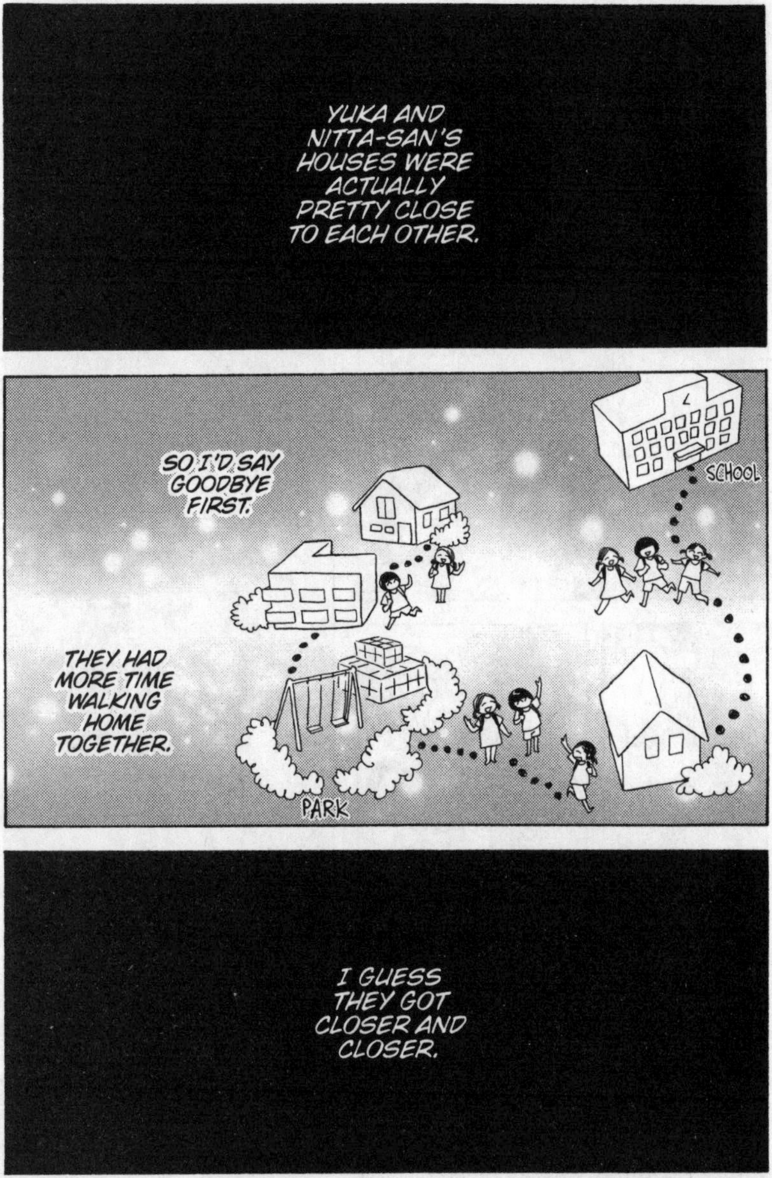
YUKA AND NITTA-SAN'S HOUSES WERE ACTUALLY PRETTY CLOSE TO EACH OTHER.
SCHOOL
SO I'D SAY GOODBYE FIRST.
THEY HAD MORE TIME WALKING HOME TOGETHER.
PARK
I GUESS THEY GOT CLOSER AND CLOSER.

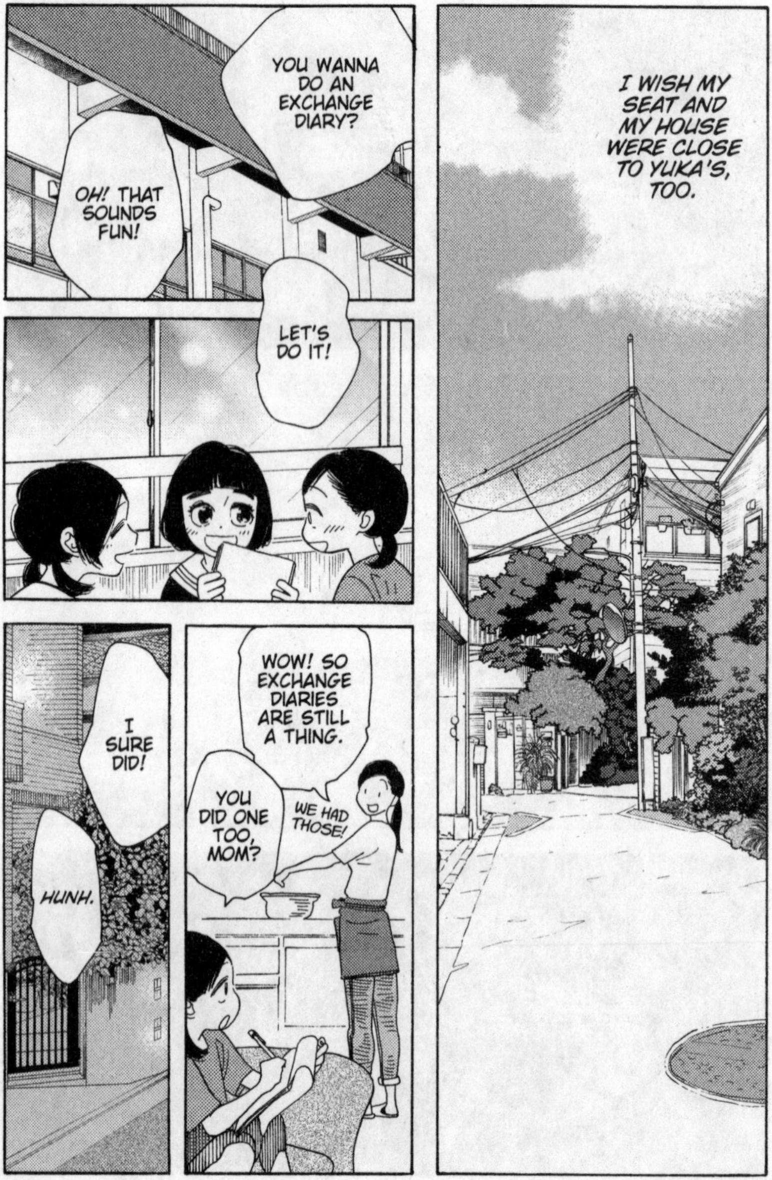
I WISH MY SEAT AND MY HOUSE WERE CLOSE TO YUKA'S, TOO.
YOU WANNA DO AN EXCHANGE DIARY?
OH! THAT SOUNDS FUN!
LET'S DO IT!
WOW! SO EXCHANGE DIARIES ARE STILL A THING.
WE HAD THOSE!
YOU DID ONE TOO, MOM?
I SURE DID!
HUNH.

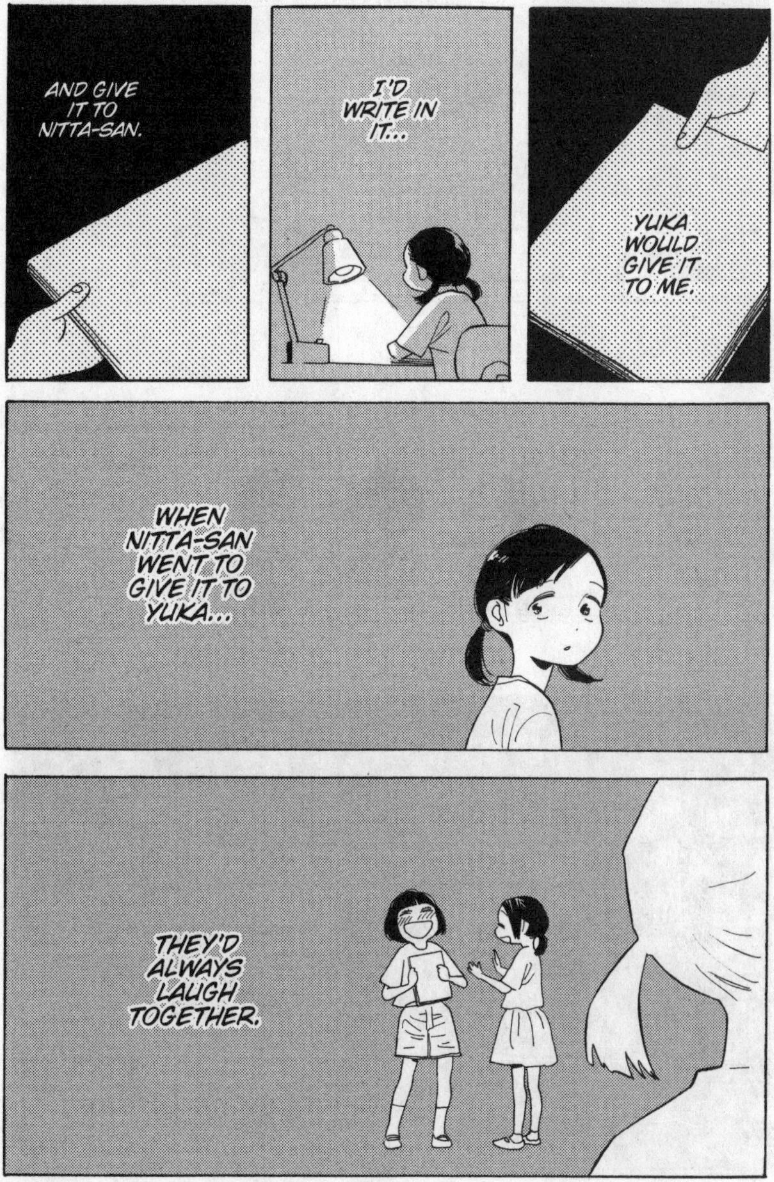
YUKA WOULD GIVE IT TO ME.
I'D WRITE IN IT...
AND GIVE IT TO NITTA-SAN.
WHEN NITTA-SAN WENT TO GIVE IT TO YUKA...
THEY'D ALWAYS LAUGH TOGETHER.

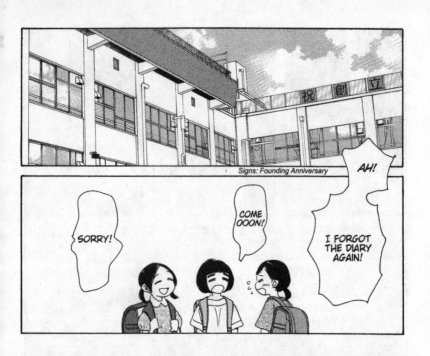

祝創立
Signs: Founding Anniversary
AH!
I FORGOT THE DIARY AGAIN!
COME OOON!
SORRY!
WHEN I KEPT FORGETTING IT AGAIN AND AGAIN...
THE DIARY JUST SORT OF NATURALLY DISAPPEARED.

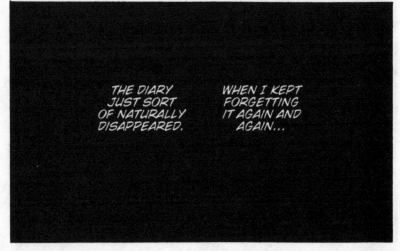

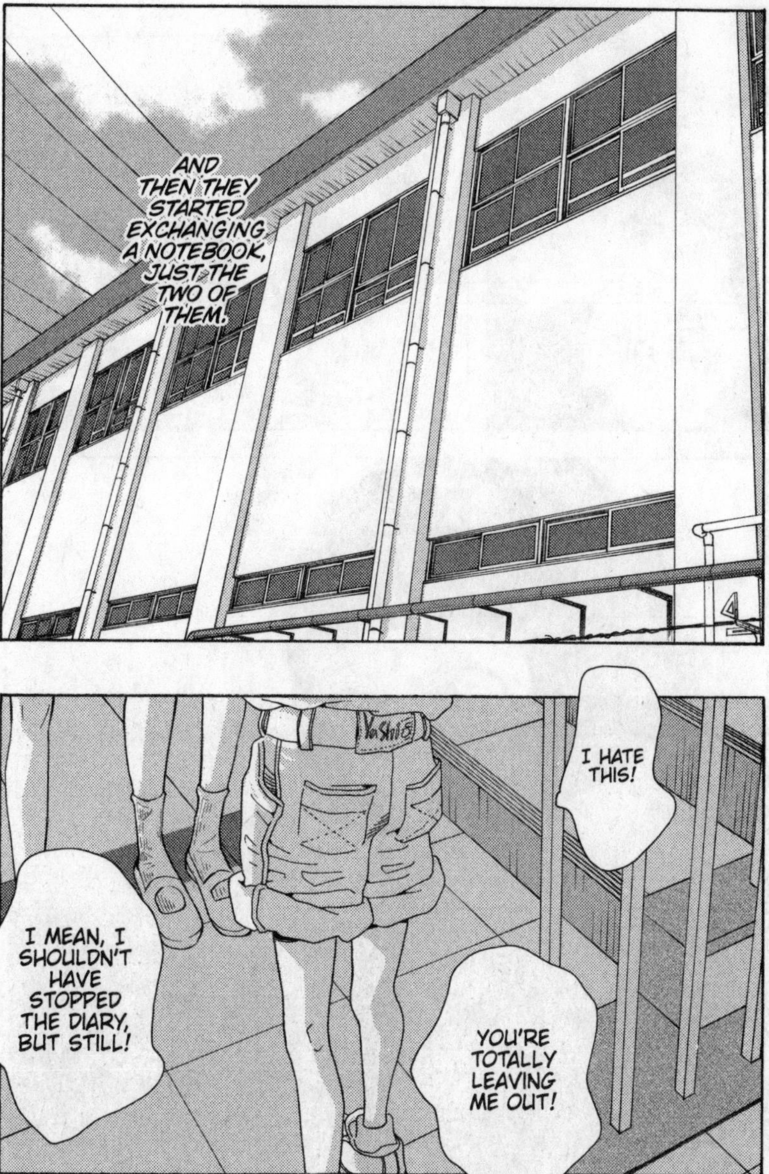
AND THEN THEY STARTED EXCHANGING A NOTEBOOK, JUST THE TWO OF THEM.
I HATE THIS!
I MEAN, I SHOULDN'T HAVE STOPPED THE DIARY, BUT STILL!
YOU'RE TOTALLY LEAVING ME OUT!

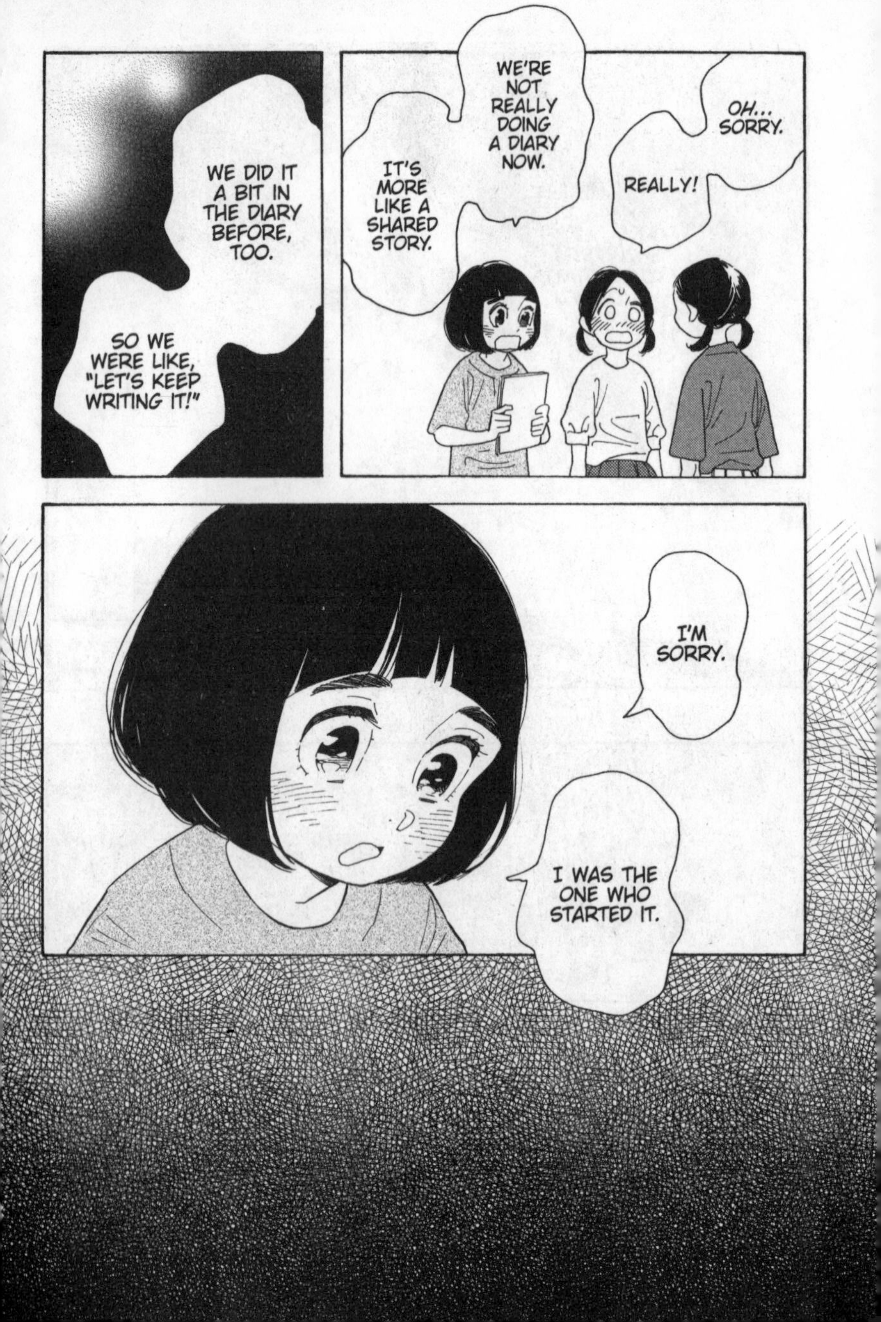
OH... SORRY.
REALLY!
WE'RE NOT REALLY DOING A DIARY NOW.
IT'S MORE LIKE A SHARED STORY.
WE DID IT A BIT IN THE DIARY BEFORE, TOO.
SO WE WERE LIKE, "LET'S KEEP WRITING IT!"
I'M SORRY.
I WAS THE ONE WHO STARTED IT.

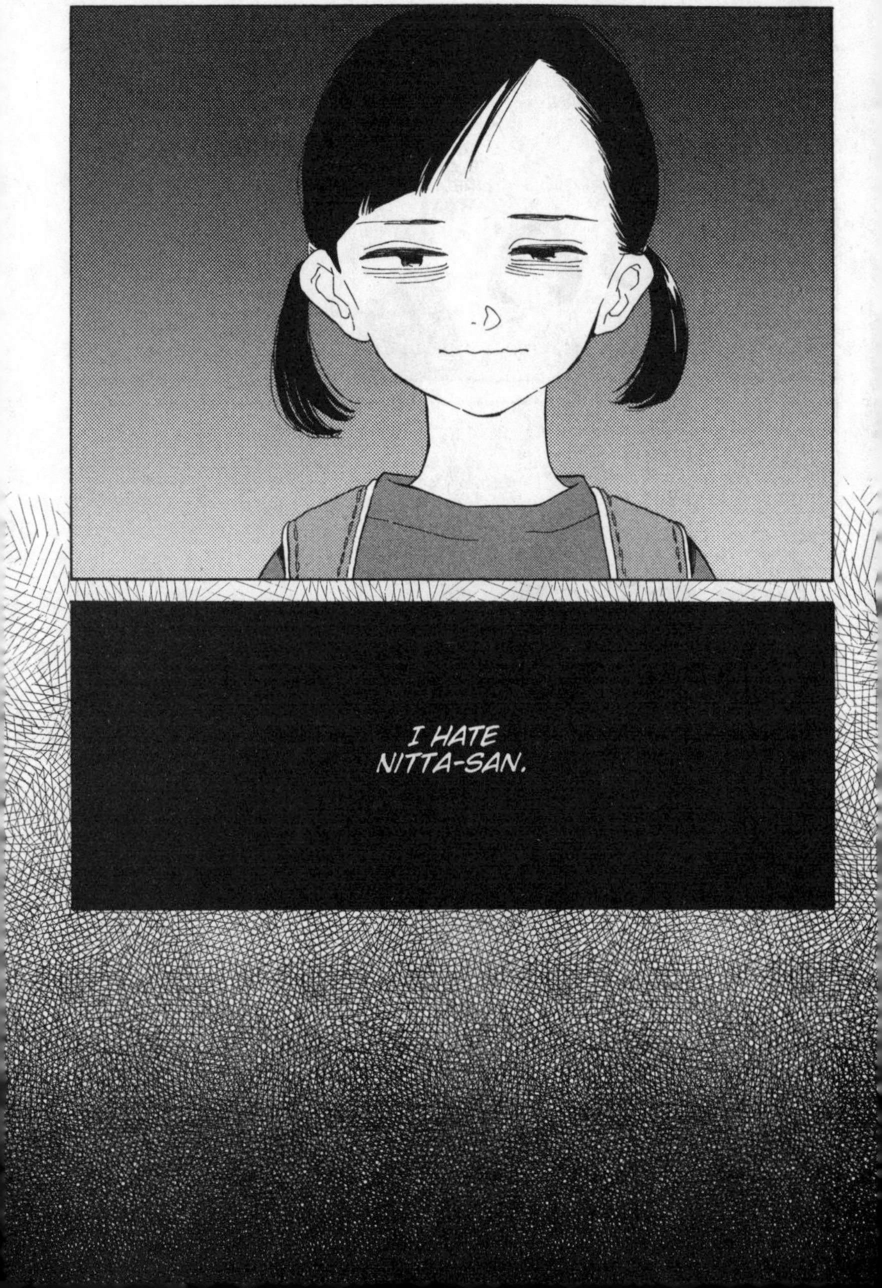
I HATE
NITTA-SAN.

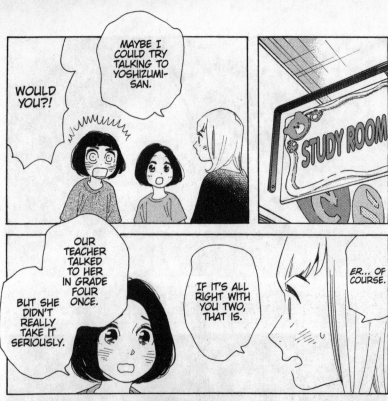

STUDY ROOM
MAYBE I COULD TRY TALKING TO YOSHIZUMI-SAN.
WOULD YOU?!
ER... OF COURSE.
IF IT'S ALL RIGHT WITH YOU TWO, THAT IS.
OUR TEACHER TALKED TO HER IN GRADE FOUR ONCE.
BUT SHE DIDN'T REALLY TAKE IT SERIOUSLY.
THAT'S WHY YUKA'S A LITTLE SCARED OF PEOPLE NOW.
M-MANA!
QUIT IT!
SO WHO HAD GRADE FOUR LAST YEAR...?
KOTANI-SENSEI, HM?

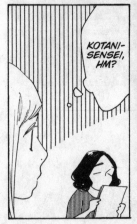

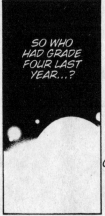

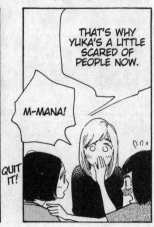

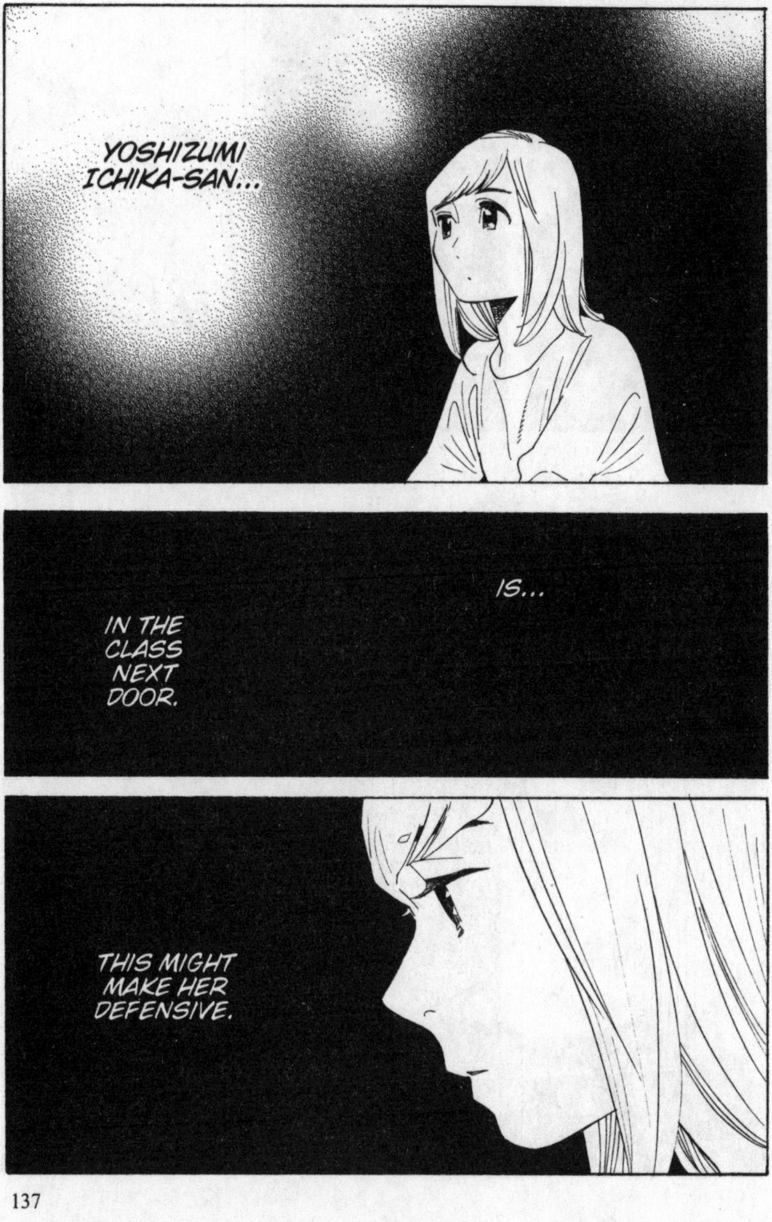
YOSHIZUMI ICHIKA-SAN...
IS...
IN THE CLASS NEXT DOOR.
THIS MIGHT MAKE HER DEFENSIVE.

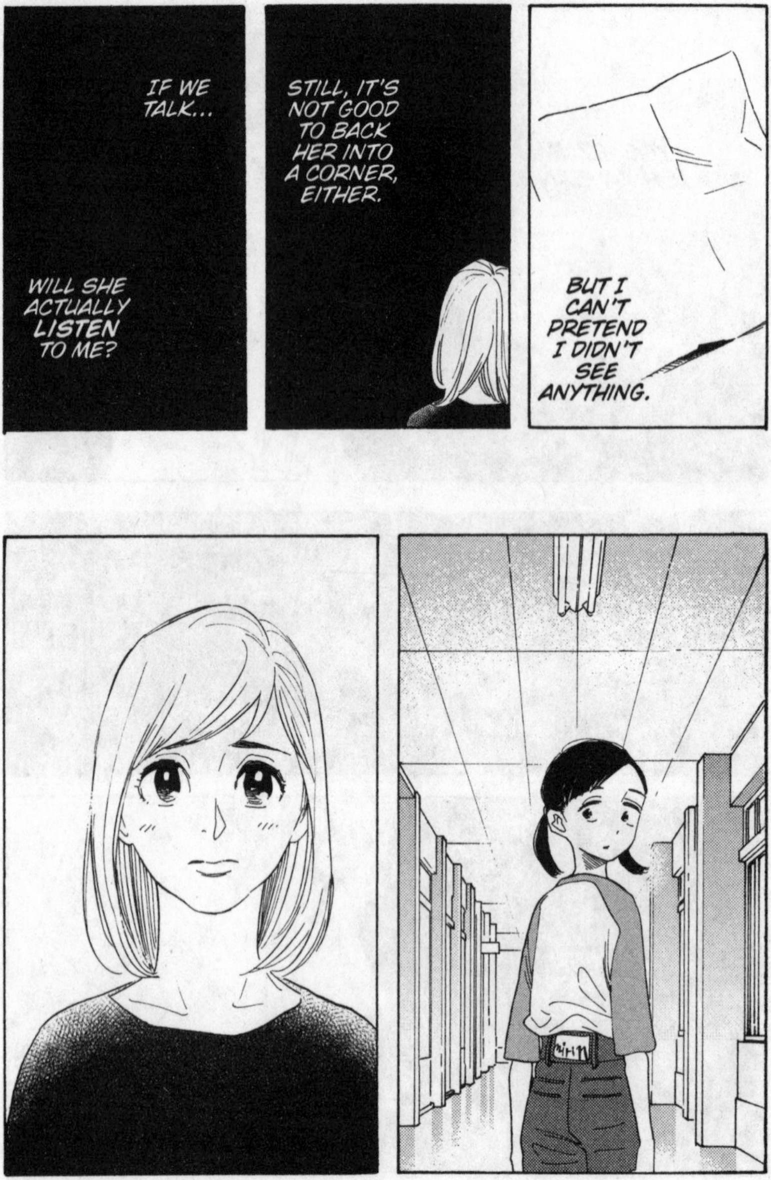
BUT I CAN'T PRETEND I DIDN'T SEE ANYTHING.
STILL, IT'S NOT GOOD TO BACK HER INTO A CORNER, EITHER.
IF WE TALK...
WILL SHE ACTUALLY LISTEN TO ME?

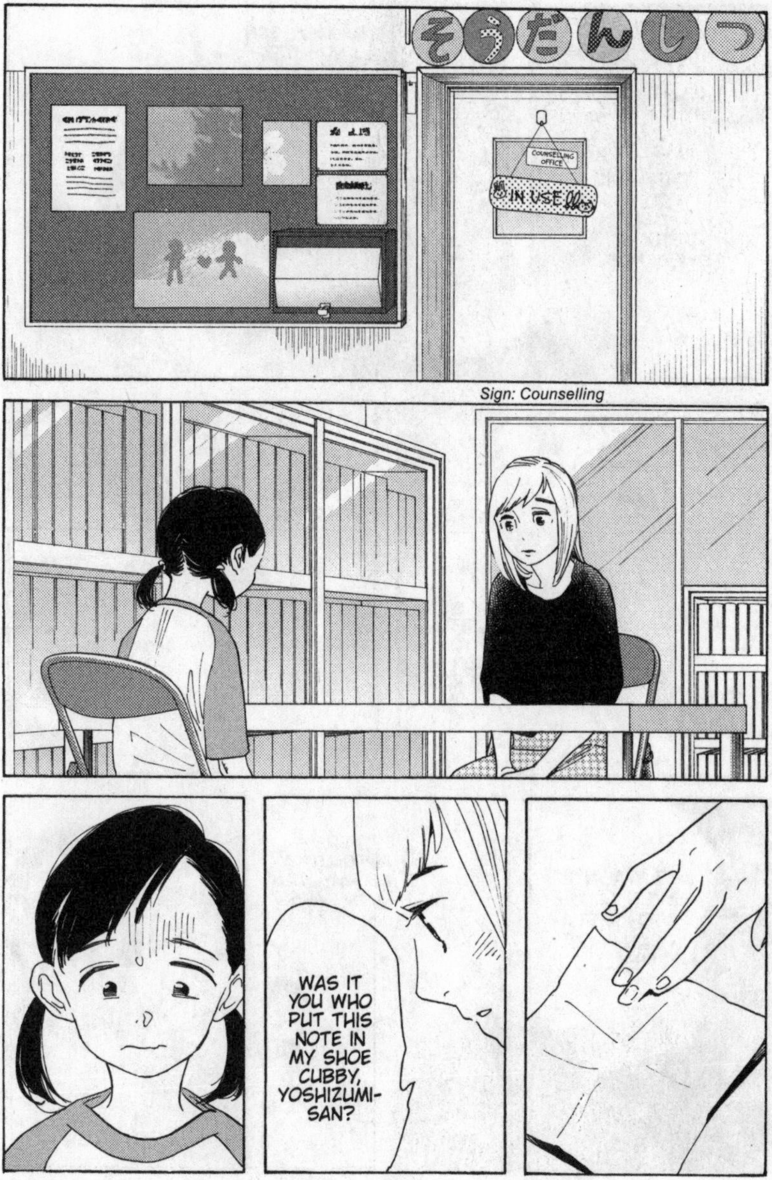
そうだんしつ
COUNSELLING OFFICE
IN USE
Sign: Counselling
WAS IT YOU WHO PUT THIS NOTE IN MY SHOE CUBBY, YOSHIZUMI-SAN?

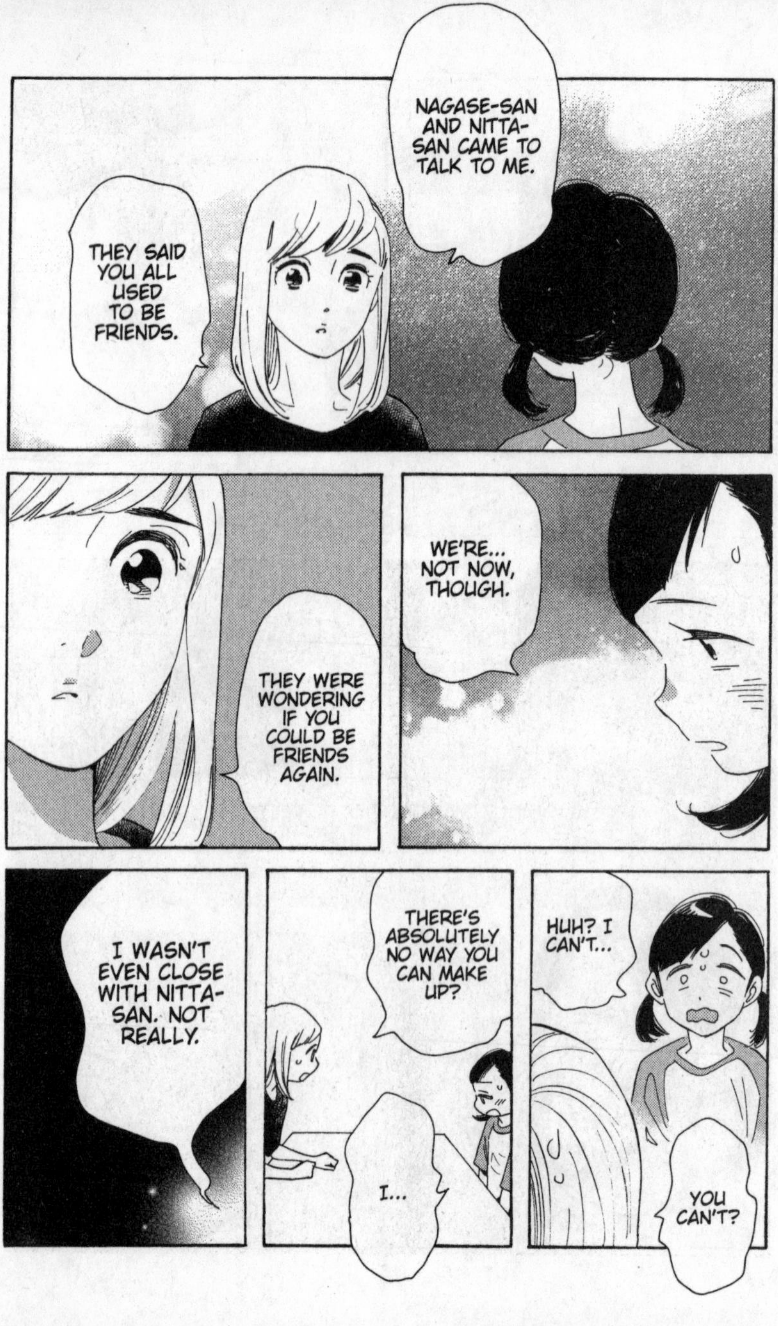
NAGASE-SAN AND NITTA-SAN CAME TO TALK TO ME.
THEY SAID YOU ALL USED TO BE FRIENDS.
WE'RE... NOT NOW, THOUGH.
THEY WERE WONDERING IF YOU COULD BE FRIENDS AGAIN.
HUH? I CAN'T...
YOU CAN'T?
THERE'S ABSOLUTELY NO WAY YOU CAN MAKE UP?
I...
I WASN'T EVEN CLOSE WITH NITTA-SAN. NOT REALLY.

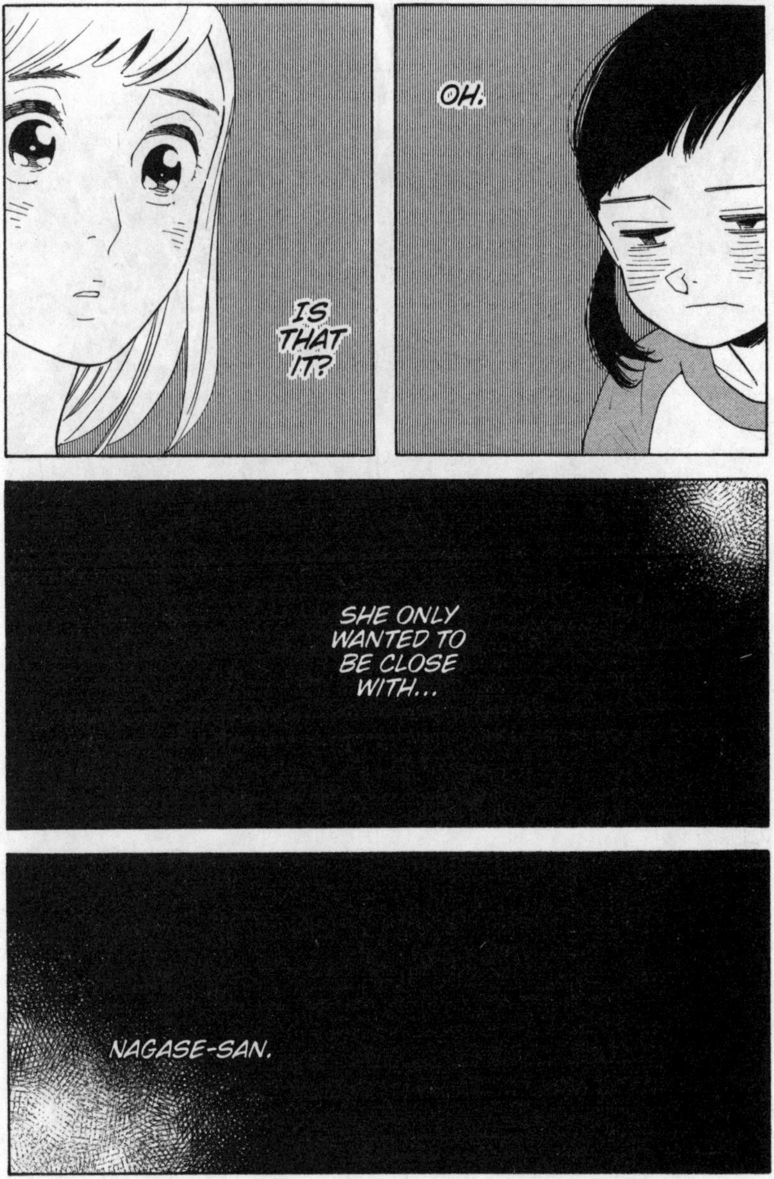
OH.
IS THAT IT?
SHE ONLY WANTED TO BE CLOSE WITH...
NAGASE-SAN.

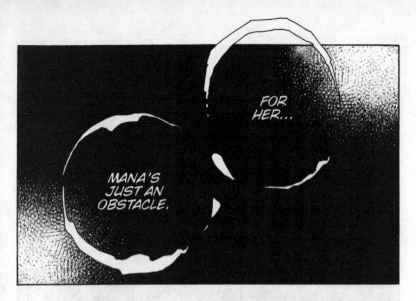

FOR HER...
MANA'S JUST AN OBSTACLE.
I WAS THIS WAY WHEN I WAS YOUNG, TOO.
IT'S SUCH A SMALL THING.
BUT NOT SMALL AT ALL.

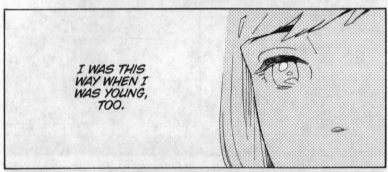

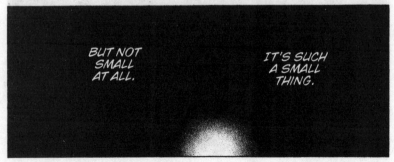

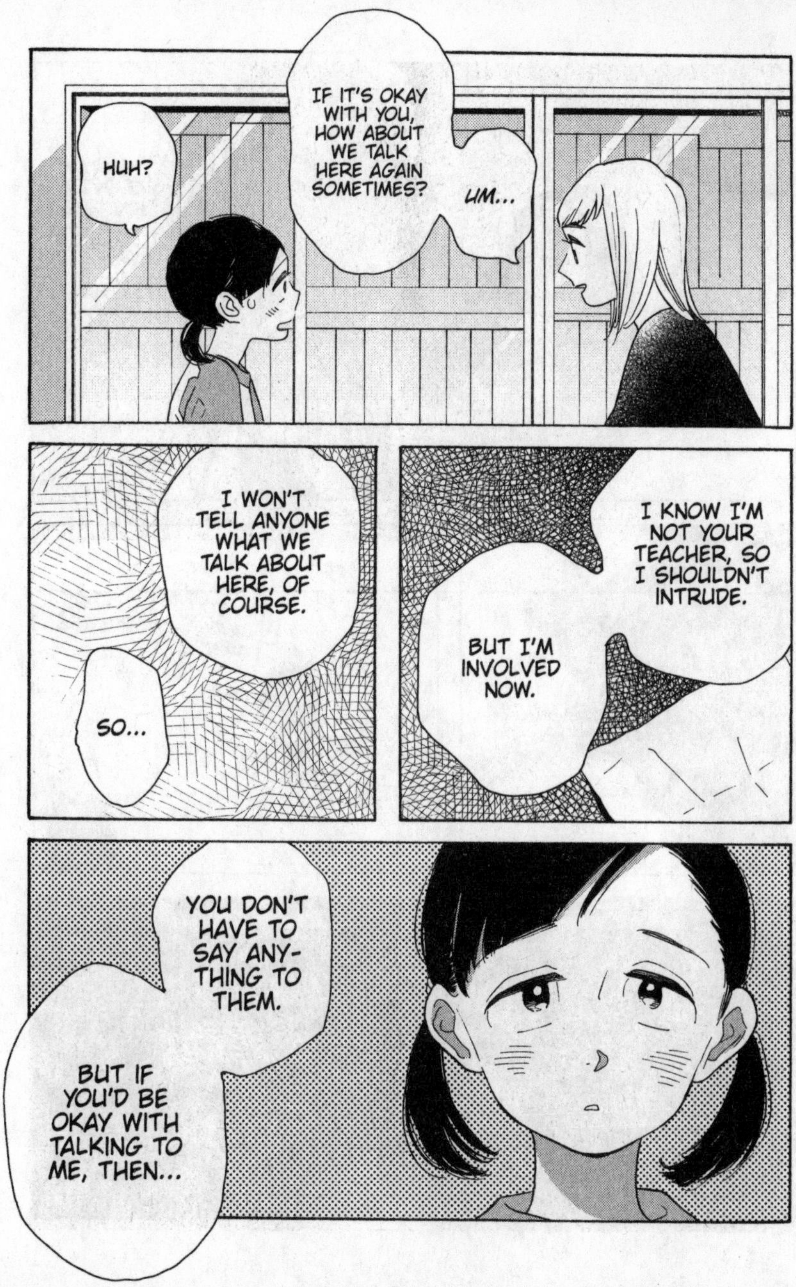
UM...
IF IT'S OKAY WITH YOU, HOW ABOUT WE TALK HERE AGAIN SOMETIMES?
HUH?
I KNOW I'M NOT YOUR TEACHER, SO I SHOULDN'T INTRUDE.
BUT I'M INVOLVED NOW.
I WON'T TELL ANYONE WHAT WE TALK ABOUT HERE, OF COURSE.
SO...
YOU DON'T HAVE TO SAY ANY-THING TO THEM.
BUT IF YOU'D BE OKAY WITH TALKING TO ME, THEN...

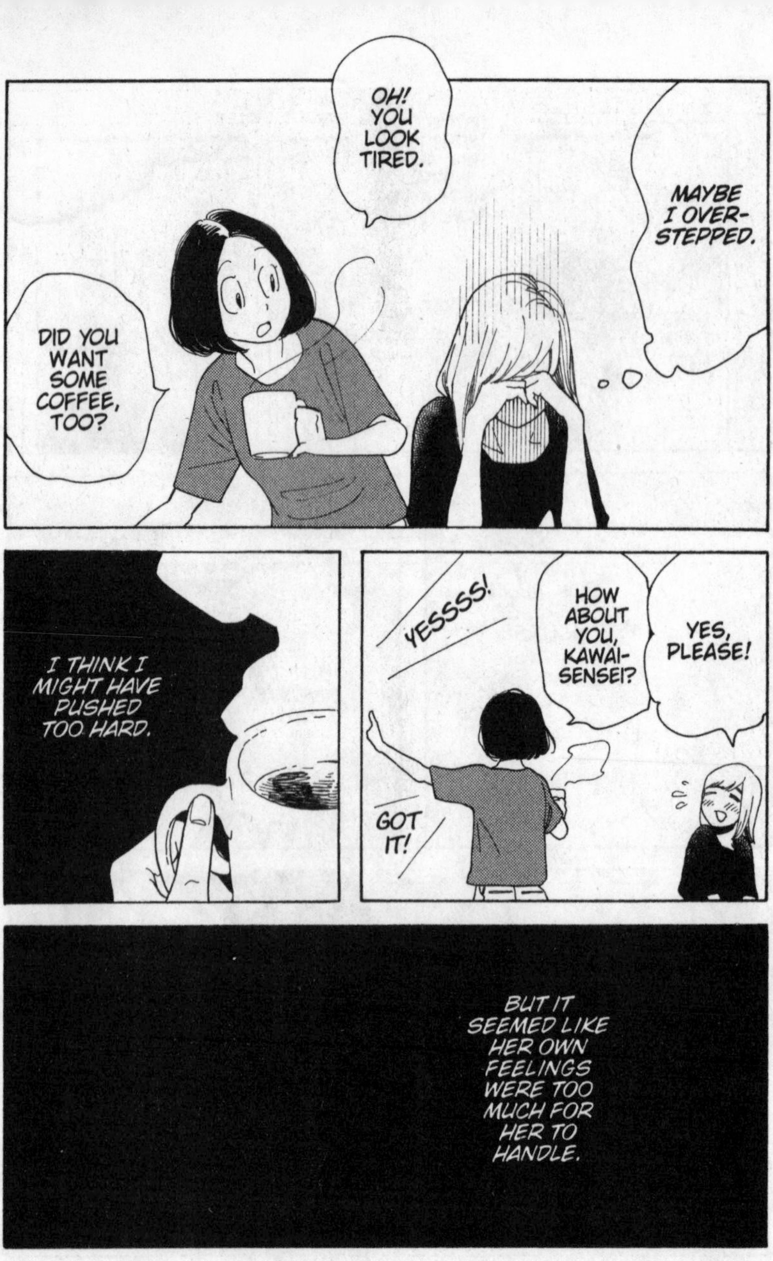
MAYBE I OVER-STEPPED.
OH! YOU LOOK TIRED.
DID YOU WANT SOME COFFEE, TOO?
HOW ABOUT YOU, KAWAI-SENSEI?
YES, PLEASE!
YESSSS!
GOT IT!
I THINK I MIGHT HAVE PUSHED TOO HARD.
BUT IT SEEMED LIKE HER OWN FEELINGS WERE TOO MUCH FOR HER TO HANDLE.

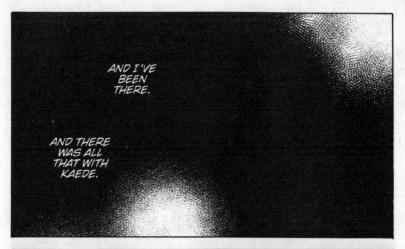

AND I'VE BEEN THERE.

AND THERE WAS ALL THAT WITH KAEDE.

I'M SURE EVERYONE'S BEEN THROUGH THIS MORE OR LESS.

OKUBO-SENSEI?

BUT MAYBE ADULTS WANT TO HIDE THIS FROM KIDS.

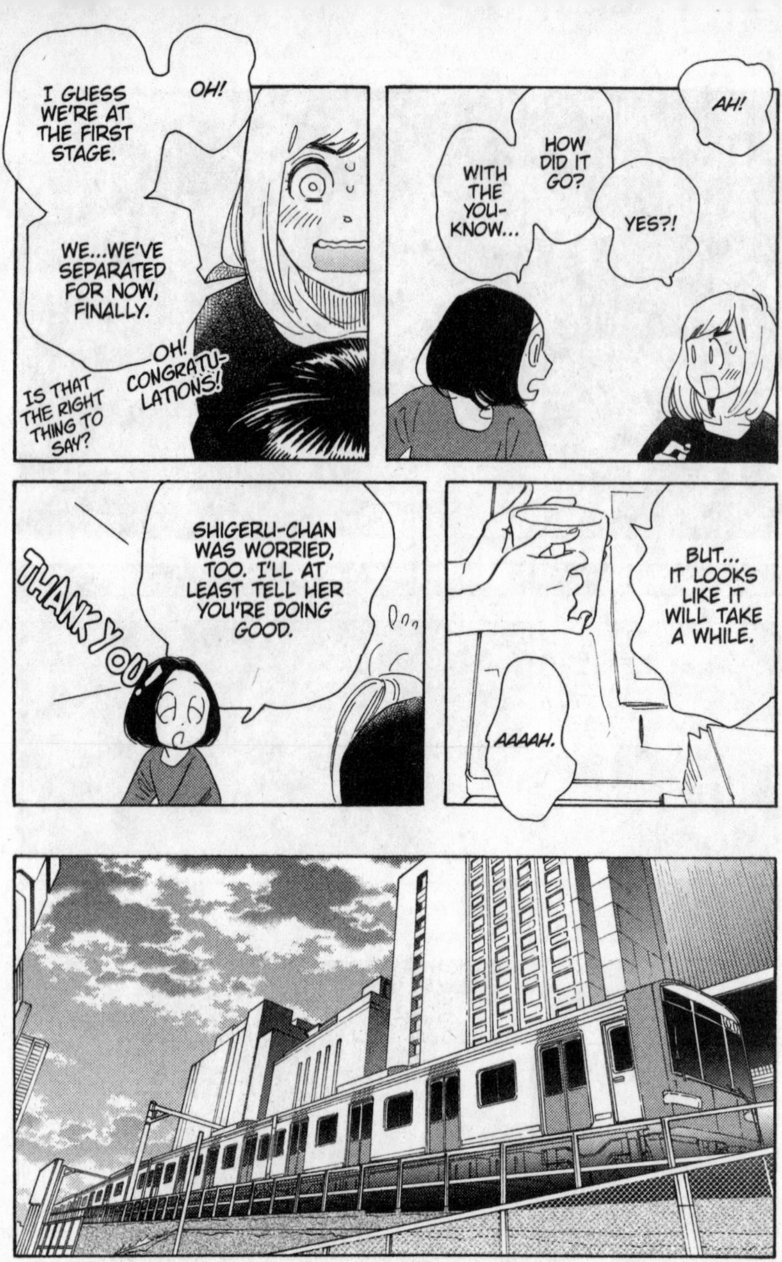
AH!
HOW DID IT GO? WITH THE YOU-KNOW...
YES?!
OH!
I GUESS WE'RE AT THE FIRST STAGE.
WE...WE'VE SEPARATED FOR NOW, FINALLY.
OH! CONGRATU-LATIONS!
IS THAT THE RIGHT THING TO SAY?
BUT... IT LOOKS LIKE IT WILL TAKE A WHILE.
AAAAH.
SHIGERU-CHAN WAS WORRIED, TOO. I'LL AT LEAST TELL HER YOU'RE DOING GOOD.
THANK YOU!

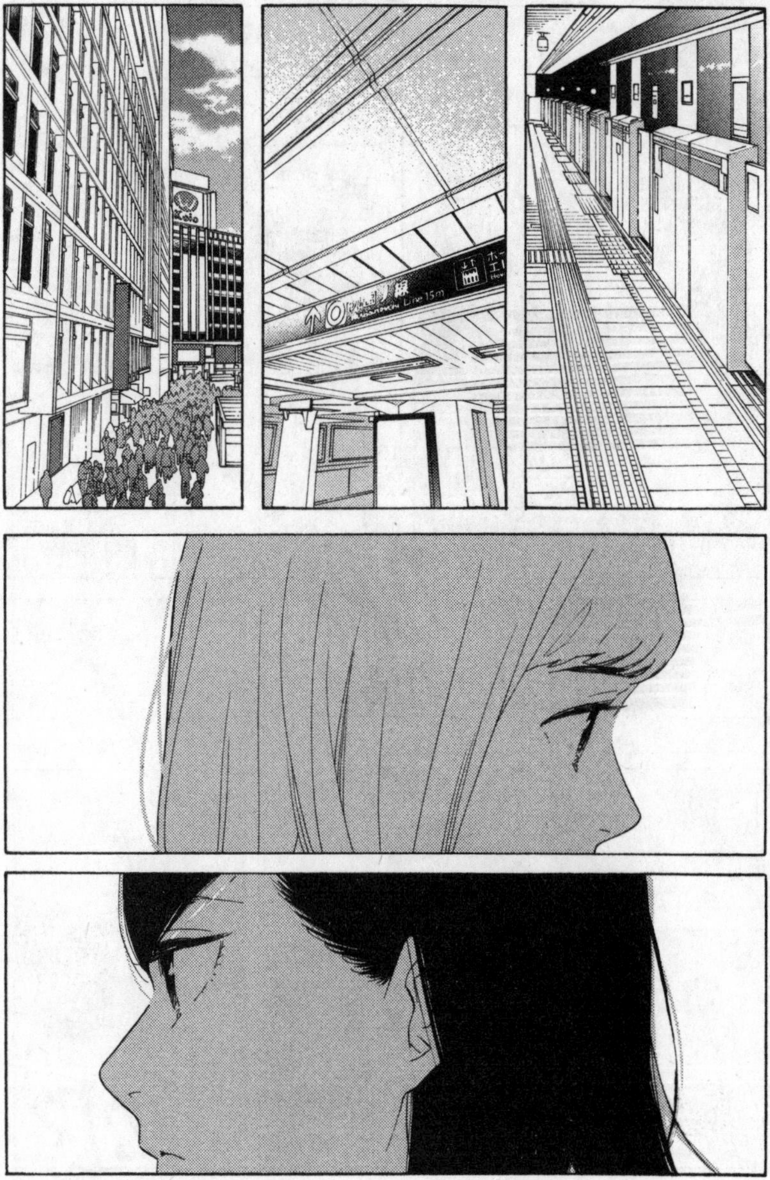
線
Line 15m
Keio

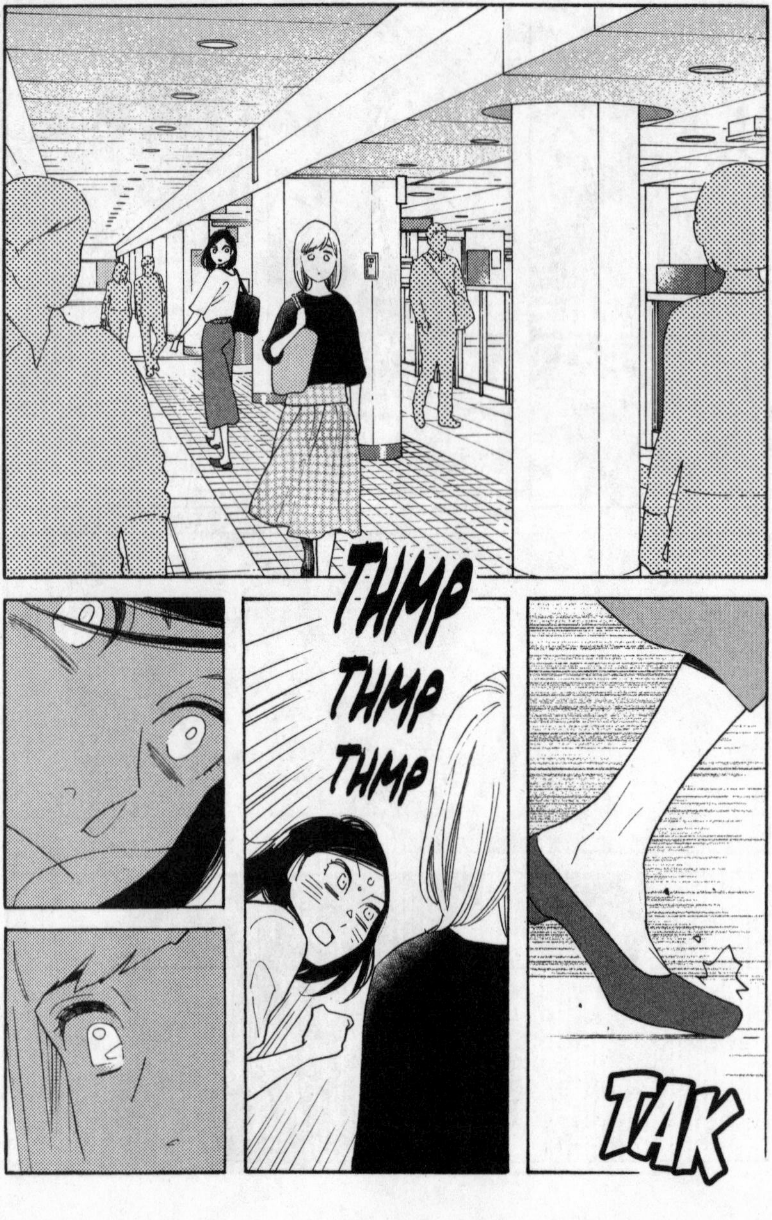
TAK
THMP
THMP
THMP

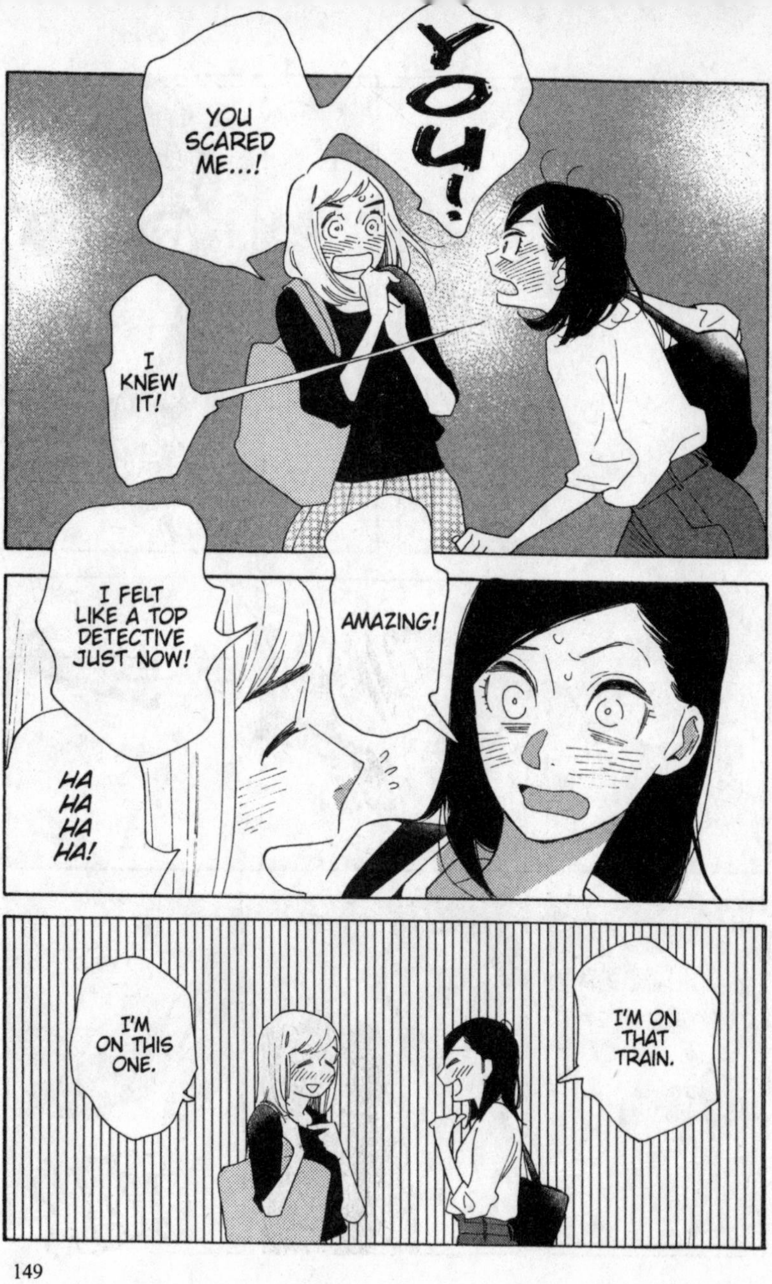
YOU!
YOU SCARED ME...!
I KNEW IT!
AMAZING!
I FELT LIKE A TOP DETECTIVE JUST NOW!
HA HA HA HA!
I'M ON THAT TRAIN.
I'M ON THIS ONE.

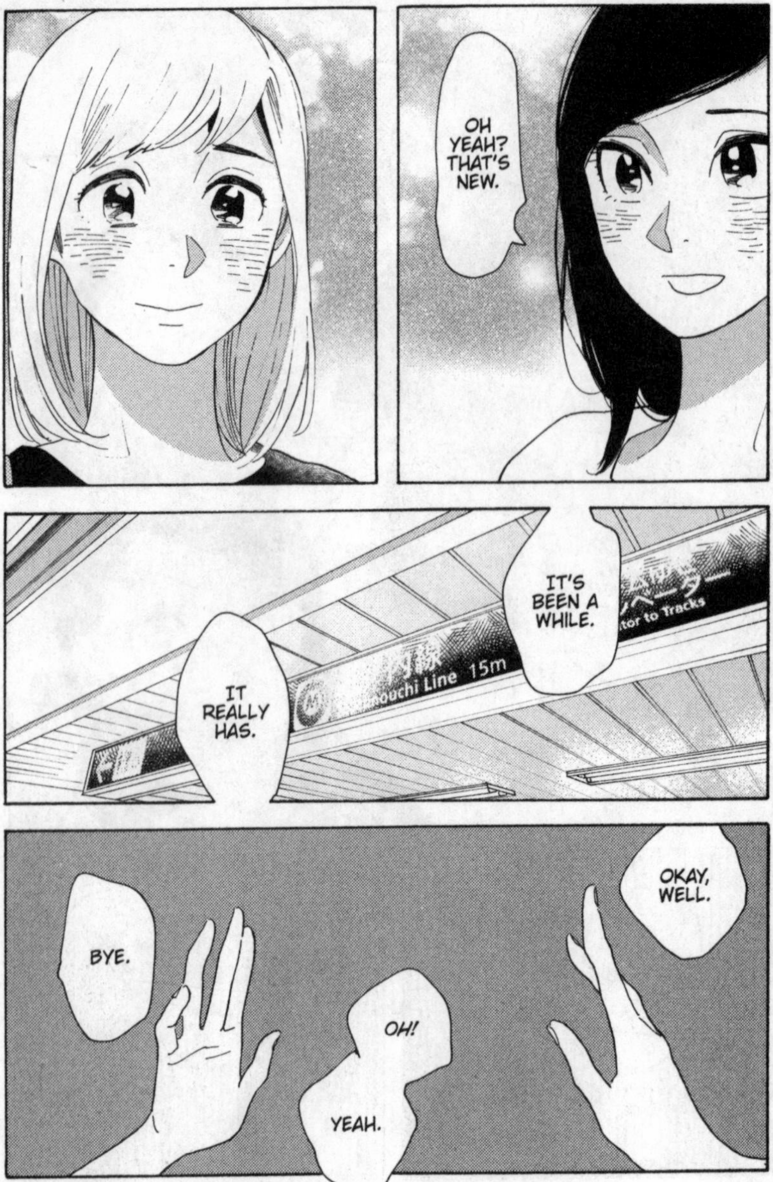
OH YEAH? THAT'S NEW.
IT'S BEEN A WHILE.
IT REALLY HAS.
OKAY, WELL.
OH!
YEAH.
BYE.

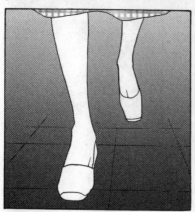

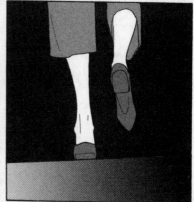

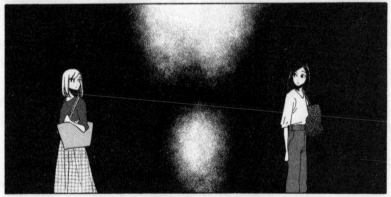

HA HA!
WE BOTH LOOKED AT THE SAME TIME, HUH?!

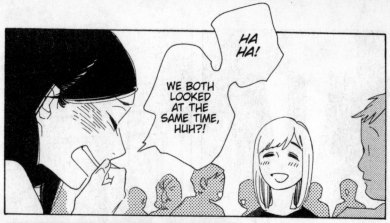

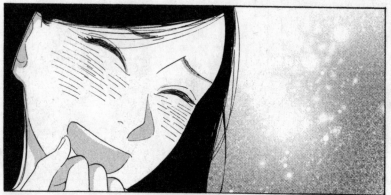

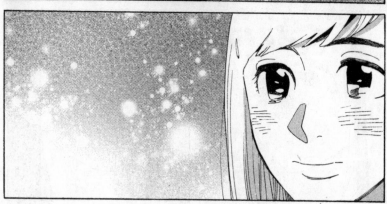

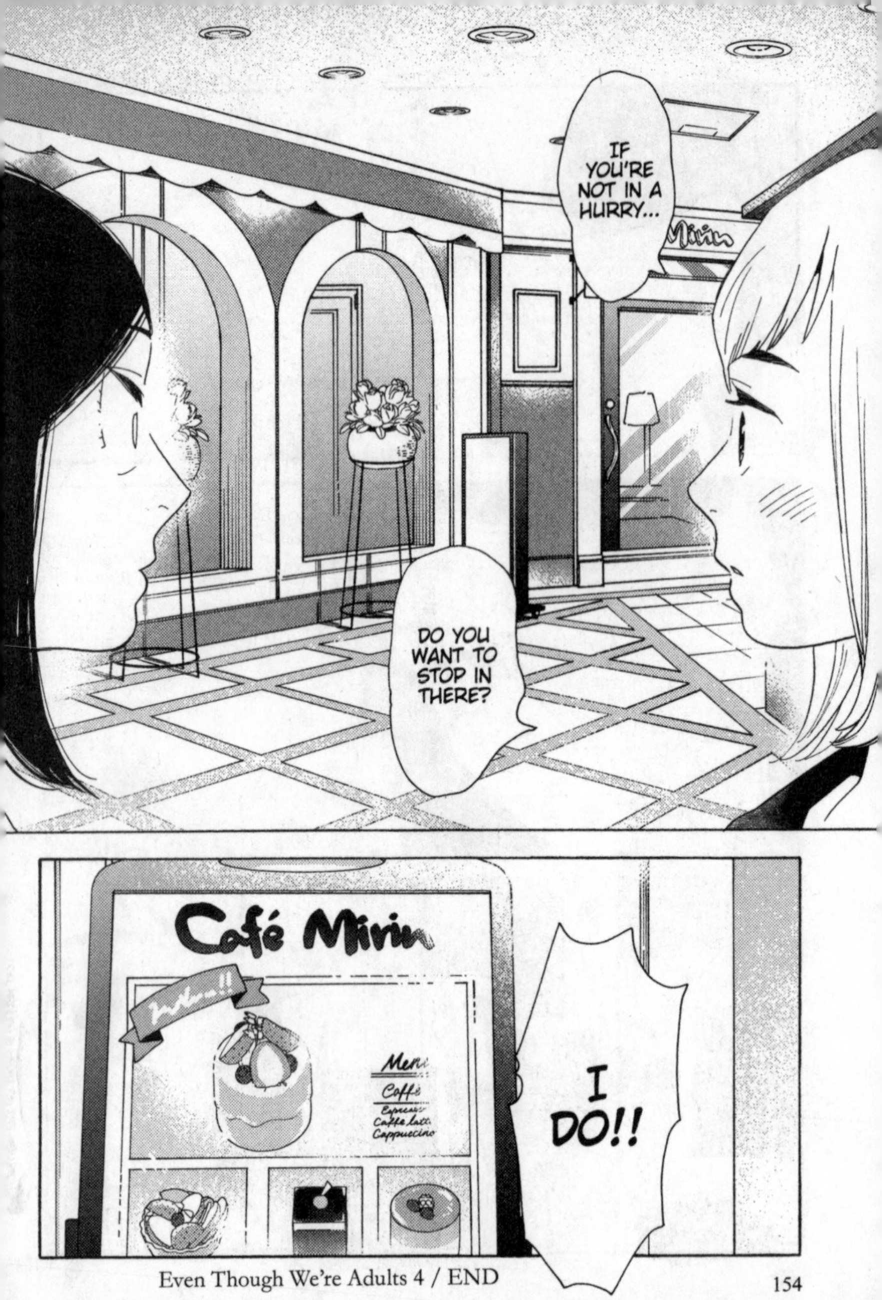
Mirin
IF YOU'RE NOT IN A HURRY...
DO YOU WANT TO STOP IN THERE?
I DO!!
Café Mirin
Menu
Caffè
Caffe latte
Cappuccino

Even Though We're Adults 4 / END

THANKS AS ALWAYS TO O-KURA-SAN, S-MOTO-SAN ISHIDEDEN-SAN, EVERYONE AT KOHEI NAKATA DESIGN OFFICE, MY EDITOR O-MURA-JOSHI, ALL YOU READERS, AND EVERYONE INVOLVED WITH THE BOOK!!

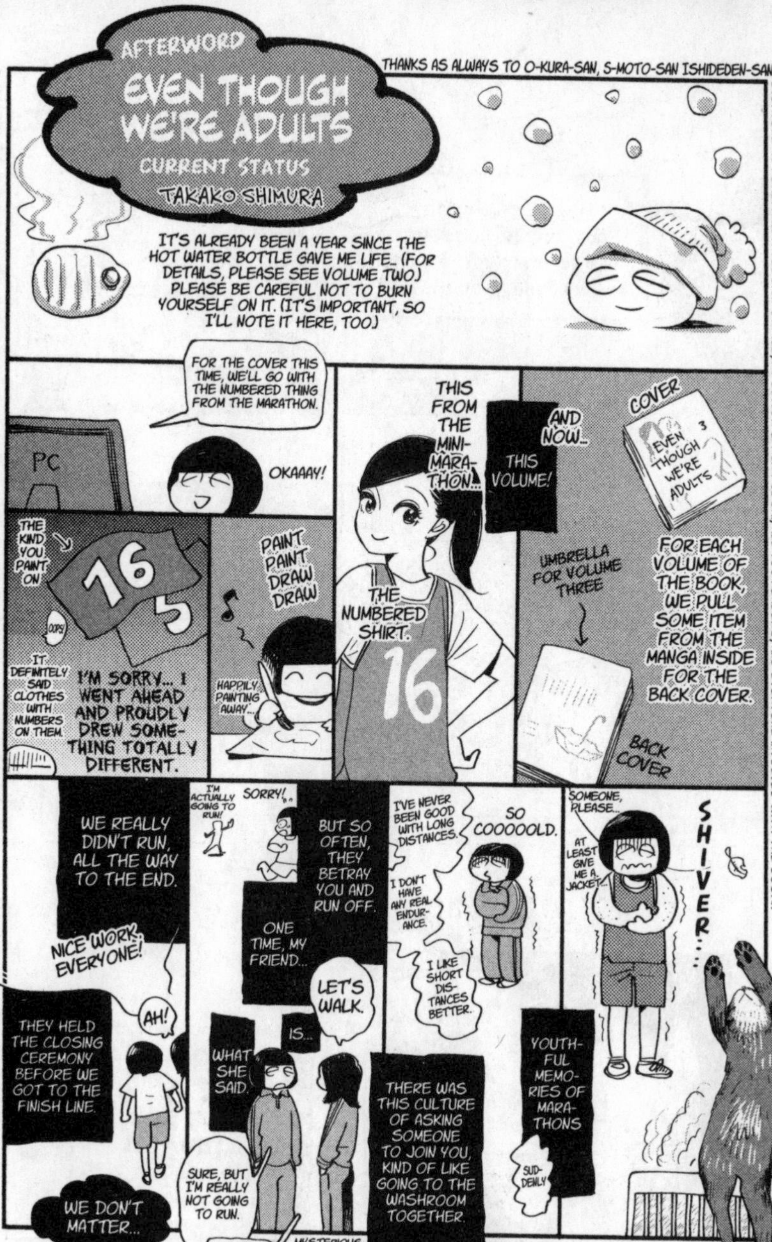

AFTERWORD
EVEN THOUGH WE'RE ADULTS
CURRENT STATUS
TAKAKO SHIMURA
IT'S ALREADY BEEN A YEAR SINCE THE HOT WATER BOTTLE GAVE ME LIFE... (FOR DETAILS, PLEASE SEE VOLUME TWO.) PLEASE BE CAREFUL NOT TO BURN YOURSELF ON IT. (IT'S IMPORTANT, SO I'LL NOTE IT HERE, TOO.)
COVER
AND NOW... THIS VOLUME!
EVEN THOUGH WE'RE ADULTS 3
FOR EACH VOLUME OF THE BOOK, WE PULL SOME ITEM FROM THE MANGA INSIDE FOR THE BACK COVER.
UMBRELLA FOR VOLUME THREE
BACK COVER
THIS FROM THE MINI-MARATHON...
THE NUMBERED SHIRT.
16
FOR THE COVER THIS TIME, WE'LL GO WITH THE NUMBERED THING FROM THE MARATHON.
PC
OKAAAY!
PAINT PAINT DRAW DRAW
HAPPILY PAINTING AWAY...
THE KIND YOU PAINT ON
16
OOPS!
IT DEFINITELY SAID CLOTHES WITH NUMBERS ON THEM.
I'M SORRY... I WENT AHEAD AND PROUDLY DREW SOMETHING TOTALLY DIFFERENT.
SHIVER...
SOMEONE, PLEASE...
AT LEAST GIVE ME A JACKET...
YOUTHFUL MEMORIES OF MARATHONS
SO COOOOOLD.
I'VE NEVER BEEN GOOD WITH LONG DISTANCES.
I DON'T HAVE ANY REAL ENDURANCE.
I LIKE SHORT DISTANCES BETTER.
SUDDENLY
THERE WAS THIS CULTURE OF ASKING SOMEONE TO JOIN YOU, KIND OF LIKE GOING TO THE WASHROOM TOGETHER.
SORRY!
I'M ACTUALLY GOING TO RUN!
BUT SO OFTEN, THEY BETRAY YOU AND RUN OFF.
ONE TIME, MY FRIEND...
LET'S WALK.
IS...
WHAT SHE SAID.
SURE, BUT I'M REALLY NOT GOING TO RUN.
THERE'S NO WAY I'M RUNNING EITHER.
MYSTERIOUS RESOLVE.
WE REALLY DIDN'T RUN, ALL THE WAY TO THE END.
NICE WORK, EVERYONE!
AH!
THEY HELD THE CLOSING CEREMONY BEFORE WE GOT TO THE FINISH LINE.
WE DON'T MATTER...

CAT MELTING IN FRONT OF THE HEATER

I SPOKE TO YAMAMOTO SHIZU-SENSEI, UESUGI TAKAKO-SENSEI, SAKO MAKO-SENSEI, AND WAKAMATSU MIZUKI-SENSEI ABOUT DIVORCE ISSUES!

THANK YOU SO MUCH!

Next issue...

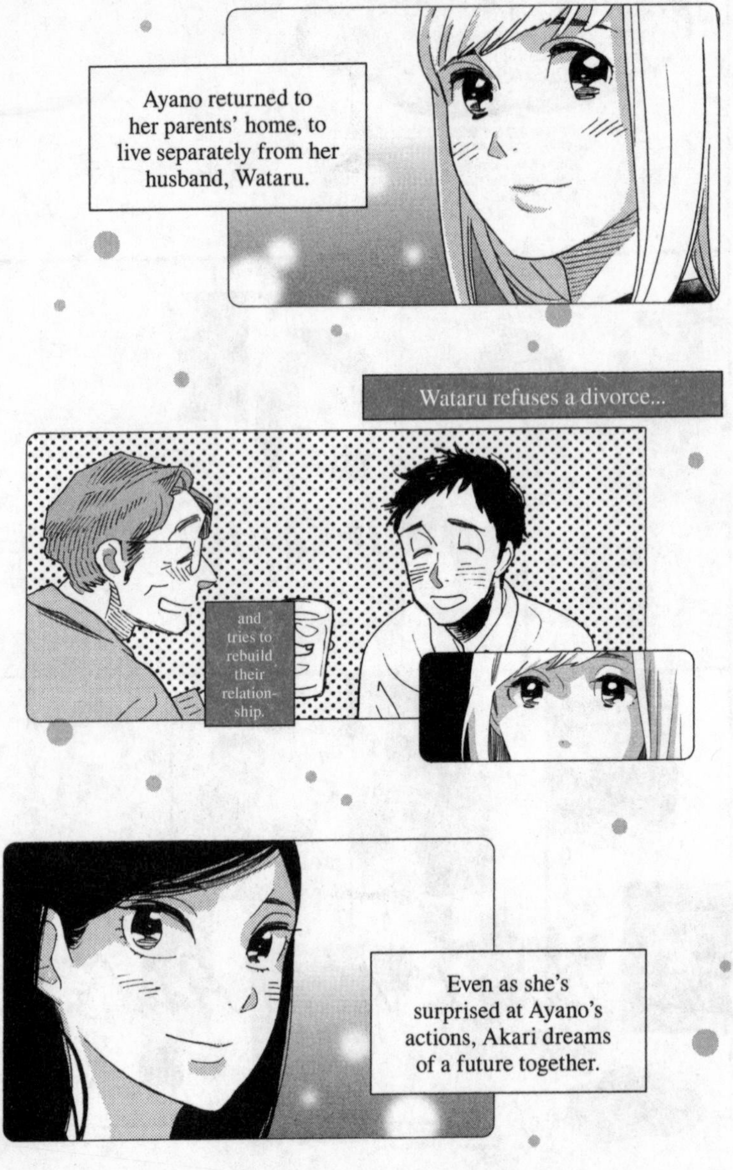
Ayano returned to her parents' home, to live separately from her husband, Wataru.
Wataru refuses a divorce...
and tries to rebuild their relation-ship.
Even as she's surprised at Ayano's actions, Akari dreams of a future together.

Trying to figure life out...

as well as a love that's out of our control.

Even Though We're Adults 5

On sale soon!

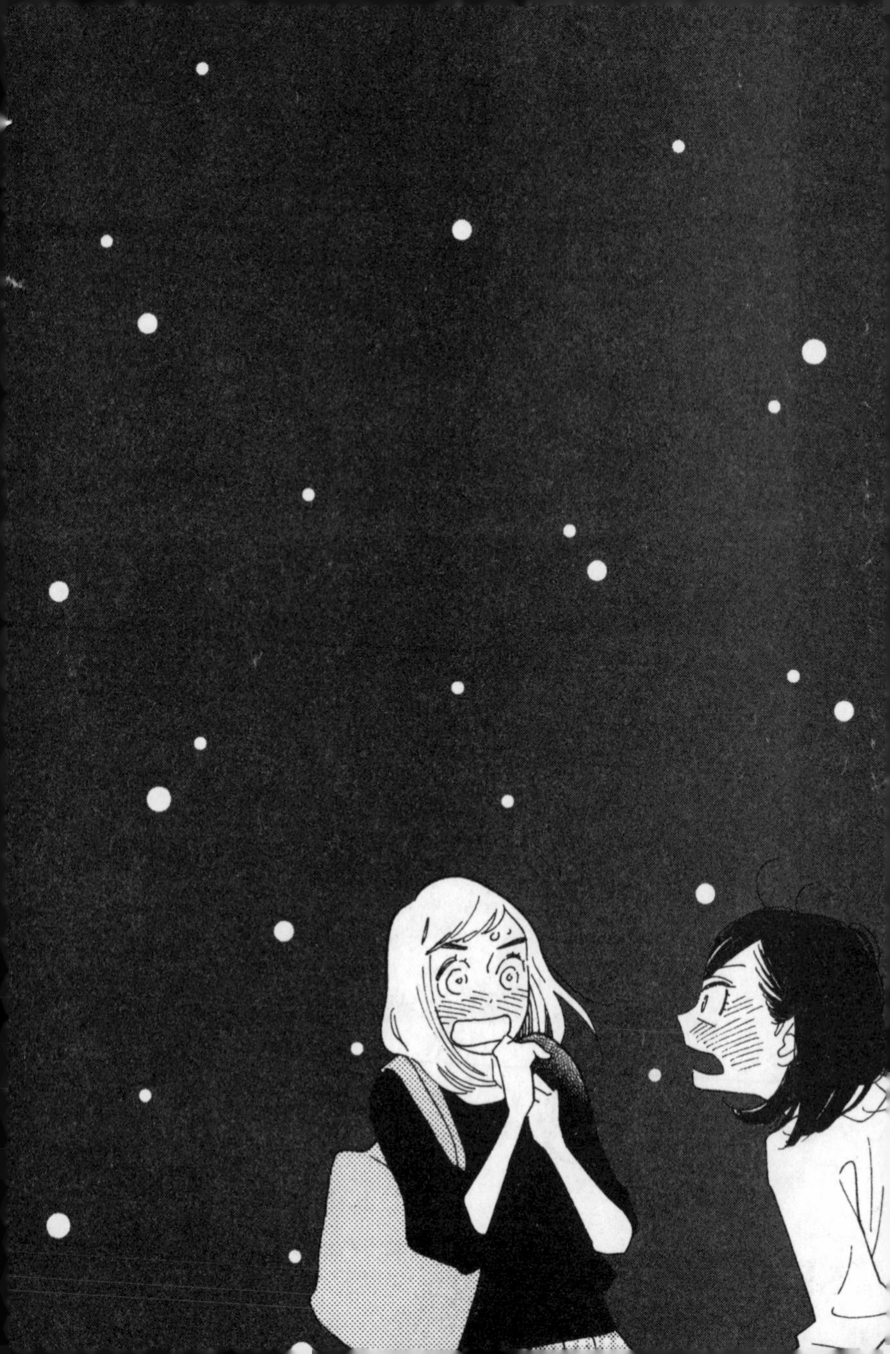

SEVEN SEAS ENTERTAINMENT PRESENTS

Even Though We're Adults

story and art by TAKAKO SHIMURA

VOLUME 4

TRANSLATION
Jocelyne Allen

ADAPTATION
Claudie Summers

LETTERING AND RETOUCH
Rina Mapa

COVER DESIGN
H. Qi

PROOFREADER
Dawn Davis

EDITOR
Shannon Fay

PRINT MANAGER
Rhiannon Rasmussen-Silverstein

PRODUCTION MANAGER
Lissa Pattillo

EDITOR-IN-CHIEF
Julie Davis

ASSOCIATE PUBLISHER
Adam Arnold

PUBLISHER
Jason DeAngelis

Seven Seas press and purchase enquiries can be sent to Marketing Manager
Lianne Sentar at press@gomanga.com. Information regarding the distribution
and purchase of digital editions is available from Digital Manager CK Russell
at digital@gomanga.com.

Seven Seas and the Seven Seas logo are trademarks of
Seven Seas Entertainment. All rights reserved.

ISBN: 978-1-63858-131-4

Printed in Canada

First Printing: April 2022

10 9 8 7 6 5 4 3 2 1

FOLLOW US ONLINE: **www.sevenseasentertainment.com**

READING DIRECTIONS

This book reads from **_right to left_**, Japanese style.
If this is your first time reading manga, you start
reading from the top right panel on each page and
take it from there. If you get lost, just follow the
numbered diagram here. It may seem backwards at
first, but you'll get the hang of it! Have fun!!

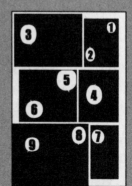